Racial Care

Racial Care

On Asian American Suffering and Survival

JAMES MCMASTER

Duke University Press   *Durham and London*   2025

© 2025 DUKE UNIVERSITY PRESS. All rights reserved
Project Editor: Ihsan Taylor
Typeset in Garamond Premier Pro by Copperline Book Services

Library of Congress Cataloging-in-Publication Data
Names: McMaster, James, [date] author.
Title: Racial care : on Asian American suffering and survival /
James McMaster.
Description: Durham : Duke University Press, 2025. |
Includes bibliographical references and index.
Identifiers: LCCN 2025008335 (print)
LCCN 2025008336 (ebook)
ISBN 9781478032830 (paperback)
ISBN 9781478029397 (hardcover)
ISBN 9781478061595 (ebook)
Subjects: LCSH: Asian Americans—Social conditions. | Asian
Americans—Race identity. | Race discrimination—United States. |
Asian Americans—Psychology. | Performance art—Social aspects—
United States. | United States—Race relations.
Classification: LCC E184.A75 M42 2025 (print) | LCC E184.A75 (ebook)
LC record available at https://lccn.loc.gov/2025008335
LC ebook record available at https://lccn.loc.gov/2025008336

Cover art: Illustration by Jess X. Snow.

Contents

Acknowledgments
vii

INTRODUCTION
Racial Care: March 2020
1

1 REVOLTING SELF-CARE
29

2 THE RACIALIZED HOLDING ENVIRONMENT
57

3 RACIAL EMOTIONAL LABOR
77

4 DEHUMANIST CARE
101

CONCLUSION
Racial Care: June 2020
125

Notes   Bibliography   Index
135   153   163

Acknowledgments

My favorite part of any scholarly monograph is its acknowledgments section. It's a peek behind the scenes, a tour through where the secrets are kept. Academic labor is often isolating. We are incentivized to act as if our work is ours and ours alone. Many of us uphold the fantasy of singular genius in exchange for more money and job security. But the beautiful thing about a book's acknowledgments is that they kindly permit us to drop the charade of individual authorship. They let us lay bare the web of relations, caring and otherwise, that have made it all possible.

So much became possible for me when I entered the Department of Performance Studies at New York University as a PhD student. That place and its people made me who I needed to become to write the book you are reading, to live the life I live now. What I owe them is incalculable. The model of mentorship set for me by my dissertation adviser, Karen Shimakawa, is one I will spend my career trying to approximate. Tavia Nyong'o took me under his wing and into the queerer corners of our fields; for this I have always been grateful. Ann Pellegrini and Malik Gaines were dream committee members by any measure. David Eng and Martin Manalansan were rigorous outside readers of the research that would become this book. Nicole Cusick, Laura Elena Fortez, and Noel Rodriguez supported me in innumerable ways. And to Barbara Browning, Lisa Duggan, Jonathan Flatley, Jack Halberstam, Deborah Kapchan, André Lepecki, Agnes Magtoto, Fred Moten, Paul Preciado, Dean Saranilio, Richard Schechner, Diana Taylor, Alexandra T. Vazquez, Mariellen Sanford, and Hentyle Yapp: thank you for being my teachers.

My colossal luck continued after graduate school when I landed a job at the University of Wisconsin–Madison. I am indebted to the staff in the Department of Gender and Women's Studies and the program in Asian American studies—Jamie Lynn Gaitrix, Jessica Montez, Em Morris, Nhung Nguyen, Su-Ann Rose, Lyddia Ruch-Doll, and Diane Walton—whose work enabled mine. The graduate students in my early-pandemic care theory seminar were nothing short of inspirational. Chris Barcelos, Leslie Bow, Anna Campbell, Jill Casid, Cindy I-Fen Cheng, Peggy Choy, Laurie Beth Clarke, Finn Enke, Katherine Jensen, Judith Houck, Monica Kim, Maria Lepowski, Bill Limpisathian, Keisha Lindsay, Lori Kido Lopez, Jenna Loyd, Annie Menzel, Aurora Santiago Ortiz, Michael Peterson, Ellen Samuels, Jesse Waggoner, Morris Young, and Timothy Yu all taught me how to do my job with integrity, generosity, and rigor. Sami Schalk showed me how to navigate the tenure track without losing myself or my commitments. Ramzi Fawaz has been a shimmering example of intellectual investment and exchange. And Christine Garlough's capacious, inclusive, and worldmaking mentorship has meant nothing less than everything.

Then there are my colleagues at the George Washington University, my comrades in Washington, DC. Thank you for your warm welcome, for your generosity and your solidarity, for helping this book across the finish line. My most heartfelt gratitude goes to Emily Bock, Patricia Chu, Jamie Cohen-Cole, Manuel Cuellar, Kavita Daiya, Holly Duggan, Maria Frawley, Tom Guglielmo, Jonathan Hsy, Nicole Ivy, Jennifer James, Andy Johnson, Alexa Joubin, Antonio López, Melani McAlister, David Mitchell, Dara Orenstein, Suleiman Osman, Chet'la Sebree, Gayle Wald, Akae Wright, Dwayne Kwaysee Wright, Orian Zakai, and the many other wonderful people in the Departments of American Studies and English. I would also like to thank the graduate students who have taken my seminars, from whom I have learned so much. Libby Anker's mentorship, and her feedback on my writing at a key moment, kept me afloat and moving forward. And I owe so much to Theo Gonsalvez, Robert McRuer, and Lily Wong who generously offered their expertise to a late-stage manuscript incubator. The book is much better because of them.

The list of people who have supported this writing over the years is very long and yet certainly incomplete. Some of the people who have made the list may not even realize the impact they have had on the words in this book. To me, their impact is undeniable. To Francis Tanglao Aguas, Luis Rincon Alba, Kadji Amin, Marc Arthur, Crystal Baik, Christine Balance, Nick Bazzano, Bobby Benedicto, Lauren Berlant, Taylor Black, AB Brown, Michelle Castañeda, Joshua Chambers-Letson, Mel Chen, Andrea Long Chu, Lawrence-Minh Bùi Davis, Iyko Day, Cynthia Delgado, Natalia Duong, Chris A. Eng, Valerie Francisco-Menchavez, Donatella Galella, Joshua Javier Guzmán, Maurice Hamington, Brian Herrera, Leon Hilton, Hi'ilei Julia Kawehipuaakahaopulani Hobart, Kelly Howe, Michelle Huang, Vivian Huang, Douglas Ishii, E. Patrick Johnson, Ronak Kapadia, Kareem Khubchandani, Jina B. Kim, Jinah Kim, Christopher J. Lee, James Kyung-Jin Lee, Josephine Lee, Summer Kim Lee, Eng-Beng Lim, Caleb Luna, D. Soyini Madison, Hil Malatino, Justin Mann, Brandon Masterson, Patrick McKelvey, Shawn Metzger, Christine Mok, Will Mosley, José Esteban Muñoz, Amber Musser, Cheryl Naruse, Fiona Ngô, Nguyen Tan Hoang, Mimi Thi Nguyen, erin Khuê Ninh, Lakshmi Padmanabhan, Roy Pérez, Ethan Philbrick, Iván Ramos, Sarah Richter, Takeo Rivera, Ramón Rivera-Servera, Shireen Roshanravan, Chad Shomura, Elizabeth Son, Eric Stanley, Anna Storti, Karen Tongson, Joan Tronto, Tara Willis, Danielle Wong, and Patricia Ybarra: thank you, thank you, thank you. I also reserve special thanks for Charles O. Anderson, Paul Bonin-Rodriguez, Charlotte Canning, Ann Cvetkovich, Omi Osun Joni L. Jones, Matt Richardson, Rebecca Rossen, and especially Laura Gutiérrez for what they taught me while I studied at the University of Texas at Austin, the place where the seed of this book was first planted.

A few writing groups were willing to get into the nitty-gritty with me, reading and responding to drafts, keeping me honest and on time. To Mimi Khúc and Simi Kang: thank you for taking me in, for keeping me close. To Jennifer Nelson, Eileen Lagman, Kristina Huang, Juliet Huynh, Nadia Chana, and LiLi Johnson: thank you for your brilliance and for bringing much needed warmth to Madison's pandemic-era winters. To Patricia Nguyen, Lily Mengesha, and Olivia Michiko Gagnon, my treasured co-traveler since graduate school: thank you for friendship, for our retreats, and for many conferences to come.

This book simply would not exist without the artists, organizers, and others whose works have enabled its arguments: Adriel Luis, Mark Aguhar, Michael Aguhar, Kimberly Alidio, Julia Cho, kt shorb, Jess X. Snow, Kristina Wong, Kabzuag Vaj, and Kit Yan. I hope you will find my work worthy of you.

This book would also not exist without the editors who have helped me to craft it into something worth reading. I recommend Craig Willse to anyone in need of developmental editing. I came to him with a bundle of ideas and he taught me how to tie them together into a coherent whole. I am also eternally indebted to Elizabeth Ault, Benjamin Kossak, Ihsan Taylor, and the rest of the staff at Duke University Press. That Elizabeth always seemed to believe in this book was enough for me to believe in it, too. I am grateful to her and my anonymous reviewers for forcing me to rise to a level of accomplishment I did not know I could reach.

Finally, I owe everything to my family and friends. My father, Bill McMaster, passed away shortly after I started my PhD program. He never knew me as a professor or as a published author, but I know he would have had tears in his eyes if he ever got to hold this book. Thank you, father. For everything. Forever.

Yolanda Kostenko swooped in to save me from my father's death by shielding me from the work it required. I would not have made it this far without her. Giselle Tongi-Walters has been a fairy godmother through it all. Roxy Schoenfeld and Kimmy Fanok have been there from the beginning, making me laugh, lifting me up, keeping me honest and weird. Ron Cabral, Nicolo Cabral, Nicole Cabral, Kyle Cabral, and my mother, Avie Cabral, have indelibly shaped who I am and how I think. My mother especially has never faltered as a model of unconditional love. Teresita Alavata—the singularly beloved "Auntie Tess"—knows everything there is to know about care and lives like it. I am who I am, this book is what it is, because of her. And to York Chow, my heart and my home: when work and the world feel impossible, your love makes me want to go on.

Introduction

RACIAL CARE: MARCH 2020

"The only way to survive is by taking care of one another, by recreating our relationships to one another." —GRACE LEE BOGGS

It was March 2020. The coronavirus pandemic was just beginning, and Asian people across the settler colonial United States—once again cast as alien invaders and vectors of contagion—were being spit on, punched in the face, kicked from behind, and refused service.[1] Anti-Asian slurs were everywhere. Broken bones were, too. And women and elders were especially vulnerable to both. I will never forget the video of the woman in Brooklyn who was doused in acid while taking out her trash. Neither will I forget the morning I woke to an email from a colleague telling me that two xenophobic messages had been chalked onto the ground at the edges of the campus where we both worked in Madison, Wisconsin: "IT'S FROM CHINA #CHINESEVIRUS" and "FUCK THE CHINESE

GOVERNMENT." The former statement's hashtag was, of course, a direct quote from then-President Donald Trump, a cheap shot fired amid new Cold War tensions with China. According to the Stop AAPI Hate Project, more than 650 acts of anti-Asian violence were reported that month. This number would rise to over 2,800 by the end of that year.[2] And many months after that, a white man with a gun would steal eight lives near Atlanta, Georgia, six of them belonging to Asian women hypersexualized by their service work. None wholly escaped the violence of that long moment. Those who didn't feel the blows of it directly, on their bodies, felt the winds of it in the air, as fear, anxiety, abjection, depression, or some other sort of affective suffering. To be made to anticipate violence is already to experience violence. Everyone in that moment needed so much care.

In April of 2020, as if to meet that need for care with the urgency it deserved, the Smithsonian Asian Pacific American Center produced *Care Package: Poems, Meditations, Films, and Other Cultural Nutrients for Times Like This*. Curated "with love" by Adriel Luis, *Care Package* was an online exhibition that promised to aid its assumed Asian American audience with the management of "uncertainty, anxiety, and grief through vision, reflection, and healing."[3] The exhibit sought to live up to its name by collecting and uplifting creative works crafted by Asian Americans and Pacific Islanders in an attempt to stem the psychosocial suffering caused by the pandemic and the COVID-era anti-Asian racism that came with it. A guided meditation by the Korean-Japanese artist Naoko Wowsugi invited its listeners to sip some mamaki tea and engage in "a healing ritual of crying," an act of self-care. *Afterearth*, a short film by Jess X. Snow and Kit Yan, depicted women, queers, and trans people of Asian and Indigenous heritage attempting, through their individual art practices, to engage in responsible caring relations with the environment amid ongoing and impending climate disaster. A kitchen collective contributed some family recipes. An artist-theorist duo offered their zine. Some musicians put forth a sound bath. Some poets did what only poets can do, and on and on. Whereas the national atmosphere of so-called anti-Asian hate produced uncountable care need among Asians in the United States, the many aesthetic works assembled in and as *Care Package* aimed to tend to that need through the creative provision of cultural nourishment.

Care Package is exemplary of the strategies I seek to identify, describe, and analyze throughout the pages to come. The book you are reading takes up, as its primary work, an examination of the ways that twenty-first-century Asian American artists have used aesthetic means to survive, contest, and improve their neglected position within an unjust distribution of what I call *racial care*. The feminist theorists Berenice Fisher and Joan Tronto teach us that care "includes everything that we do to maintain, continue, and repair our 'world' so that we can live in it as well as possible."⁴ This definition has proven durable and influential within the scholarship on care, even as it has been criticized as overbroad. But it is precisely the capaciousness of Fisher and Tronto's definition that makes it a useful model for my purposes here. As I define it, racial care includes everything we do to sustain racialized subjects through whatever suffering may converge on their particular location within the white supremacist, anti-Black, and settler colonial capitalist order of the United States. I privilege the aesthetic performance of racial care because, as I will show and as *Care Package* illustrates, the aesthetic is the realm within which minoritarian cultural production acts upon our senses in order to soothe racial suffering at the level of affect. It is the realm within which artists and other world-makers work to unsettle the widely held attachments and ideologies that preserve inequalities of racial care. And it is also the realm within which the ordinary performance of racial care, so often obscured in the course of everyday life, is made most widely available to sense perception.

Quotidian acts of racial care come in many forms. Racial care can be an outstretched hand, a pep talk, or a gesture of solidarity. It shows up when sentences and bodies are bent toward educated sensitivity. It happens when material needs are met through dedicated effort. Racial care can travel across lines of racial difference. It can even travel up and down the racial hierarchy, performable by people of every race and ethnicity. But it cannot, lost in a post-racial fantasy, disavow the fact of racial difference. And it also cannot, in every instance, be about feeling good. Like surgery, racial care can be both painful and lifesaving. It can be both reactive and proactive, preventive. And like any kind of care, it can also be exhausting. This is true for racial care passed diligently between loved ones. It is also true for people of color performing emotional labor for white fragility, caring for the racially advantaged by sparing them a shattering confrontation with their own racial culpability.⁵ In these latter cases the "care" in "racial care" resembles the care one might take while tiptoeing atop creaky floorboards as others sleep lightly nearby. This sort of racial care shields minoritarian subjects from racial backlash, but it also exacerbates the need for other forms of racial care—the sort that sustain and enrich minoritarian life. And while the range of activity that I am calling racial care cannot be thought apart from the formal economy of paid care work, in what follows I aim to deepen our understanding of what Evelyn Nakano Glenn has called "the racialized division of reproductive labor" by placing my focus elsewhere.⁶

My mission in this book is to illuminate the *informal* activities of racial care that are enacted, often under the radar of scholarly attention, in the registers of aesthetic encounter, social interaction, and affective exchange. My method is to close read performances of racial care in everyday life as well as in theater, poetry, visual art, and film in order to lay bare the almost infrared, psychosocial field of racial caring relations as well as the position Asian Americans occupy within that field. I seek to expose the neglect and need for racial care experienced by Asian Americans under neoliberal capitalism and white supremacy. And I seek to do so while remaining attentive to the caring responsibilities Asian Americans must meet in relation to other minoritarian groups, responsibilities that are imposed on Asian American subjects by their unique location within the racial–colonial order of the United States. All this is to support a single argument, crystallized in the following thesis: while Asian Americans inhabit an unsustainably neglected situation on the field of racial care, they can and have altered that situation by seeking recourse, across scales of existence, to both minoritarian aesthetics and movement organizing. Ultimately, like *Care Package*, *Racial Care* is a study of what Asian American artists, organizers, and other world-makers do for one another when the going gets tough and the tough are tired of living life against the whipping winds of racism.

Racism: "the state sanctioned or extralegal production and exploitation of group-differentiated vulnerability to premature death."[7] This is Ruth Wilson Gilmore's definition. We could also say, racism: that which produces a need for racial care. When racism detonates across a nation, or in a room, racial care is how we keep each other alive and well amid the fallout. It is the labor people of color must perform for one another when the shiv of racial violence gets under the skin and all that can be felt is the slow, serrated tearing of one's soft interiority. The specific violences racial care redresses can be physical, a boot on the neck; but they need not be. "Affective violence," to use Dorinne Kondo's poignant term, hurts too.[8] Subtle harms add up and whisper out for racial care.[9] An incomplete list of salient slights:

> a suspect glance; a Halloween costume; a telling scoff; an arcane turn of phrase; "where are you really from?"; yellowface; being undocumented; being underestimated; being overestimated; being desexualized; being hypersexualized; being deemed a terrorist; being hyperexploited; being shunned; being ignored; being unduly celebrated; being rejected for what you are; being mistaken for another othered person; being assaulted; being interned; being criminalized; being multiply marginalized and having one's back used as a bridge; being burdened by all of the extra work; being exhausted because, miraculously, one has kept kind through all of it, or because one hasn't.

Each of these items, to the extent that it bears the stench of racism, can quickly become a source of care need—cause for racial care in the psychosocial register, by which I mean the zone of relationality and performativity, affect and attachment. Each also, insofar as it indexes a way of being that shouldn't be, provides a negative example against which to imagine a better ethics and politics of racial care, one rooted in the ontological interdependence of all life and made manifest in art, organizing, and ordinary existence.

None of this, however, is to romanticize racial care as the anti-racist antidote par excellence, because the imperative to perform racial care often becomes a burden that accelerates our dying. From 2006 to 2015, the performance artist Kristina Wong went on tour with her semi-autobiographical one-woman show, *Wong Flew over the Cuckoo's Nest*, a meditation on the high rates of depression and suicide among Asian American women. The show finds Wong playing a character—in her words, "an overachieving martyr and people pleaser"—who shares her name.[10] Near the top of the performance, Wong makes a promise: all Asian American women will be saved from suicidal ideation by the end of the show. Though it is obvious that Wong the performer recognizes how ridiculous such a promise is, Wong the character seems to make the promise in earnest. And, with an eye toward fulfilling this promise, she spends the bulk of the show engaging in various performances of racial care.

One crucial moment of the piece finds Wong attempting, in accordance with her overachieving and audience-pleasing persona, to tell the story of every single Asian American woman who has ever experienced depression or suicidal ideation. Wong starts by inhabiting a thirty-three-year-old Korean American woman named Angie. She performs a monologue that evokes the specter of postpartum depression: "Stop crying! I should have never had this baby!" Then suddenly she drops that character and assumes another, a sixty-year-old Cambodian American woman dealing with the traumatic inheritances of war.[11] Then Wong becomes another woman, then another woman, then another, until she is finally overwhelmed by the number of stories she has promised to tell. She is crushed beneath the weight of them.

In this moment, as in others, the performance of racial care on display in *Wong Flew over the Cuckoo's Nest*, however well intentioned, is itself revealed to be debilitating, depressing, and life-draining. In a postmortem about her time on tour, Wong writes that she "marketed [*Wong Flew over the Cuckoo's Nest*] as a 'funny show about depression.'" She "touted the show's ability to bring 'healing' and 'conversation' to a national crisis that wasn't being addressed enough."[12] If *Wong Flew over the Cuckoo's Nest* is a show about the need Asian American women have for racial care, it is also a show that promised intraracial care to neglected Asian American audience members who might themselves have unmet racial care needs. After performances of the show, as Wong tells it, women would approach her "in tears, speaking very candidly about their own frail emotional health," and Wong could only "hold them and hug them and listen through [her] exhausted and jaded ears."[13] "The world I had created onstage was so consuming, it followed me offstage," Wong confesses. "I would never recommend, even to the world's most self-hating masochist, touring any semi-autobiographical solo theater show for years."[14] Especially not, she writes, if the subject matter so directly implicates the hardest parts of one's own life. Wong's experience with *Wong Flew over the Cuckoo's Nest* exposes the costs and benefits of performing racial care. Racial care saps life at the same time as it saves lives. And the truth is: none of us is above this core contradiction.

None of us is exempt from navigating the space between the need for racial care and the responsibility to perform it. We are all entangled in relations of racial care, though not all of us move through the world with an awareness of this fact. The risk of inflicting racial harm, perhaps unconsciously, is a risk that all of us are running all of the time. But only some of us take sincere, competent, and socially conscious care around race as we interact with the world. Some others try, but only to avoid trouble, cancellation, consequences. And still others refuse even the thought of racial care outright—that is, if they have any conscious thought of racially marked sociality at all. This is all to say that most people move through the world creating more need for racial care than they labor to relieve. And if more racial care need is being created than is being relieved, it follows that more racial care is needed than is being received. This is a life-defining fact of material reality. My intention in naming it is not to lay blame at the feet of incompletely autonomous individuals but rather to give definition to the relational field within which the need for racial care among Asian Americans continues to accrue, often without acknowledgment. To this end, I work within and against established approaches to the study of care.

Toward a Minoritarian Care Theory

Often when scholars make explicit reference to "care theory," they are referring to the feminist school of thought known as the ethics of care. The origins of this field are typically traced to two important books. The first is Carol Gilligan's *In a Different Voice: Psychological Theory and Women's Development* (1982), and the second is Joan Tronto's *Moral Boundaries: A Political Argument for an Ethics of Care* (1993). Gilligan's book challenged a masculinist, justice-based morality valuing autonomy and rights in favor of an ethics of care rooted in the maintenance of human connection and forged from the stuff of femininity, motherhood, and emotion. Tronto's book shifted the field away from reifying the association between women and care in order to position care as a matter of concern in all areas of life. Tronto pushed the field past the intimate arrangements of the private sphere, positioning the allocation of care and care labor as a public matter to be addressed politically. As a result, care ethics has become a promising theoretical framework through which to study "everything we do to maintain, continue, and repair our world." The *care* in care ethics refers capaciously to a feeling (affect/attachment) and a doing (labor/performance). The *ethics* in care ethics is relational, situated, and rooted in the ontological assumption that all living beings, precious and vulnerable, exist in interdependent relation with one another. Tied together, these terms assist us in considering how the responsibility to perform caring labor should be assigned, to whom, and to whose benefit. An ethic of care asks us to be attentive to the need for care, wherever and whenever it may emerge.

And yet, for all this promise, care ethics has a race problem. The language in which care ethics has historically been written has been a racially unmarked one. And this has resulted in an ethics of care that struggles to conceive of racial competence as an essential element of any caring relation.[15] Whereas gender has typically been assumed as the field's a priori axis of analysis, race has emerged across the discourse most often as an additive or secondary concern.[16] A similar claim can be made in relation to another feminist outpost of care theory of importance to this project: social reproduction feminism, which has historically placed primary focus on the gendered divisions of labor that define the maintenance of life under capitalism—more on this in chapter 3. What would happen if race were assumed as the organizing category of care theory, and in a way that would bring gender and other genres of social difference along for the ride? *Racial Care* is written as one possible answer to this question. Some within care ethics and social reproduction theory have turned to intersectionality as a corrective to their fields' implicit whiteness. This development is heartening in that it foregrounds the inextricability of oppressive systems.[17] But the analytic of intersectionality alone is not enough to enable these feminist discourses to account for the deeply embedded material realities and psychosocial patterns that produce an excess of need for racial care within disenfranchised and disregarded Asian diasporic worlds.[18]

To rise to these realities, *Racial Care* braids care ethics and social reproduction feminism with other strands of care theory. Queer and trans thinkers remind us to reject the heteronormative impulse to cast caring labor as a private performance essentially aligned with the family, femininity, or womanhood. They remind us, too, to cultivate what Hil Malatino has named "an infrapolitical ethics of care," which calls attention to those minor "community practices" that attempt both to support political movement and to alleviate trans and queer suffering, racial, affective, and otherwise.[19] The field of critical disability studies and the movements for disability justice shift care theory in a similar direction by bringing focus to racialized disablement and debilitation.[20] Disabled care theory casts disabled people not only as care receivers (objects of care) but also as care providers (subjects of care). In the former discussions, the provision of care is commonly cast as coercive, a potential site of confinement, abuse, and exhaustion. In the latter, care comes into view as a kind of work that circulates unevenly and differentially through communities crowded with multiply marginalized people of color, all of whom exist in an invisibilized web of interdependence. Notably Asian diasporic writers and cultural workers are well-represented within these care theoretical lineages: Leah Lakshmi Piepzna-Samarasinha, Mimi Khúc, and Mia Mingus to name only three.[21] And from the vantage point of the crip queer Asian diasporic feminism discernible in their work, any ethics of care worthy of the name would need to be anti-carceral, anti-colonial, anti-imperial, radically relational, and written in pursuit of what Akemi Nishida calls "care justice," a political vision in which caring relations are arranged in a way that fosters the flourishing of all life on Earth, human and nonhuman.[22] This book follows in step with this tradition of care theorizing, forging a minoritarian approach to the study of Asian American racial care from the insights of feminist, queer, trans, and crip of color critique.[23]

In doing so, *Racial Care* aims to intervene upon a twenty-first-century critical scene in which care has become a key term with which to respond to the deepening crises of racial capitalism. The events of 2020 have only intensified a more general turn among artists, organizers, and scholars toward the practice of what Hiʻilei Julia Kawehipuaakahaopulani Hobart and Tamara Kneese have called "radical care," those "vital but underappreciated strategies for enduring precarious worlds."[24] Surging interest in mutual aid, reproductive justice, and trans care would all fall under the heading of radical care.[25] As would a range of abolitionist discourses: family abolition, with its emphasis on communizing care, as well as prison and police abolition, with their emphases on healing and transformative justice.[26] *Racial Care* draws from all these resources and more, including Black and Indigenous studies, posthumanism, the new materialisms, and psychoanalysis. While these many areas of care theory overlap, this fact is sparsely acknowledged, and critical conversations about care too often remain siloed. This keeps care theory from cohering into an intellectual tradition capable of rising to the political, economic, social, and psychic crises it aims to address. For this reason I set a table with this book at which these diverse discourses might meaningfully break bread, get to know one another, and think together toward a radical ethics of racial care.

The Asian American Case

What is the history of racial care in the Asian American case? This question is an essential one because racial care's appearance in the world changes in accordance with shifting material conditions. These conditions have, over time, included formal legal exclusions from citizenship and property ownership; US imperial warfare and its orientalist domestic impacts; dynamic regimes of border enforcement, policing, and incarceration; technological advancements around mobility, communication, and computation; alterations to the infrastructures of higher education; and the ever-evolving imperatives of capital accumulation, both nationally and globally. While this book does not promise a comprehensive account of racial caring relations amid these changing circumstances, it does invite us to reread familiar flashpoints of Asian American history for the insights they can offer around racial care's life in the *longue durée*.

Consider, for example, the racial disparities in care experienced by those who were held captive at the Angel Island Immigration Station during the era of Chinese exclusion (1882–1943).[27] The Chinese migrants detained at Angel Island, sometimes for years, received inferior food and accommodations compared to their European counterparts. They were also often subject to more extensive and invasive medical testing. Faced with such conditions of carceral care and neglect, detainees wrote poems on the walls of the detention center. These poems often acted as windows into the psychic suffering their authors experienced. They served as evidence of a widespread need for racial care. Detainees addressed this need in a variety of ways, many of which are imagined in Genny Lim's play *Paper Angels*. A work of historical fiction, *Paper Angels* follows a group of Chinese detainees who care for one another not only by meeting each other's need for emotional support in the face of border violence but also by running interference with guards, keeping one another's secrets, and securing coaching papers designed to guide other detainees through scrutinizing interrogations. All these microsocial acts express a radical ethics of racial care rooted by necessity in fugitivity, a historically specific ethics crafted in response to a macropolitical-economic context in which a national desire for white supremacist consolidation outweighed the ruling class demand for cheap Chinese labor.

The mid-twentieth century reality of Japanese internment also highlights how the logic of anti-Asian excludability central to the US racial-colonial order has historically shaped racial care for Asian Americans. Over 120,000 people of Japanese descent left their homes, jobs, schools, and communities behind when the US government forced them into concentration camps during World War II. Livelihoods were lost. Families were separated. Homes were abandoned or hastily sold for less than they were worth. Racial care quickly became about ameliorating the inhumane conditions of camp life in diverse ways. Imagine, for example, the moral and emotional support passed tearfully between prisoners after word of Hiroshima and Nagasaki reached the camps. Think of Christmas celebrations, sporting events, and other activities made possible through the socially reproductive labors required to build and sustain community while incarcerated. Those held in Manzanar constructed community gardens to make everyday life more bearable. They built ironing rooms that they also used as hair salons, infrastructures of care and social exchange. Recall the legal effort launched in the name of Mitsuye Endo, which would eventually lead to the closure of the camps. All of this responded to the need for racial care, a need that would persist even after camp life ended. Newly freed, Japanese Americans found that the capacities available to them for reproducing their personal, familial, and collective lives had been devastated, though they worked to rebuild these capacities by establishing community-oriented employment agencies and by demanding racial care from the state in the form of reparations. Like the era of Chinese exclusion, Japanese wartime incarceration makes clear how the distribution of racial care in the United States has historically taken shape in response to the militarized machinations of a white supremacist carceral state at once antagonistic and indifferent to Asian diasporic needs.

But these oppressive tendencies would face a fundamental challenge from the liberation movements of the 1960s and 1970s, which sought to radically restructure the way caring relations in the United States were arranged. Drawing energy from the feminist, civil rights, and anti-war movements, the Third World Liberation Front (TWLF) student strikes of 1968 demanded that San Francisco State University transform itself to support minoritarian education. A Black-led interracial coalition, the TWLF took its name from the National Liberation Front of North Vietnam, a sign of the group's opposition to US imperial intervention in the region. As a result of the TWLF student strikes, the term *Asian American* emerged to allow Asians in the United States to consolidate political power across national and ethnic difference. Since then, Asian American studies has proliferated as a justice-oriented scholarly field; queer and trans Asian Americans have, over decades, cultivated infrastructures of social life and community care at regional and national scales;[28] and a decentralized Asian American left has crystallized across a range of political organizations and cultural institutions.[29]

Collectively, these histories and contemporary efforts constellate into a renewed outline for a radical ethics of racial care in the Asian American case, one that requires Asians in the United States to act in internationalist, interracial, and intersectional solidarity to meet their own and others' interconnected care needs.

This book builds on this framework to challenge the ways that neoliberalism and white supremacy have colluded to tame and domesticate both the liberation movements of the post–World War II period and the vision for racial care those movements advanced. From the perspective of care theory, neoliberalism is an economic, cultural, and moral formation premised on the disavowal of the ontological interdependence of all things. Care theory has long been critical of neoliberalism's ableist, individualist ethos of personal responsibility; its upward distribution of wealth; the privatization of childcare, eldercare, and health care; the shredding of the social safety net; and the generalization of precarity for all people.[30] But this care theoretical critique, while powerful, can be bolstered through critical engagement with another aspect of neoliberalism—one exposed by scholars such as Grace Kyungwon Hong, Roderick Ferguson, and Jodi Melamed[31]—namely, the way neoliberalism has historically sustained itself through the multiculturalist incorporation and affirmation of minority difference.

To minoritarian subjects deemed respectable, neoliberalism holds out the promise of privilege on the condition that they disavow their affirmative duty to enter ethically into racial caring relations with those most in need of racial care. Figures like Hillary Clinton, Barack Obama, and Kamala Harris are paradigmatic of the way women and people of color have been recruited to serve neoliberal and nationalist interests, interests opposed to an emancipatory politics. We have also watched, in the early twenty-first century, as some gays, lesbians, and others identified with the queer community have abandoned what Cathy Cohen has called "the radical potential of queer politics" rooted in redistribution and liberation for an incrementalist and individualist political tendency compatible with capitalism that seeks little more than access to normative institutions like the family and the military.[32] And according to David Mitchell and Sharon Snyder, the disabled, too, are welcomed by neoliberalism into the biopolitical fold "as long as [they do] not demand an excessive degree of change from relatively inflexible institutions, environments, and norms of belonging."[33]

The Asian American model minority must also be regarded as a figure of neoliberal incorporation. As erin Khuê Ninh has argued, the model minority is best understood not through the orthodoxy of myth but as racialization and social role.[34] It is an identity defined by the aspirational pursuit of a neoliberal success frame that places a premium on excellent grades, elite education, and high-income-earning professions. It is an identity that pursues, above all—and often at the expense of others—the individualist accumulation of human capital. Think here about the Asian American undergraduates who, under white guidance, delivered a death-blow to affirmative action. Think of all the white-collar Asian Americans seeking corporate solutions to problems better solved by social movements. The examples are myriad, and they gesture toward the neoliberal and racial knots we can begin to loosen by locating Asian Americanist care theory in the recent past.

Accounting for racial care's many lives across time will need to be a collective project, but *Racial Care* initiates that project with a specific focus on the racial crises and culture wars associated with the Obama-Trump years (2007–21). Common sense links the incorporative impulse of neoliberal multiculturalism with the post-racial fantasies that suffused the Obama era. The first Trump years, meanwhile, were most often understood as representing a rising white supremacist revanchism, a reactionary culture shift away from racial progress. In reality, the age of Obama-Trump is best apprehended as a flashpoint of what Dylan Rodriguez has called "multiculturalist white supremacy."[35] This term asks us to understand white supremacy not as an exceptionally hateful right-wing ideology that has periodically receded with the rise of official state anti-racisms but as a very much unexceptional "violence of aspiration" and "logic of social organization" that has long operated in tandem with neoliberal multiculturalism to sustain racial capitalism and racial-colonial domination by recruiting a diverse range of minoritarian subjects as "living evidence" of social progress.[36]

Situating *Racial Care* in the Obama-Trump years forces care theory's critique of neoliberalism to engage more deeply with questions of race by bringing forward what neoliberalism and white supremacy share. And what they share is a multiculturalist mechanism of Faustian inclusion, one that lures Asian American model minorities and other assimilative minoritarian subjects toward performances of self that align with whiteness and US capitalist culture while providing cover for anti-Blackness and racial-colonial violence in the process. Care theory, in turn, offers to Asian American studies a clearer vantage on what model minoritism is and does. The pressure that model minoritism applies to Asian American subjects to perform and achieve at such a high level often induces in them intense experiences of stress, anxiety, depression, aggression, overall unwellness, even suicidal ideation.[37] At the same time, model minoritism names an aspiration for uplift under racial capitalism and for inclusion under white nationalism that is ultimately antithetical to the project of racial care. This is core to model minoritism's violence: it simultaneously produces the need for sustaining relations of racial care and a disavowal of that need rooted in an imperative of individual advancement.

The other reason for situating this study in the early twenty-first century has to do with the overlapping crises that overwhelm this period. In addition to a global pandemic and elevated rates of depression among Asian American women, the age of Obama-Trump also witnessed an avalanche of femme suicides, mass shootings, concentration camps, climate catastrophe, and unending police killings. After Lauren Berlant, we can call this a time of "crisis ordinariness." It was a time during which the reproduction of life was hardly distinguishable from the attrition of life, and the need for racial care built up like carbon in the atmosphere.[38] In addition to Wong and the contributors to *Care Package*, the artists and writers I discuss across my chapters include the Tumblr-famous figure Mark Aguhar; the poet Kimberly Alidio; the playwright Julia Cho and the other theater artists behind her play *Office Hour*; an experimental theater troupe called the Generic Ensemble Company; Kit Yan and Jess X. Snow, each a poet and a filmmaker; and finally all the artists featured in Yan and Snow's film *Afterearth*. The works put forth by this diverse collection of Asian diasporic cultural producers amount to an archive that is illustrative of racial care's spatially and temporally situated forms but not at all exhaustive of them. Each of these works is in conversation with at least one of the ongoing crises I have listed above, and this is key to why I selected them for inclusion in this study. It is in proximity to crisis that the demand for racial care is most acute and the performance of racial care most available for critical analysis.

Moreover, against background conditions of crisis ordinariness—with the psychosocial field so dense with vulnerability and precarity, depression and anxiety—so much of our small-scale social conflict has been made into fodder for a large-scale culture war waged over the arrangement of racial caring relations. This is due in large part to the emergence and dominance of social media throughout the period on which I focus. Debates over self-care and collective care, call out and cancel culture, emotional labor and white fragility, separatism and solidarity: all of these are taken up throughout this book as historically situated skirmishes over the racial distribution of psychosocial reproductive labor, by which I mean the work it takes to keep people of color well despite abjection under racial capitalism.[39] We tend to fight these culture wars when we cannot win structural alterations to formal caring relations through the official channels of settler governance—channels that are undeniably oligarchical and hardly able to work at all for working people. As Lisa Lowe argues, "It is through culture, rather than government, that alternative forms of subjectivity, collectivity, and public life are imagined."[40] Some aspects of racial sociality might be bettered with changes to law or shifts in economic hierarchy, but others will only be altered through transformations of desire, reversals in currents of stigmatization, and other shifts in social norms.[41] Culture names the site at which these alterations, through aesthetic means, might be made. And so, at stake in the racial care culture wars is nothing less than this: the terms according to which racial care needs will be met, racial care responsibilities allocated, racial care labor performed, and racial caring relations arranged.

Because Asian Americans have historically been cast as relatively privileged racial minorities, these issues are of special salience in their case. Buttressed by the actual existence of model minority subjects recruited under multiculturalist white supremacy, model minority racialization masks the inequality that exists within the unwieldy category of "Asian America" by running roughshod over what Lowe has famously called its "heterogeneity, hybridity, and multiplicity."[42] Those Asian American groups that do meet the metrics of model minority status are deemed too fortunate to require racial care. Those that do not are left to shiver in the model minority's shadow where they struggle for the disaggregation of demographic data to make their need for racial care legible as such. Some Asian Americans are kept or cast out of model minority status altogether by the anti-Black, Islamophobic, and xenophobic impulses of the carceral state and other people. They are left to whither with other names like "criminal," "terrorist," "illegal." And this harm, too, is obscured by the thought-image of the model minority, as are other historical instances of carceral, imperial, colonial, capitalist, and white supremacist violence enacted against Asian peoples, structurally and interpersonally, both within the United States and outside it. While these insights are obvious within Asian American studies, when routed through care theory, they reveal the ways in which model minority racialization renders Asian Americans as subjects without struggle, subjects unworthy of racial care and solidarity in the present, subjects whose needs can be met after others' needs are met first.

Anti-Asian Neglect

In *Racial Care*, I use the language of *anti-Asian neglect* to account for the ways in which model minority racialization frames Asian Americans as racial subjects without care need, deemed to be doing just fine, or well enough, at least for now. This, to be sure, is precisely the narrative that *Wong Flew over the Cuckoo's Nest* sought to combat. The very premise of that solo show is that the psychic strife facing Asian American women is neglected, obscured by a model minority fantasy upheld by Asians and non-Asians alike. It is this structural circumstance that leads Wong to write and perform the show and to be drained by it. *Wong Flew over the Cuckoo's Nest* is both about anti-Asian neglect and against it. What I am suggesting is not that Asian Americans are more neglected than other racialized groups but that they are *uniquely* neglected as a function of the way they have been racialized under neoliberal multiculturalist white supremacy; that this neglect is compounded by gendered and sexual subordination; and that both these realities produce debilitating and sometimes deadly psychosocial outcomes for the subjects at the center of this study.

Neglect is irreducible to more familiar categories like invisibility and erasure. The answer to neglect is not visibility, representation, or state recognition. The answer to neglect, as this book's conclusion will make clear, is abolition, another world of just caring relations. Neglect is care's dialectical other. And, like care, it is also something one can feel. We might say that the affective outcome of anti-Asian neglect is Asian American loneliness, a feeling I discuss at greater length in my second chapter. To feel neglected is to feel lonely, uncared for; it is to feel that one's needs go ignored and unmet; that one is not worth enough, or pained enough, to magnetize to oneself the caring attention and attachments of others. Anti-Asian neglect is why the suffering produced by anti-Asian racism yields hardly any outcry for Asian Americans. It is why so few non-Asians feel responsible for literacy in Asian American histories and causes. Anti-Asian neglect operates passively and impersonally. It operates without malice or notice. It allows only for scattered expressions of sympathy and solidarity, measly rations of racial care.

It is true that there are abundant resources in the world, and if these resources were not as hoarded and withheld as they are under racial capitalism, working people might have an easier time reproducing their lives. But it is also true, on a microsocial scale, that each of us has only so much attention and labor-power to offer one another. And this means that racial care, at least the sort that operates in a psychosocial register, is a finite resource. Decisions must always be made about where racial care should be directed given limitations in capacity. We make these decisions, most often, based on an assessment of care need. Where is the need for care most urgent? Where can our care have the most meaningful, lasting impact? Whose needs must take priority and why?

This question of priority is central to theories of racial and colonial comparison and relation, which means we can read such theories to better understand the logic according to which racial care is distributed in the United States. Black-nonblack, Native-settler: these are widely held to be the structuring binaries of the US racial-colonial order. One outcome of this binary thinking is that Asianness enters the conversation only belatedly, after Blackness and Indigeneity, as a triangulated third category of subjects uniquely complicit with the violences of anti-Blackness and settler colonialism. Another outcome, as Iyko Day observes, is that this binary approach to racial and colonial analysis has sometimes yielded a certain "exceptionalism" within afropessimist Black studies and settler colonial studies "whereby both the Native and the black body signify a genocidal limit concept."[43] These claims to exceptional suffering then shape and sustain the logic of ontological and political priority according to which racial care is so often meted out.

Crucially, this logic of priority exists not only in critical theory but also in the left and liberal common sense of the Obama-Trump years. According to the *New York Times*, the acronym BIPOC (Black, Indigenous, people of color) first appeared on social media in 2013 and quickly became "ubiquitous" online among those invested in racial sensitivity and racial justice.[44] It emerged as a corrective to the phrase "people of color" and its acronym POC, which neglect to account either for the singularity of anti-Blackness or for the way that Indigeneity, though still a racializing category, is distinguished from other racialized modes of being in the world in part because of its relationship to land-based struggles for sovereignty. Many have argued that BIPOC is valuable insofar as it offers an inclusive way to refer to non-whiteness in the US context. Others have rejected the term, arguing that it flattens all manner of racial, colonial, and diasporic difference, often in a way that mistakes multicultural inclusion for liberation. But most important for this study is the observation that BIPOC reveals and reinforces the same logic of priority expressed by theorists of race and settler colonialism.

In BIPOC, those with exceptional claims to victimhood and suffering come first, and those pained subjects who supposedly lack such claims, namely non-white and non-Black (im)migrants and refugees, come last and lumped together. The acronym lends support to Summer Kim Lee's suggestion that Asian Americans "occupy the time of the after, the polite accommodating phrase 'after you.'"[45] As POC—and this is especially true on the minoritarian left—Asian American care needs are often considered only after the needs of those more impacted by the gratuitous violences of anti-Blackness and settler colonialism, which are framed as the conditions of possibility for the United States as such and for Asian America by extension. It may not be the case that theorists of anti-Blackness and settler colonialism are engaging in a heightened iteration of the oppression Olympics when advancing their exceptionalist claims, but it is nevertheless true that these theories help us to see why the impulse to play such games exists. For better and worse, it is through exceptional claims to suffering that finite social and material resources are so often secured, including the resource of racial care. Without this kind of claim and with its model minority reputation alive and well, the Asian American case amounts to little more than an afterthought in the US political imagination.[46]

This places Asian Americans in a double bind. A radical ethics of racial care in the Asian American case must contend with the claims to priority that theorists of anti-Blackness and settler colonialism have advanced. At a minimum, such claims communicate a profound and disproportionate experience of care need within Black and Indigenous worlds. The ontological assumption of interdependence on which care theory is based requires Asian Americans to be attentive and responsive to those needs in their situated, material manifestations. So does the relational ontology of Asian American racialization. And yet, while Asian Americans may, in individual cases and localized contexts, receive racial care in return, anti-Asian neglect means that such care is rarely motivated by a structurally determined ethical imperative. Asian Americans are unique in that the fantasy of their categorical privilege produces a certain ethico-political pressure for them to show up in solidarity with other oppressed racial groups.[47] But the same fantasy forecloses on an expectation of reciprocity when Asian Americans fall victim to racial violence. "Asians for X," but rarely the reverse.[48] To speak these dynamics aloud is not to engage in "what aboutism" nor even to lodge a request for more attention from other minoritized groups. Rather, my aim is to establish that anti-Asian neglect, that constant and enduring mode of anti-Asian violence, is as much a side-effect of anti-Blackness and settler colonialism as it is an effect of model minority racialization. I expand upon this claim in the later sections of this book. While tracking the ways that Asian Americans have engaged in relations of care with Indigenous artists and Black organizers, I suggest in my final chapter and conclusion that Asian Americans will not know life without racial neglect until after settler colonialism and anti-Blackness have been brought to their respective ends.

By contrast and echoing the histories of racial care articulated above, the early portions of this book tend to the ways in which neglected Asian Americans have taken care of themselves when no one else would. My first chapter finds a Chicago-based Filipina American artist performing self-care on the internet as a way to survive racism, fatphobia, and anti-trans/queer vitriol in community with others. My second chapter observes a Korean American teacher in Virginia tasked with providing racial care during office hours to her Korean American student when he cannot find it anywhere else. My third chapter attends to a musical mounted by a Texas-based theater ensemble to study the care passed between its queer Asian American characters in the forms of song, dance, and silence. Location matters here, as most Asian Americans (55 percent) live in only five states.[49] The rest are scattered across the country, many in places where anti-Asian neglect is exacerbated by racial and ethnic isolation and an accompanying inability to mount demographic arguments for material resources, cultural programming, and political recognition.

Additionally, even when there are other Asians around, there are no guarantees that racial proximity will lead to the provision of racial care. Whether as a concept or a coalition, Asian America is unstable and incoherent. The limits of the term are also limits on racial care in the Asian American case. In 2012, nearly two-thirds of Asians in the United States (62 percent) identified most strongly with their countries of familial origin, and only one-in-five identified strongly with Asian Americanness.[50] As Jay Caspian Kang writes, "[It is] hard to blame anyone for not caring enough about Asian Americans, because nobody—most of all Asian Americans—really believes that Asian America actually exists."[51] Moreover, issues related to language retention and linguistic diversity set Asian Americans apart from other minoritarian groups, which points to another reason why Asian Americans might struggle to receive racial care even from one another. In the Asian American case, racial care is often asked to traverse profound difference. It often requires certain cultural and linguistic proficiencies to achieve its desired effects. Then there are the many brutal histories of colonization and wars fought within Asia that continue to divide the Asian diaspora today, making it difficult for racial care to reach across ethnic and national differences. And all this impacts multiply marginalized Asian Americans the most. Such subjects experience compounded neglect, even as they are also exposed to misogyny, homophobia, transphobia, and ableism in addition to anti-Asian racism and xenophobia. All this is to say: Asian Americans, especially multiply marginalized Asian Americans, inhabit an unsustainable situation with respect to racial care. They are structurally neglected and at the same time burdened by that neglect with the labor of sustaining one another through psychosocial suffering. And still, such subjects have managed in specific cases to shift these circumstances by turning to performance and performative aesthetics.

The Aesthetic Performance of Racial Care

Performance is privileged in *Racial Care* because, as Amanda Stuart Fisher argues, "It is impossible to conceive of caring practice outside the parameters of how it is performed."[52] We cannot understand the doing of care, the labor of it, except by observing how it is embodied and enacted. We cannot understand the feeling of care, what it means to care about someone or something, unless we attend to how such affective attachments are made evident, or even anew, in quotidian and aesthetic performance. We need to be able to account for the performativity of care, the scripts of social reproduction within which minoritarian subjects are constantly navigating international, racial, gendered, and (dis)abled divisions of labor as well as the social norms and roles that these divisions smuggle into everyday life.[53] If we cannot understand care in these terms, then we are left ill-equipped to discuss imbalances and injustices in the field of racial caring relations. And if we cannot have these discussions, then we are less able to strategize to sustain minoritarian life. Care theory, therefore, needs performance studies: its methodological protocols; the tools it offers for engaging with embodiment, situatedness, and social interaction; its tactics for attending to the ephemeral and the fleeting; and most of all its belief in the aesthetic's ability to secure "More Life" for minoritarian subjects by soothing their psychosocial suffering.[54]

In the Asian American case, the patterns and textures of such suffering have been the subject of more than two decades of Asian Americanist affect theory. Scholars have written entire books about "racial melancholia," "national abjection," "racist love," "model minority masochism," and other forms of racial feeling that emerge from Asian American contexts.[55] Crafted from the paradigms of psychoanalysis, its own kind of care theory, these categories cast Asian American affective life as something that must be survived and endured. According to this discourse, Asians in the United States are abject. They are hated and eminently excludable. They are admired and yet always at a loss for belonging, and always on some level grieving that loss and the other losses that follow from it. They are also isolated, lonely, and often proximate to suicidal ideation—at least they are in this book. And all this is why *Racial Care* turns its attention to cultural production. Asian American artists and writers are everywhere attempting to address these neglected forms of unspectacular suffering through all manner of aesthetic means.

Much of the art and writing considered in this book aims to provide direct aid to Asian American subjects in need of racial care. The aesthetic interventions included in *Care Package* operate in this way. Wowsugi's guided meditation, for instance, provides its potential listeners with self-care instructions to follow should they wish to feel otherwise amid an atmosphere of exacerbated anti-Asian violence. "Between You and You," a poem read and written by Shame-Ali Nayeem and set to music by Qais Essar, speaks in the second person to transform solitude into something sustaining: "You found your reflection in the mud. You honored the way you loved, the way your heart broke, how life became living, became generative, regenerative, magic." In many ways, the strategies used in *Care Package* to attend to Asian American needs seem inspired by strategies used years earlier in a similar project titled *Open in Emergency*, a multimedia special issue of the *Asian American Literary Review* guest-edited by Mimi Khúc.

Like Care Package, *Open in Emergency* employed a range of writing, visual art, and "interactive mini-projects" to explore the "structures of care" through which Asian Americans survive psychosocial unwellness.[56] It was a kind of first aid kit and, like *Care Package*, a convincing counterargument to Tronto's assertion that "to create a work of art," or to engage in "creative activity," is not to engage in caring activity.[57]

The reality is that we often meet our psychosocial needs for racial care by engaging with aesthetic objects and creative works. We make songs into warm showers where we can cry in peace; we weave poems into handkerchiefs with which to wipe those tears; and we build plays into cradles where we might rest and feel held. These observations, in some ways, merely evoke the affinity for reparation within minoritarian performance studies, which can be traced back to Eve Sedgwick's preoccupation with "the many ways selves and communities succeed in extracting sustenance from the objects of a culture—even of a culture whose avowed desire has often been not to sustain them."[58] However, by formalizing reparative relations as caring relations, performance studies is better able to attend to the function of aesthetic work within the psychosocial field of need, responsibility, and obligation that I am here associating with racial care.

In this vein, the work of Kristina Wong is again instructive. On March 23, 2020, Wong created a Facebook group for friends and acquaintances who wanted to help fight the pandemic by constructing and distributing homemade masks. That Facebook group would give rise to a collective consisting mainly of Asian American women that would come to be known as the Auntie Sewing Squad. The name sought to honor aunties as caregiving figures whose contributions exceed the nuclear family even as they remain essential to all kinds of kinship formations.[59] The Auntie Sewing Squad's task was simple: to provide what the state had failed to provide and to do so for those most vulnerable to the effects of the pandemic. The group was a model of mutual aid rooted in a crip queer Asian diasporic feminism—explicitly politicized, anti-capitalist, anti-heteropatriarchal, radically relational, and deeply devoted to the solidaristic performance of racial care.

The group was also the centerpiece of a solo performance that Wong would perform at the New York Theatre Workshop between October 25, 2021, and November 21, 2021. An eventual finalist for the Pulitzer Prize in drama, *Sweatshop Overlord* was something of a first draft of COVID-era history. The show, directed by Chay Yew, follows Wong and the Auntie Sewing Squad as they do the work of racial care not only amid pandemic conditions but amid the many crises of the long 2020: the murder of George Floyd, the uprisings that followed, the death of Ruth Bader Ginsburg, the death of legendary Asian American photographer Corky Lee from COVID-19, the January 6 insurrection, and more. Through it all,

Wong is dressed as something like a sewing soldier armed with scissors, thread, pins, elastic, and the like. She performs on a set that feels makeshift, a visual representation of her personal sewing space made mostly of yarn, masks, and similar materials. Surrounded by these soft symbols of feminized labor, Wong frames the pandemic as a war and mask-making as an essential element of the war effort. And if Wong and the rest of the Auntie Sewing Squad waged war against COVID-19 transmission in anti-Asian times, *Sweatshop Overlord* extended that effort as a contribution to the ongoing culture wars being waged over racial care.

Like *Care Package*, *Sweatshop Overlord* offered its audiences an affective experience of direct psychosocial aid. For me and for many others, the show marked a first return to the theater after many months of isolation, avoidance, and COVID-anxiety. It mattered very much that the theater required masks and proof of vaccination, but it also mattered that the show was explicitly about masks and mask-making. The production participated in a then-waning ethos of care in pandemic times, and it did so while helping its audiences process together the many traumas they had all experienced separately. In this way, the solo performance became a collective occasion for healing. And because the show so centered Asian American feminism, it also transformed the New York Theatre Workshop into what in my second chapter I term a *racialized holding environment*, an affective architecture assembled from the stuff of racial care to combat the effects of anti-Asian neglect.

Moreover, by performing (showing doing) on stage the invisibilized labor performed (doing) by the Auntie Sewing Squad, *Sweatshop Overlord* was able both to make legible existing needs for racial care and to model the replicable relations of racial care the group engaged in to meet those needs. Over the course of their real-world mutual aid effort, the Auntie Sewing Squad sent masks to "asylum seekers, Indigenous communities on reservations, people newly released on parole, transgender immigrants, urban farming coop members, trafficking victims, and low-income BIPOC communities."[60] And over the course of *Sweatshop Overlord*, Wong names many of these constituencies explicitly, raising her audiences' awareness of structural disparities and the exacerbated need for care produced by them. Additionally, while spotlighting these outward-facing relations of racial care, the show also foregrounded the lateral and inward-facing relations of care that existed among the Auntie Sewing Squad's members. Wong speaks, for instance, of a system of "Auntie Care," which began as an internal pizza fund and grew into a community care effort. Shannon Jackson has argued that socially engaged performances like Wong's are especially valuable because they lay bare the relations of care that are the conditions of possibility for their own existence. *Sweatshop Overlord* lends itself to this sort of "revelation of interdependent support" precisely because it was born out of the lived reality of such support in pandemic times.⁶¹ It is a one-woman show that defies the fantasy of individual accomplishment in favor of a radical rendering of mutual aid that both exposes unmet needs for racial care and offers relational models through which to meet those needs ethically. In this way, Wong makes use of the unique capacities of live performance to shift arrangements of racial care toward an anti-colonial, interracial, and intraracial impulse for solidarity.

The end of *Sweatshop Overlord* finds Wong at an outdoor celebration alongside many of the aunties she has been working with throughout the pandemic. At this point in the 2020 timeline, vaccine distribution has begun in the United States, and the supply of masks is finally able to meet demand. The aunties' work is over, and Wong delivers a speech to mark the occasion. In the world of the play, she speaks to the aunties in attendance, but in the world of the theater, she speaks to the audience:

> You are my family of would-be strangers. Alone in our homes we were not essential, but we became essential for each other's survival.... We attempted to fight the odds for the love of people we will never know. Friends. We have survived until this moment. Who are the people who helped you survive this? What do you hope for as we move forward? Will you be generous in more than times of crisis?

These lines, which strategically speak in both the second person and the first-person plural, attempt to hail the audience as members of the Auntie Sewing Squad. They usher the audience into a care ethical imaginary by using the co-presence of the moment to implicate them in the web of solidaristic racial caring relations that constitute the very substance of the show.

In sum, the provision of direct affective aid; the exposure of unmet need; the representation of racial caring relations; the implication of audiences within those relations: each of these is a contribution that aesthetic performances and performative aesthetics can make to the struggle over racial care. They are evident to varying degrees not only in *Sweatshop Overlord* but also in *Wong Flew over the Cuckoo's Nest, Care Package,* and the range of work discussed across *Racial Care*. Each of the artists under examination in this book deploys the aesthetic as a material force with the capacity to bring about the ethical impulses of attentiveness and responsibility in potential providers of racial care. Aesthetic works are uniquely able to elicit our attention and point it toward unaddressed racial care needs. They also gain access to our psyches through our senses, and there they can stir up new feelings of investment in persons and communities once foreign to the imagination.

The poems and visual artwork I analyze in this book function in this way, in a register of queer performativity. They are queer because the work is created by queers for queers and because the work aims to redistribute attention and attachment toward neglected, nonnormative subjects. They are works that seek to intervene at the level of what Kandice Chuh calls "sensibility," which refers to both "what is held to be reasonable and what is viscerally experienced."[62] They attempt to induce a reader or viewer to care about and for subjects, objects, and issues they may not have previously.

The plays and films that I analyze in what follows function similarly. As collaborative and time-based media, they are also uniquely able, as *Sweatshop Overlord* demonstrates, to depict the provision and reception of quotidian racial care. Plays and films model embodied, durational relations that might then be studied and scrutinized in the light cast by a minoritarian care ethics. In this light we are tasked with determining which aspects of a given relation of racial care we might wish to adjust, which we would reject outright, and which we would like to adopt in our lived realities. This is all to say that aesthetic encounters can lead us to act differently. We might adjust our use of language, learn what not to say or do, and even develop the capacity to intervene in scenes or infrastructures of racial harm. We might learn to perform racial care otherwise and even better.

Additionally, while artists and organizers are care theorists in their own right, scholars of caring performance have their own roles to play in the struggle at hand. In addition to enacting and representing racial care through their writing, it is the scholar's task to search social reality and the aesthetic realm for racial care's incipient or invisibilized forms. To delineate a new form of care is to sketch the mental blueprint for a replicable arrangement of caring relation, or a pattern of caring performance, that has taken discrete shape in response to a specific need or set of needs.[63] Throughout this book, I will demonstrate that as-yet undescribed forms of racial care are modeled, transmitted, and proliferated through aesthetic forms. In this, I follow the example set by Leah Lakshmi Piepzna-Samarasinha's delineation of the social form she calls the "care web" in her book *Care Work: Dreaming Disability Justice*.[64] A care web, Piepzna-Samarasinha tells us, emerges when a group of people, often sick or disabled, comes together to provide one another with life-sustaining support without relying on the state, the family form, or paid attendants. Part of the reason the care web is such an exemplary form of care is in how it upholds the values of interdependence and coalition that lie at the heart of this book's relational politics, even as it always entails the risk of backsliding into unfairness, resentments, and other vexed realities of everyday caring relation. The thing about care webs is that they can be studied and, ultimately, replicated by anyone who needs what they afford. Each one offers a template or set of protocols, a form according to which we might arrange and enact more just caring relations.

Each of this book's chapters puts forth a form of racial care that has thus far eluded description, and I have ordered these chapters according to the relational scale at which their most central forms are performed. *Racial Care* begins with the study of the care of the self, and its final chapter focuses on care in the ecological context of global climate catastrophe. In between, I analyze the caring relation that emerges between a pair of individuals, a teacher and her student, and I follow that analysis with another about the collective care that can connect members of an ensemble cast. The arc of the book is organized in this way, according to a logic of ascending scale, because its chapters are meant to relate to one another as concentric circles. In order to speak about care at a planetary scale, one must first be able to think capaciously about self, interpersonal, and collective care. The problem of self-care persists inside the problem of care between two people, which persists inside the problem of collective care, which persists inside the problem of planetary care. This is partly because the crises that bring about the need for self-care remain relevant within the institutional and national crises that bring about the need for collective care, and so on. In other words, by organizing my chapters as I have, I am mounting a formal argument that winning a just arrangement of racial caring relations will require us to think and act nimbly across these scalar registers. The result is a complex and cumulative, rather than merely additive, approach to the study of racial care.

Chapter 1, "Revolting Self-Care," is at once a defense of self-care and an attempt to reimagine the concept so that it is no longer considered the antithesis to collective forms of racial care but rather an essential aspect of them. At the center of the chapter is a deep engagement with the trans/queer Filipina artist Mark Aguhar, specifically the aesthetic work she posted to the social media site Tumblr, where she blogged under the handle Call Out Queen. By framing Aguhar's online aesthetic performance as an act of what Michel Foucault calls "the care of the self," I seek in this chapter to outline a less individualizing performance of self-care for minoritarian subjects. Specifically, I use the term *revolting self-care* to give name to a process by which minoritarian subjects might obliterate their identification with and desire for those who are conventionally deemed worthy of care in order to reorient their capacities for racial care toward more oppressed others. And through a reading of Kimberly Alidio's poetic appraisal of Mark Aguhar's online aesthetics of existence, my first chapter argues further that the performance of revolting self-care, aided as it is by networked social media, also has the potential to generate collective online contexts in which isolated minoritarian subjects might find sustenance. Aguhar's multiply marginalized position in the social allows me to show how issues of racial care are all tangled up in issues of gendered embodiment, sexual desire, and psychosocial debilitation. Thus, my minoritarian approach to Asian American racial care is most thoroughly established in this first chapter.

My middle two chapters shift the focus of *Racial Care* from the care of the self to performances of collective care conducted at two scales: the dyad and the ensemble. If chapter 1's study of revolting self-care reveals how Asian Americans might reorient their racial care away from the privileged to the oppressed, my second and third chapters reveal what happens when racial care is passed, both successfully and unsuccessfully, among Asian American subjects in more social circumstances. In chapter 2, "The Racialized Holding Environment," I offer a close reading of Julia Cho's *Office Hour*, a play based on the events that led up to the Virginia Tech massacre of 2007. *Office Hour* focuses on a Korean American adjunct instructor named Gina and the regular meetings she has in her office with a Korean American student named Dennis, the play's stand-in for the Virginia Tech shooter. By analyzing the racial care that Gina performs for her student alongside the institutional conditions that oblige her to do so, this second chapter outlines "the racialized holding environment" as a dyadic form of racial care calibrated for both the pedagogical context of academic office hours and the creative context of the theatrical encounter. I adapt this concept from the psychoanalyst D. W. Winnicott's theory of the "holding environment"—that affective architecture actuated for the infant by the mother through a good-enough performance of care—so that it might be more attentive to race relations and the psychosocial suffering that they often induce for Asian Americans.

Chapter 3, "Racial Emotional Labor," expands my second chapter's consideration of collective racial care by scaling up in two ways. Whereas chapter 2 analyzed care between two people, chapter 3 analyzes care as it can occur among an ensemble of Asian American actors. And whereas chapter 2 remained within the institutional context of the neoliberal university, chapter 3 investigates how the state and national norms produce certain needs and obligations related to racial care for Asian American subjects. To do this, the chapter juxtaposes two Asian American afterlives of Gilbert and Sullivan's racist opera, *The Mikado*. Through an analysis of my own experience as an ensemble member in *The Mikado*, I develop a theory of racial emotional labor, an obligatory form of care performed by the Asian American subject for fragile white subjects in order to avoid the violence that often follows when whiteness is forced to confront its racial culpabilities. And through an analysis of the Austin-based Generic Ensemble Company's *The Mikado: Reclaimed*, a theatrical response to Gilbert and Sullivan's original opera devised by an entirely Asian American ensemble,

I suggest that the mandate to perform racial emotional labor is not just about maintaining the fantasy of white racial innocence on an interpersonal scale. Instead, I show that in certain cases it can be about maintaining the fantasy of national innocence as well. Whereas most forms of racial care described in this book are aimed primarily at sustaining Asian American life, racial emotional labor emerges as a form of care that functions, first and foremost, to constrain Asian American life—and to do so at multiple scales of relation. The solution on offer to this problem, the second form of care at the center of this chapter, is the minoritarian team, which is given in and as a collaborative effort to rehearse alternative social protocols better suited to multiply marginalized social actors.

Taken together, my second and third chapters reveal the unique capacities of Asian American theater to affect and effect relations of racial care. Both chapters are organized around plays whose primary action finds Asian Americans acting under duress to keep themselves alive. These productions are useful for my purposes not just because they model racial care but because in doing so they mount, in Diana Taylor's words, "vital acts of transfer" in live social space.[65] In this, theatrical performances both draw on and deepen the repertoire of racial care, allowing racial care's needed forms to proliferate and permeate the register of everyday activity where they might be repeated and, in this repetition, imperfectly preserved in perpetuity. Previous studies of care in performance have emphasized the unique capacities of social practice art and applied theater to both reveal and engender sustaining infrastructures of caring relation.[66] I extend this work to argue, in my second chapter, that Asian American theatrical productions and the theater spaces they claim can function as holding environments, as respites for Asian American spectators in need of social shelter. And with a nod toward the essentially collaborative nature of theater, my third chapter argues further that the collective context of theatrical rehearsal can be a vibrant site within which to imagine and practice relations of racial care anew. As Maurice Hamington argues, "Caring skills can be exercised and honed, just as actors improve their skills."[67] Asian American theater has a central place in this book because its social and aesthetic affordances are unique in their potential to aid in the project of sustaining minoritarian life.

And yet, each of my first three chapters ends in death. The forms of racial care covered in these chapters are all attempts to compensate for the attrition Asian Americans experience as the cost of living an abject life, and they all ultimately fail—that is, if one is wont to count premature death as a failure of psychosocial reproduction. The people who populate the first three chapters of this book are all killed: by the state, by negligent institutions, by one another, and by suicide.

My fourth and final chapter, "Dehumanist Care," argues that in order to establish relations of racial care capable of sustaining Asian American life, we need to stretch the collective forms of care articulated in my first three chapters toward something that we might, following Julietta Singh, call "dehumanist" inasmuch as it opposes sovereign mastery in all its colonial and human exceptionalist forms. The chapter begins with a close reading of Snow and Yan's film *Afterearth* in order to adapt Melanie Klein's theory of "reparation" for an ethico-politics of care that decenters the human while prioritizing the decolonial. I assemble this dehumanist ethico-politics from the insights of Indigenous studies as well as from the work of scholars like Singh and Maria Puig de la Bellacasa. After my reading of *Afterearth*, the chapter continues by considering Snow's work on the death of the honey bee. This reading contends that the aesthetic enactments of racial care advanced by Snow's poetry and illustrations have the performative power to shift our senses toward a more just distribution of racial care, one that would require the human to give in to dehumanist grief, which is also to say decolonial coalition with nonhuman kin.

This final chapter is followed by a conclusion that shifts *Racial Care*'s focus from the aesthetic realm to the stuff of social movements. Specifically, the conclusion analyzes the caring solidarities that appear in the protest activity of Freedom Inc., a Southeast Asian, Black, and LGBTQIA+ organization fighting for abolition and gender justice in Madison, Wisconsin. Building on my final chapter's consideration of the responsibilities related to care that Asian Americans bear in relation to Indigenous peoples and epistemologies, this last section of my book considers the difference anti-Blackness makes to an Asian Americanist approach to racial care. Thus, to close this book with a path toward Asian and Black caring coalition, this conclusion gestures toward an abolitionist horizon for racial caring relations.

Relations of racial care can often feel intractably structured to dim the light of minoritarian life, but my move in this book is to insist that they can be imagined and inhabited otherwise. In the end, there are no legal remedies that would solve the problem of racial care for good. And even if we were to wake up under "communist social reproduction" tomorrow, its survival would still depend on our ability to navigate relations of racial care as ethically as possible.[68] As Marx said, "From each according to [their] ability, to each according to [their] need."[69] So much about our current arrangement of racial caring relations is sustained almost ineffably in social and cultural life, in the registers of ideology, affect, attachment, and sensibility. So much is lived out, without scrutiny, as the inevitable unfolding of normative social competition and political disappointment. As long as white supremacy, anti-Blackness, settler colonialism, and capitalism continue to structure psychosocial life, as long as cisheteropatriarchal violence and systemic debilitation are unevenly distributed along racial lines, racial care will persist as a perennial problem both for those who need it and for those who have little choice but to provide it to others.

My claim is that Asian Americans can and have altered relations of racial care for the better by seeking recourse, across scales of existence, to both minoritarian aesthetics and to movement organizing. There is no guarantee that these strategies will save us, but we know that we will not make it to a concrete utopia—and many of us will not make it to tomorrow—unless we pursue them. As Grace Lee Boggs puts it in the epigraph that opened this introduction, "The only way to survive is by taking care of one another, by recreating our relationships to one another."[70] The task before us is to take up the tools we have at our disposal and to cultivate infrastructures for racial care rooted in mutual aid and mutual defense. The aesthetic can assist us in this task if we wield it like a weapon in the racial care culture wars, mobilizing affect in order to mobilize more racial care and new forms of racial care for neglected Asian Americans and other minoritarian subjects. This work will not be easy, but it is our ethical and political obligation as interdependent beings trapped on a crisis-ridden planet. Racial care is what we must perform for one another when the world wears us down to hold itself up. And so, at the end of the world, we begin.

I

Revolting Self-Care

These are the axes:

1
Bodies are inherently valid

2
Remember death

3
Be ugly

4
Know beauty

5
It is complicated

6
Empathy

7
Choice

8
Reconstruct, reify

9
Respect, negotiate
—MARK AGUHAR

I still remember how I felt after reading Mark Aguhar's axes for the first time. Recognition and validation gave way to inspiration and aspiration—it was literally easier to draw breath. Here were nine principles about which a better world might turn: axes. Or else, here were nine rhetorical weapons, tools with which to chop, hack, or cut through the arborescent: axes. Here were words to live by, sacred script and profane scripture, gifted by a queer and transfeminine Filipino American who relished in her fatness and her fire. Whenever I have shown Aguhar's axes to friends and strangers, I have noticed a similar shift in them, a release into a trans/queer of color communitas too infrequently felt. The axes teach us many things. Among them, this: Mark Aguhar was an artist who had a way of making the world feel survivable for those who were never meant to survive.[1]

I first encountered Aguhar on Tumblr, the microblogging platform and social media site founded in 2007. Tumblr was a special place back then. Most of its early users were young, between the ages of fifteen and thirty-four. And, as scholars have shown, these youths turned the site into fertile ground for the advancement of "black feminist theory, LGBTQ+/nonbinary identity formation, disability and chronic pain collectivities, critical media culture, and alternative body erotics and porn."[2] As the United States entered the Obama-era with its centrist pragmatism, neoliberal multiculturalism, and white supremacist revanchism, it also entered what the *New York Times* would eventually call "the age of Tumblr activism." This was a moment marked by a growing minoritarian consciousness and counterculture, a moment that cannot be adequately understood absent an analysis of Mark Aguhar and her artwork.

Aguhar entered Tumblr in 2010 with a blog initially titled, "notheretomakefriends." Operating under the handle Call Out Queen, she used the site as an online performance and gallery space. Tumblr distinguished itself from the other microblogging and social media platforms of its time by enabling users to post images, animated GIFs, videos, and text-only posts. These affordances were what allowed Aguhar's multimedia art practice to take center stage on the site. To scroll through Aguhar's blog was, and still is, to scroll past images of highly sexual watercolor paintings, textile-patterned illustrations, BDSM-style sculptures made from rope, video-based performances, and text-based works like "The Axes." Many of these creations circulated widely thanks to Tumblr's innovative "reblog" function, which predated the streamlining of Twitter's "retweet" function and allowed users to republish others' posts on their own blogs for their own followers. Much of this chapter's work will be to close read Aguhar's Tumblr-based art for insights into its capacity to provide cultural nourishment to multiply marginalized Asian Americans and other minoritarian subjects.

But a close reading like this cannot be done without attending to the way Aguhar's blog served not just as a display case for her artwork but also as an archive of her everyday life experiences. Aguhar's artist statement describes her work as "a continuous exploration of queer expression and what it means to have grown up gay on the internet." So if one wishes to understand Aguhar's online art practice, one must do so in relation to her more quotidian contributions to minoritarian culture. These contributions include the countless selfies that appear on her blog, filled as they are with body affirmation and stylish experimentation. They also include the many minor musings she posted about identity, desire, power, popular culture, her artistic influences, and her theoretical inspirations. Across her blog, Aguhar invokes artists like Wu Tsang, Juliana Huxtable, Ryan Trecartin, and Nick Cave. The thinkers she cites include Michel Foucault, Judith Butler, José Esteban Muñoz, and Richard Fung. She also shares details of an even more personal nature to her blog. Some focus on her friendships and her family. Others highlight her time spent living in Houston and then Chicago, where she pursued her MFA in Studio Arts. Still others expose Aguhar's very real struggle to endure the harshness of a world unable to appreciate all that she was, a struggle she often carried out through aesthetic means.

This book lays bare the existence of something called *racial care*, which includes everything we do to sustain racialized subjects through whatever suffering may converge on their particular location within the white supremacist, anti-Black, and settler colonial capitalist order of the United States. Quotidian performances of racial care can assume any number of forms: a listening ear, a hand to hold, a brave intervention enacted within a scene of racial violence. I argue that Asian American racialization results in both a heightened need for racial care and the neglect of that need by others. But I also suggest that Asian American subjects have compensated for their racial care deficit through art. Multiply marginalized Asian American artists, especially, are everywhere employing aesthetic strategies both to soothe their psychosocial suffering and to unsettle the widely held attachments and ideologies that preserve inequalities of racial care.

Mark Aguhar is a case in point. Much of what can be found on Aguhar's Tumblr blog documents her disproportionate experience of psychosocial violence and neglect. She is the target of verbal harassment. She is dismissed as undesirable. And these slights so often reek of the now clichéd refrain "no fats, no femmes, no Asians." This chapter studies how Aguhar endured all this online, in public, and with artistic creativity. It does so to expose how racialized hierarchies of desirability produce inequalities of care that cannot be understood apart from gender, sexuality, and body size. My argument, ultimately, is that Aguhar's Tumblr-based aesthetic performance models a yet-undescribed form of self-care, one with the potential both to sustain minoritarian life and to alter normative arrangements of racial caring relation.

The contemporary conversation about self-care typically takes the form of an argument with two sides. On one side, there are those who believe that self-care is a selfish performance of neoliberal individualism dedicated only to meeting one's own needs and pursuing one's own ambitions.[3] For many of its detractors, self-care amounts to little more than a consumerist, middle-class rejection of one's responsibility to the collective.[4] On the other side of this debate, though, there are many who believe that self-care can serve a radical political project.[5] This camp aligns with Audre Lorde's oft-cited quotation on the subject: "Caring for myself is not self-indulgence, it is self-preservation and that is an act of political warfare."[6] As Jina B. Kim and Sami Schalk remind us, because Lorde wrote these words as she waged a losing battle with cancer, they might usefully be reconsidered through the lens of crip of color critique. Doing so, Kim and Schalk argue, can help us glimpse a vision of self-care that is less individualist than "socially reproductive, productive of both a social field and a viable future and time for socially dispossessed populations."[7]

My analysis of Aguhar's performance of self-care builds upon this foundation established by Lorde, Kim, and Schalk, even as it draws its primary inspiration from another theorist of the concept. Michel Foucault frames the care of the self as "an exercise of the self on the self by which one attempts to develop and transform oneself, and to attain to a certain mode of being."[8] He draws this view from Greco-Roman antiquity and elaborates upon it in an interview titled, "The Ethics of the Concern for Self as a Practice of Freedom":

> Among the Greeks and the Romans—especially the Greeks—concern with the self and care for the self were required for right conduct and the proper practice of freedom, in order to know oneself [*se connaître*]—the familiar aspect of the *Gnothi sauton*—as well as to form oneself, to surpass oneself, to master the appetites that threaten to overwhelm one.[9]

Within this Foucauldian framework, the care of the self is best understood as a durational performance through which one can cultivate a critical attunement to one's own position within ever-changing power relations, including relations of racial care and neglect. It is an exercise of the self on the self that enables one to better conduct oneself, practice freedom, and pursue pleasure—erotic and otherwise—ethically in relation to others, for others.[10]

In casting Mark Aguhar as a practitioner of Foucauldian self-care, I aim to expand upon the work Muñoz has done to recalibrate the concept for modern-day minoritarian subjects. In *Disidentifications* and in pursuit of "a minoritarian ethics of self," Muñoz brings a Foucauldian framework to bear on the ways that Pedro Zamora cared for himself as an HIV-positive queer person of color while on MTV's *The Real World*, emphasizing "the ways in which representations of and (simultaneously) by [the minoritarian] self signal new spaces within the social."[11] Muñoz is writing about the way Zamora's televised self-care made the practice seem possible to onlookers. Aguhar's public performances of self-care carry a similar potential, but it matters that they are transmitted online rather than on television. While both Tumblr and television promise experiences of what Karen Tongson calls "remote intimacy," networked social media affords immediate access to a sociality unyielded by broadcast media.[12] Simply put, representations of and simultaneously by the minoritarian self are more frequent and available online, making new spaces within the social all the more abundant and accessible.

The next section of this chapter reads Aguhar through Foucault to propose that the aesthetic projects Aguhar posted to social media acted in service to a form of racial care that I term *revolting self-care*. Revolting self-care is an exercise on the self by the self that seeks to shift attention and attachments—one's own and others'—from the usual objects of racial care to more neglected alternatives. It is a two-pronged tactic for rearranging racial caring relations: disaffirm the desirable, affirm the ignored. Attending to the whole of Aguhar's blog, I first address the preoccupation with white male objects of desire that characterizes the blog's earlier pages. Then I take a wider view to track the various ordinary and aesthetic strategies through which Aguhar dismisses whiteness, masculinity, thinness, and all things hegemonic to instead uplift Asianness, brownness, femininity, and fatness for herself and others. After laying bare the mechanics of revolting self-care, the chapter's next section offers a close reading of Aguhar's "Litanies to My Heavenly Brown Body" to suggest that her public performance of revolting self-care makes manifest a virtual site of separatist respite for those historically neglected within hierarchies of desirability. This leads me, in the chapter's penultimate section, to offer a close reading of Kimberly Alidio's poem titled "All the Pinays are straight, all the queers are Pinoy, but some of us." One reason I take up Alidio's poem is that it situates Aguhar squarely within a Filipino frame. Another reason is that doing so illustrates how Aguhar's enactments of revolting self-care challenge the common-sense assumption that self-care and collective care are opposite or even antithetical performances.

My intention in all of this is not to idealize Aguhar. Nor is it only to uplift her as an invaluable model of minoritarian self-care. To do her honest justice I must also tarry with the aggression and ambivalence that is evident throughout Aguhar's oeuvre. And I must address her untimely loss as well. In March of 2012, at the age of twenty-four, the Call Out Queen, Mark Aguhar, took her own life. She was survived by her parents, her brother, her friends, and many others. We are still grieving the sudden loss of a queen, a loss that threatens always to leave us at a loss for words and a way forward. So many of this book's central figures die premature deaths, many of them by suicide. The final section of this chapter reckons with this reality in Aguhar's case. In the end, what is promised here is less a totalizing account of Aguhar's life or work than a humble reckoning with her dying and the strategies she utilized throughout her life to keep that death at bay, strategies that might be taken up as arms in the ongoing culture war over racial care.

Revolting Self-Care

Images of white men are scattered across the early pages of Aguhar's blog. White men kiss, they fist, they smoke, they drink, they stare into each other's eyes. One, wearing a shirt but no pants, sits on a couch and jerks off into his own mouth. Aguhar's caption reads: "this is perfect." Some of these images appear to be stills from pornographic videos. Most of the images are reblogs, not Aguhar's own creations but images she chose to reproduce on her page. Taken together, they highlight the preoccupation with white men that characterizes Aguhar's early blog. The images expose a certain attachment and attraction to white masculinity, a desire for it.

Such a desire is also evident in another set of photos both taken and posted by Aguhar to her blog in its early days. These photos are of white men wrapped by Aguhar in bondage rope. They capture the men, friends of Aguhar's, caught within the bounds of her will. Their hands are tied to their sides, behind their backs, and otherwise. On the one hand, each of these photos can be seen as an aesthetic enactment of the care of the self insofar as each tangles with Aguhar's desire for white masculinity so that, echoing Foucault, these appetites might not overwhelm her. On the other hand, these works stop short of striving for that desire's undoing. Loyal to the spirit of S&M, the ropes in the photographs function both as constraints and as erotic adornments. By submitting these men to her own aesthetic and sexual proclivities, Aguhar, in a way, submits herself to them in turn. And this view is fortified by the fact that these photos are of Aguhar's process, they are not themselves the finished art object. Aguhar would ultimately remove the men from their bondage but leave the rope sculptures intact, their knotted patterns telling the stories of the people they once held. Eventually she would display the rope sculptures on gallery walls, and there they would evoke the person they once bound. They would become monuments to the absent presence of a white masculinity around which Aguhar literally shaped her art practice.

Two of Aguhar's ink and watercolor paintings also take up her attachment to white masculinity. Their titles are characteristically provocative: *IF UR GAY I WANT 2 FUCK U* and *EVEN IF UR STR8 I STILL WANT 2 FUCK U 2* (see figures 1.1 and 1.2). Though neither piece appears in the early pages of Aguhar's blog, both are worth analyzing here as illustrations of Aguhar's multimedia engagement with her own upwardly distributed erotic attachments. Each of the two paintings juxtaposes Aguhar's body with a seemingly undifferentiated mass of (mostly) white men wearing white briefs. While in *IF UR GAY I WANT 2 FUCK U*, Aguhar is seated in lotus pose above the men, in *EVEN IF UR STR8 I STILL WANT 2 FUCK U 2*, she lies on her back beneath the men who all stand upright in a grid. Roy Pérez, a friend of Aguhar's and a leading scholar of her work, suggests that in these images, "by diagramming this erotic field[,] Aguhar draws a queer heuristic for owning, learning, and unlearning desire."[13]

To this observation we might add some others about the differing intensities at which these two paintings operate. Because of Aguhar's seated position at the top of the image, *IF UR GAY I WANT 2 FUCK U* suggests a somewhat measured negotiation of sexual desire. Everyone is in their tighty-whities, but they have other differences made all the more significant by Aguhar's use of watercolors, which traffics not in realist renderings but in relatively simplified figures differentiated only by telling details. They are not all facing the same direction. Hair color and patterns vary. Some expose their insecurities by concealing their bodies. One uses a wheelchair. Though Aguhar sits singularly atop the image while everyone around her stands, this arrangement of bodies seems to desexualize her. She looks more like a spiritual adviser than an object of desire, and perhaps this is her point. She is larger than life and yet she is neglected, unnoticed by the more normative figures in the frame. By contrast, *IF UR STR8 I STILL WANT 2 FUCK U 2* depicts Aguhar's "view from the bottom," to invoke the title of Nguyen Tan Hoang's study of Asian American sexual representation.[14] Aguhar is lying down, looking up at a hoard of heterosexual men who do not return her gaze. She is neglected by them, below them, and yet seemingly ready to bottom for them. The suggestion here is that Aguhar's sexual desires for straight men differ in aim and intensity from those she experiences in relation to gay men. It is almost as if white masculinity demands more from her—more attention, attachment, desire, submission, and so on—the whiter and more masculine it appears to be.

Things began to change, though, with a post from January 2011 titled, "TL;DR" or "Too Long, Didn't Read," in which Aguhar issues a new mission statement

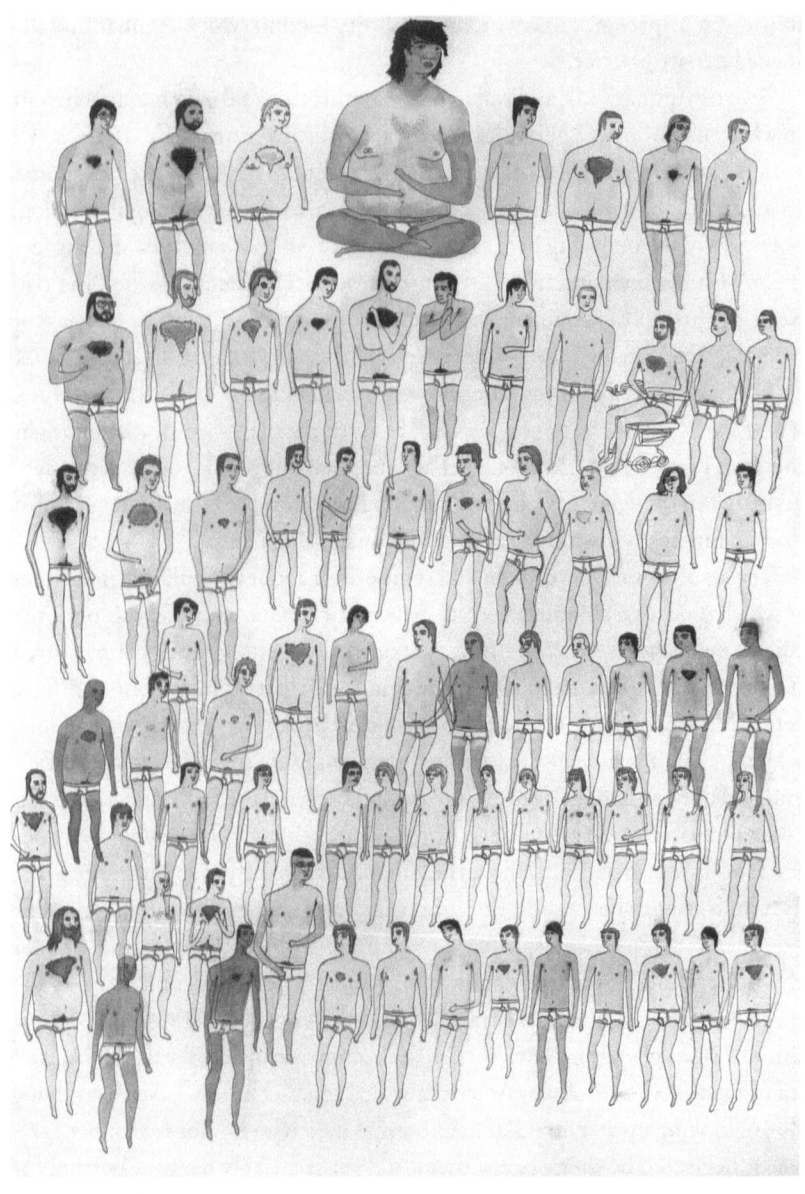

FIGURE 1.1. Mark Aguhar, *IF UR GAY I WANT 2 FUCK U* (2010). Courtesy of the Estate of Mark Aguhar.

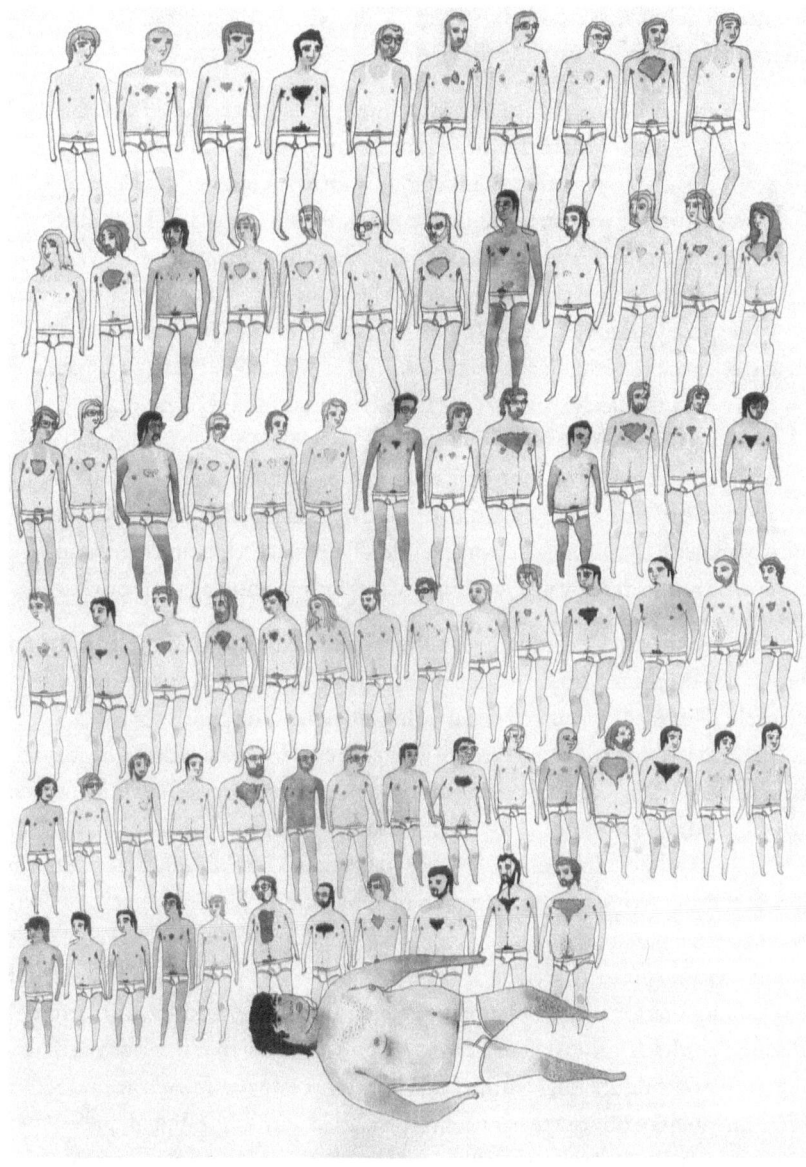

FIGURE 1.2. Mark Aguhar, *EVEN IF UR STR8 I STILL WANT 2 FUCK U 2* (2010). Courtesy of the Estate of Mark Aguhar.

for her blog, one that decidedly departed from the aesthetic strategies for dealing with desire that I just described.

> My blog has become for me a highly intentional space, and I hope that I can somehow translate the intentionality of my blog into my artwork. It really does worry me that so much of my artwork is based on gay males, when actually I feel alienated from most gay male space, and I talk about feminism but my artwork only contains a handful of female bodies.... It's not enough to say you're inclusive in the spaces you create when in fact your space is occupied mostly by white cis-male gays. If you want to create a safe space (or something approaching a safe space because safe spaces don't exist in reality) then you need to be intentional about it...
>
> I'm going to make it my goal to make my work entirely intentional in who I depict and how. I'm going to keep blogging about queers from just about every part of the spectrum other than mainstream attractive white gay males... [white gay cis-males] don't need me to help them, and I don't need to destroy my own sense of self by reproducing their privilege.

"TL;DR" approaches a Foucauldian performance of the care of the self on altered terms. It is motivated by the feeling that an erotic field can and must also be seen as a field of unevenly arranged racial caring relations. The politics of sexual desirability and relations of racial care are always deeply intertwined. Caring capacities are everywhere conscripted in service to normatively desirable white bodies, which are often also thin, able-bodied, neurotypical, and within certain queer worlds, masculine.[15] Indeed, the less one is able to successfully inhabit or perform any of these co-constituting categories of convention, the more uncertain one's access to intimate relations of care may be, racial or otherwise. "TL;DR" finds Aguhar coming into awareness of these dynamics. The post marks a new effort to challenge various forms of erotic neglect (anti-Asian, anti-fat, anti-femme) through aesthetic means. It also evinces Aguhar's sense that a performative reiteration of her desire for, identification with, and valorization of the normative ideal threatens to obliterate her when (re)enacted within the digital space of her self-presentation and self-preservation. Her subsequent choice to dismiss white masculinity and to proliferate images of conventionally undesirable queers of color on her blog should therefore be understood as a counteridentificatory self-making, worldmaking, and caretaking endeavor.

"BLOGGING FOR BROWN GURLS." Aguhar would post these words in May 2011. The statement would become the new title of her blog and serve as shorthand for the mission outlined in "TL;DR," a curatorial mission exemplary of the performance I am calling revolting self-care. To reiterate, revolting self-care is the social form of racial care that is forged when the deprioritization of the privileged is paired with minoritarian valorization. It is a performative practice that seeks to destroy and transform one's own and others' identifications with and desire for normative ideality. In this way, it is a strategy for loosening one's attachments and overcoming what Lauren Berlant calls "cruel optimism," a relation in which one's object of desire is an obstacle to one's flourishing.[16] The ethical and political promise of such an effort lies in the redistribution of the nourishing and erotic impacts of representation, desirability, and care from the elite elsewhere to those marked for neglect and death as a result of their failure to approximate normative ideals. And, crucially, revolting self-care is nothing like neoliberal individualism. Aguhar's mission statement's insistence that white men do not need her to help them implies that her care of the self is also a care for other Others, an assistive aesthetic intervention that is notably and necessarily durational, an ongoing performance of self-critical self-sustainment.

One reason I apply the category of the revolting to Aguhar's performance of self-care is to account for her revolt against normative ideality through critical counteridentificatory tactics such as destruction, disaffirmation, deflation, and dismissal. From a Foucauldian perspective, Aguhar's performance of self-care can be viewed as a "revolt of conduct."[17] Foucault defines a revolt of conduct as a movement that "seeks to escape direction by others and to define the way for each to conduct himself."[18] We can begin to attend to Aguhar's attempts at this sort of escape and redefinition by accounting for the handle she used on Tumblr: Call Out Queen.[19]

For Pérez, Aguhar's reign as Call Out Queen is best encapsulated in her enactment of "critical flippancy," which can be glimpsed in the way she responded to the many antagonistic messages she received through her blog.[20] For example, an anonymous hater sent her a private message, "You look like a whale, ok?," to which Aguhar responded, "U LOOK LYK A WHALE OK." Aguhar's capital lettering and creative misspelling mock her accuser while assuming a loud and proud posture for her allies. She performs mastery over internet communication's aesthetics as a way of marking the internet as her territory, her safer space. It is a response that seems to suggest that Aguhar views her online assailant not only as a bad person but a boring one as well. Call Out Queen, indeed. Pérez reads the flippancy in Aguhar's response—a flippancy that Aguhar herself explicitly avowed as a favored tactic in the micropolitical melee—as a discerning move to flatten anti-fatness and other assaults on social media. He writes:

> What she called flippancy was less about refusing to take things seriously and more about shutting down the mode of bad-faith elliptical debate that

reigns on the Internet in order to carry out the real talk about day to day survival under white supremacy. The Call Out Queen's way of switching registers when she needed to—from confessional, to theoretical, to capricious, to sneering—gave critical substance to her flippancy, mocking a hater while empowering the one who dared to laugh it off.[21]

Note the relay Pérez identifies in Aguhar's critical flippancy between "mocking" one's oppressor and "empowering" oneself. This balance of disaffirmation and affirmation, dismissal and uplift, is central to the form of self-care I am theorizing.

Aguhar's critically flippant participation in call-out culture is akin to the performance of what Foucault called "parrhesia." In *The Government of the Self and Others*, Foucault argues that "one cannot attend to oneself, take care of oneself, without a relationship to another person. And the role of this other is precisely to tell the truth ... and to tell it in a certain form which is precisely parrhesia."[22] Usually translated to mean "free speech" or "free spokenness," Foucault understood parrhesia as a "particular way of telling the truth" in which a speaker, by advancing a frank criticism that they believe to be true, puts herself in danger.[23] The degree of danger involved in parrhesia varies for Foucault: one might risk one's life by criticizing the decisions of a surly sovereign, or one might risk a friend's anger by naming his wrongdoing.[24] Aguhar risks the blowback of her online adversaries when she puts forth her own harsh truths, even in aesthetic form. As Christine Garlough has argued, "artistic opposition" often "requires the courage of a parrhesiastes."[25] By framing Aguhar not only as a practitioner of the care of the self but also as a performer of parrhesia, we are better able to understand her as a direct, instructive model who can help others improve their own performance of self-care. By aiding others in their performatic approximation of revolting self-care, Aguhar-as-parrhesiastes catalyzes the proliferation and development of ethical practices of freedom in the social.[26]

However, to claim, as I have, that Aguhar's actions are only *akin* to those that might pass as parrhesia is also to mark their nonidentity with parrhesia as understood in a strict sense. Aside from occasional confrontations with haters, like the one described above, Aguhar's parrhesiastic participation in call-out culture is unconventional. She does not so much call out individual white people as call out white people as a class of subjects who benefit from and reproduce the violence of white supremacy. She does not so much call out individual men as call out men as a class of subjects who benefit from and reproduce the violence of misogyny and femmephobia. She is not engaging in a disciplinary performance of panopticism as much as she is engaging in a dismissive performance deprivileging objects of unearned desire. One could cast Aguhar as an example of Sara Ahmed's "feminist killjoy," that willful figure who becomes a collective problem by exposing a problem within the collective; an "affect alien," alienated from others by (their perception of) her inappropriate affective response to a naturalized system of oppression.[27] But such a characterization may not go far enough. By the end of her life, Aguhar was avowedly anti-white and a misandrist. She had a special dislike for white gay men and for white bear culture, in particular. They bored her, failed to rise to her level, reproduced the same old exclusions and pathways of desire.

Some of the best evidence for this is provided in Aguhar's text-based art. One piece simply reads: "I HATE UR WHITE DICK." The words appear in block lettering on a torn sheet of paper, giving it the feel of a note passed in school. The letters are written in ink, each a different color, making the sentiment they express feel less hateful than playful. What might first appear to be a binary, black-and-white opposition to patriarchy and whiteness is recast as a colorful and creative counteridentification. The title of the piece, revealed in the post's caption, confirms as much: *Brown Femme Love 2011*. This is revolting self-care: an expression of hatred for white masculinity offset by a simultaneous expression of love for brown femininity. A similar dynamic unfolds in another text-based piece posted to Aguhar's blog in October 2011: "I'D RATHER BE BEAUTIFUL THAN MALE." If *Brown Femme Love 2011* expresses hatred around her oppressors, this piece expresses a preference that affirms Aguhar's transfeminine becoming. It assists Aguhar in escaping the expectations of cis-sexist gender norms in order to redefine herself otherwise. Painted using gouache and glitter, the color gradient of the piece tells the shimmering story of her own evolution away from maleness, shifting from blue on the left to pink on the right, from masculinity to femininity, from boredom to beauty. "I'D RATHER BE BEAUTIFUL THAN MALE" is an artful exercise of the self on the self inasmuch as any social media post at once invents and expresses the self. This, too, is revolting self-care.

Though less obviously self-referential than the text-based works that populate Aguhar's blog, a watercolor titled *Patriotism (asia boys)* (see figure 1.3) can also be read as an expression and enactment of revolting self-care. The piece depicts two thin and naked Asian men engaging in a sex act on a gingham picnic blanket next to a slice of apple pie. One of them, wearing a star-spangled banner bandana, lies on his back licking the head of the other's penis. The other buries his face in bandana-boy's ass. The watercolor, which is a reimagined rendering of a porn still, both depicts a sexualized scene of Asian American racial care and engages in an Asian Americanist performance of revolting self-care. It challenges the undesirability of Asianness within gay male economies of desire by uplifting what Cynthia Wu calls the "sticky rice" love relations that run between Asian

FIGURE 1.3. Mark Aguhar, *Patriotism (asia boys)* (2011). Courtesy of the Estate of Mark Aguhar.

men and sustain them.²⁸ At the same time, the ironic juxtaposition of patriotic symbolism and Asian-on-Asian gay sex locates the assimilative tendency of Asian America within the scene of homosexual eros. These are model minority gaysians who have not yet unlearned their attachments to US nationalism and who are otherwise aligned with normative beauty standards. With its simultaneous affirmation of sticky rice sexuality and disaffirmation of nationalist model minoritism, *Patriotism (asia boys)* makes apparent the ambivalence with which Aguhar uses visual art to recalibrate her own and others' racialized sexuality.

Perhaps the most paradigmatic examples of Aguhar's self-valorization, however, can be found in the embodied performances Aguhar posted to her Tumblr. In one video, a shirtless Aguhar can be seen applying a cream to her body. Her hair is tied in a small bun atop her head, and her lips are red with lipstick below a thick brown mustache. The video shows her applying the cream to her skin as she looks either into the camera or, presumably, at her own image previewed on a screen below the camera. "I Wanna Be Adored" by the Stone Roses plays in the background. Throughout the video Aguhar accentuates her breasts. She pushes them together to form a cleavage. She places her hands behind her neck, as if either baring her breasts proudly or signaling submission to an objectifying order (or both). The caption captures this ambivalence: "THE UNFORTUNATE REALITY THAT MY BODY IS A POLITICAL SITE AND MY SELF CARE IS A RADICAL ACTION." Another video features Aguhar engaging in an eroticized expression of self-care. Wearing a black tank top and bright blue lipstick, she combs her hair. Bondage rope hangs around her neck and on the wall behind her. The video's caption reads as follows: "oh u kno, just a 2¼ minute video of me brushing my hair 100 times and maybe coming close to cumming." With each stroke of her brush, Aguhar counts upward. Her voice sounds sexual as she does so and more sexual as the numbers she names get larger. She makes her performance of personal hygiene into something almost masturbatory. Through this, she affirms herself as a sexual subject, as an unconventional object of desire worthy of erotic attention, touch, and pleasure.

Aguhar's selfies similarly engage in the work of self-empowerment and auto-experimentation. They are ubiquitous across her blog, depicting the artist in close-up, testing new makeup and hairstyles, showing the world what beauty might look like if only it were recognized as such. In one especially potent display of this sort, the Call Out Queen is faceless and on all fours.[29] She wears a white, mesh crop top and sunset-colored short shorts, intentionally showing off the fatness of her belly. The caption to this photo is saturated with vulnerability to and rage against the seemingly endless anti-fatness she faces, stating, "the sins of my body are punishable by constant public derision."[30] But the caption professes a self-certain empowerment because of that same anti-fatness. Aguhar writes, "I'm glad my body continues to have such amazing public power; who else is as legendary as me."[31] The photo elucidates the transmogrification of suffering into empowerment that is captured within the caption. Against those who would punish her fat embodiment, Aguhar flaunts her fatness. If fatness makes her revolting in the eyes of unkind others, it is also the substance of Aguhar's revolt against such misperceptions. She objectifies herself in the image in order to recast herself more appropriately. Once an object of disgust, she is here, in this self-portrait, an object of desire. Her pose suggests sexual readiness, bottomhood.

For Foucault, the care of the self is a creative activity through which the subject can cultivate a particular "style of living" or "aesthetics of existence," one that may diverge from normative standards of embodiment and ethics.[32] As the above-described selfie shows, Aguhar's aesthetics of existence, like her performance of self-care, might best be described as revolting. A revolting aesthetics of existence valorizes abject ways of being a self in the world. These ways of being may be viewed as beautiful or, as Mia Mingus puts it, as "magnificent" by those who know better.[33] But they are also, as Judith Butler suggests, "unsupported by the regime of truth."[34] In cultivating a revolting aesthetics of existence, Aguhar becomes a force that unsettles normative subjectivity and conduct even as she also avails herself of abjection—that ongoing process by which outcasts are cast out by those seeking to produce themselves as subjects within normative regimes of intelligibility. But if this fact implies unavoidable psychosocial suffering for Aguhar-as-abject, it also presents her endurance as a source of inspiration for those similarly experiencing abjection.

Virtual Separatism

Revolting self-care is a minoritarian form of racial care characterized by the simultaneous disaffirmation of the normatively desirable and a generous valorization of the normatively undesirable. The practice is perhaps best encapsulated by what is arguably Aguhar's most famous work: "Litanies to My Heavenly Brown Body." The piece is divided into two parts. The first part performs the rage, pain, and resentment that fuels the disaffirmation in Aguhar's oeuvre. It speaks directly to the reader and begins as a commentary on the relationship between racialization and desirability under white supremacy. The first line, "FUCK YOUR WHITENESS," is immediately followed by the line "FUCK YOUR BEAUTY," suggesting a correlation between the two categories. The next lines—"FUCK YOUR CHEST HAIR" and "FUCK YOUR BEARD"—give the sense that Aguhar may be speaking mainly to men, her primary oppressors and objects of desire. Then the phrase "FUCK YOUR ATTRACTIVE FATNESS" appears just after the lines "FUCK YOUR THINNESS" and "FUCK YOUR MUSCLES." The discrepancy among these three lines confirms that Aguhar is speaking across a range of traits rather than about any idealized individual. She is shouting down genres of embodiment other than her own, white genres of embodiment united by their honored place within gay male economies of desire: muscle jocks, thin twinks, and the fat, hairy, bearded men who fit comfortably within the beauty standards associated with bear culture.

Aguhar's issue, in other words, is with the way certain racialized expressions of masculinity make their bearers more desirable and therefore more likely to receive specific social resources within certain queer worlds. Such resources include the attention and attachments of others; platonic, romantic, and sexual advances; and the life-sustaining resource of racial care. We see Aguhar's frustration with this reality in the lines that appear later in part one of "Litanies," lines like "FUCK THE AMOUNT OF EFFORT I EXERT TO GET LESS THAN ENOUGH CONSIDERATION" and "FUCK THAT I CAN'T EXPECT ANYTHING FROM ANYONE." These exclamations evince an awareness of an underexamined aspect of caring relations: the unevenly distributed labors of self whose function is partly to attract care to oneself when the need for it arises.[35] Disabled thinkers often refer to this issue in terms of likability.[36] Some disabled people might be less likely to receive care because, for example, their chronic pain might make them irritable in a way that others find difficult to be around.

Aguhar's work locates this issue of attracting care in relation to desirability. Again, whiteness, maleness, thinness, the right kind of fatness: these sometimes overlapping qualities can attract desire to those subjects held within their privileged embrace ("FUCK THAT YOU CAN DEMAND ATTENTION"). They then hoard that desire and harness it to structure relations of care in a way that provides a surplus of attention, affirmation, and pleasure to the privileged, leaving many minoritarian subjects to experience deficits in these areas ("FUCK THAT I'M WILLING TO GIVE YOU WHAT I CAN'T HAVE"). This leaves subjects like Aguhar with two divergent options, each a version of the care of the self ("FUCK YOUR JUDGING ME FOR SELF CARE"). One option is to do the work of aligning oneself with the norms of desirability. Such work might entail any number of activities related to personal hygiene and style, diet and exercise, financial advancement, cultural literacy, and so on. The other option is to engage in the work of revolting self-care by divesting from normative desirability to instead redefine beauty and redirect social resources to those usually denied access to them. As Aguhar once put it on her blog, "ENVISION THE EROTIC POTENTIALITY OF FLIPPING THE WHITE MAN'S SCRIPT."

Aguhar helps us to do just this in part two of "Litanies," which returns us to her practice of minoritarian valorization. In this part of the piece she uplifts the oppressed and the marginalized, the neglected and unwanted: "BLESSED ARE THE PEOPLE OF COLOR MY BELOVED KITH AND KIN," "BLESSED ARE THE TRANS," and "BLESSED ARE THE HOT FAT GIRLS." And the list of blessed peoples goes on, extending generously to "sex workers," "genderqueers," "sissies," "high femmes," "boi dykes," "the disabled," and "kinksters." She even bestows blessings upon "the dis-identifiers" in a likely nod to Muñoz and the artists he uplifted throughout his career. Indeed, it is in this Muñozian spirit that this second part of Aguhar's piece makes use of the litany form. She clearly references the Christian Bible's beatitudes only to disidentify with them—to work on, with, and against them. By bestowing her blessings onto less fortunate others, Aguhar casts herself as a Christlike figure with the power to remap the realms of the sacred and the profane, the holy and the unholy, the cared for and the uncared for. With this observation, we are again invited to consider Aguhar as a parrhesiastes tasked with aiding others in the care of the self.

As Foucault writes, parrhesia can be viewed as "a virtue, duty, and technique which should be found in the person who spiritually directs others and helps them to constitute a relationship to self."[37] This is what Aguhar does for her followers with "Litanies." The piece seeks to shift its reader's relationship to self by modeling the practice of revolting self-care and, in the process, expressing a separatist structure of feelings to which others can become attuned. Part one of "Litanies" functions as a "Do Not Enter" sign for the privileged, and part two acts as a welcome mat for the marginalized. In this way, the piece invites minoritarian subjects to feel as Aguhar does about normative regimes of desirability. It aims to induce in others a desire for a separatist space-time free from the tyrannies of white masculinity, however temporary, provisional, or mediated that space-time might be.

Aguhar's affinity for separatism is well documented throughout her Tumblr posts. In one post from 2011, she describes an experience with anti-Asian racism. A man turns to her and says, "UGH! Are you CHINESE or something?" To this Aguhar responds with critical flippancy, "No, what I am is prettier than you!" She ends the post with a simple declaration: "'SEPARATISM IS JUST SO MUCH EASIER." Another post from around the same time describes the "SIMULTANEOUS JOY AND RAGE" Aguhar experiences when in "BROWN QUEER SPACE." The joy emerges from the fact of being "IN A SPACE WHERE I DON'T HAVE TO CHOOSE WHO I AM." The rage comes from "HOW OFTEN I HAVE TO MAKE THAT CHOICE." This post, too, includes a comment on Aguhar's experience of Asian racialization. "WHEN A WHITE PERSON APPROACHES ME THEY HAVE TO PREFACE OUR CONVERSATION WITH THEIR FETISHIZATION OF ASIANS," Aguhar writes, "AND WHEN I LOOK AT THEM, I JUST SEE A HUMAN BEING." Both these examples show that Aguhar's attraction to separatism responds to the racialized desire to be safe from the threat of anti-Asian racisms both negligent and sexual. They also help to clarify what makes Aguhar's evocation of separatism useful for the larger project of Asian American racial care.

Consider that any approximation of separatism that Aguhar's aesthetics might produce on Tumblr diverges from the usual understandings of the term. Rather than a separatism that privileges singular axes of identitarian sameness, Aguhar's is a minoritarian separatism-in-difference posed against a majoritarian public sphere. And rather than a separatism that requires in-person contact, Aguhar's performance of revolting self-care—through "Litanies" and elsewhere—gives rise to an ephemeral, contingent, and contested experience of virtual separatism. This virtual separatism is defined by the feeling and fantasy that one is a part of a social world that, thankfully, stands apart from normative ideality. It is a space-time paradoxically rendered both possible and impossible by the nonspace of networked social media, one in which the threat of racial harm is crowded out by the promise of racial care. And to those inclined to believe that all separatisms are virtual in the sense of being porous and penetrated by uninvited interlopers, I would simply say that Aguhar's is unique in that its existence on social media enables an alleviation of minoritarian isolation by allowing the neglected increased access to aesthetic and social sustenance, wherever they may be.

This observation complicates and supplements theories that are skeptical of social media's value for left politics. In *Blog Theory*, Jodi Dean rightly asserts both that digital social networks circulate affect and that "affective networks produce feelings of community, or what we might call 'community without community,'" virtual separatism by another, less particular name.[38] But Dean errs when she argues that this affective circulation does little more than reify "communicative capitalism," or "that economic-ideological form wherein reflexivity captures creativity and resistance so as to enrich the few as it placates and diverts the many."[39] To make her point Dean references blogs and social networks that are "by and for teenage girls."[40] Though she concedes that such networks "produce affective spaces where [teenage girls] express themselves, share their feelings, and reach out with a little hope that someone will be touched and reach back," this brief acknowledgment of the caring relations potentiated by networked social media ultimately slips into a paranoid reading of feminized blogging as a marketing of social life.[41] Dean admits that affective labor—especially that performed by women, often for little or no pay—"produces social networks" and feelings of "vitality and security, or care and belonging."[42] But to present a picture of digital social media as a technology of capture alone, Dean chooses to discount the value of care as an affective force and relational practice. She reduces a mediated ecology of care to so many "contributions" that, for her, amount neither to critical thinking nor to political action but instead to "communication for its own sake."[43] With this move she disavows a view that positions the online performance of care *as political*, reifying an old, deeply gendered rendering of what constitutes the political as such.

Aguhar's work asks us to depart from Dean on this point. Her performance of revolting self-care, and the experience of virtual separatism it produces, cannot in any way be thought outside the political. This is evident in the effect it has on Aguhar's minoritarian followers. Consider, for example, the following anonymous message received privately and then posted publicly by Aguhar to her Tumblr blog:

> "Anonymous asked: your blog is a major part of me being able to feel like I am capable of living in the world as a whole person with all the rage and barbed beauty of being brown and fat and a fucking... post-queen femme faggot. I wish I wasn't afraid to post this non anon[ymously]."

As this message makes clear, revolting self-care is nothing less than a matter of life and death. It makes living feel possible for those who may never have known such possibility. And the very intimate affective public of virtual separatism is nothing less than a bastion within the permanent war of the present. It is a source of psychosocial sustenance for minoritarian subjects. This is true not only for queer and trans people of color cast out of desirability, living in lonely isolation. It is also true, as Valerie Francisco-Menchavez reminds us, for Filipino and other diasporic subjects, especially migrant workers and the undocumented, who often live at great distance from loved ones with little recourse for return.[44] It is true, too, for the fat and/or disabled who, due to physical or emotional exhaustion or immobility, often rely on social media for social life. And it is finally true, to quote Aguhar's "Litanies" just once more, for the "BELOVED WHO I DIDN'T DESCRIBE, I COULDN'T DESCRIBE, WILL LEARN TO DESCRIBE AND RESPECT AND LOVE."

"The Care of the Self for Others"

To further clarify the relation of revolting self-care to what is commonly called collective care, it is useful at this point to turn to Kimberly Alidio's poem, "All the Pinays are straight, all the queers are Pinoy, but some of us." The poem's title is a reference to *All the Women Are White, All the Men Are Black, But Some of Us Are Brave: Black Women's Studies*, a volume published by the Feminist Press in 1982 and edited by Gloria T. Hull, Patricia Bell Scott, and Barbara Smith. A landmark work of Black feminism, the book features such notable writers and writings as Alice Walker and the Combahee River Collective's "A Black Feminist Statement." When I asked Alidio why a poem that seemed primarily a memorial to Mark Aguhar takes its title from a decades-old collection of writings arguing for a new "Black women's studies," she wrote to me in an email that "the poem is an homage to Mark Aguhar, the Mongrel Coalition Against Gringpo, and to Black feminism. It's a non-hierarchical lineage of call-outs."[45] The lineage of call-outs in which Alidio situates her poem is also the lineage of call-outs that I wish to gather under the signs of revolting self-care and virtual separatism. It is a lineage that spans poetry, performance, and a range of platforms—political, digital, and otherwise. It is a lineage to which this writing and I (and likely you) are deeply indebted. While my turn to Alidio's poem at this point is motivated by a desire to delve into the Pinay particularities of Aguhar's performance of racial care, this desire has little relation to impulses of identitarian territoriality. In the same correspondence in which she explained her poem's title, Alidio wrote the following: "I hope there'll be a space of life/death/connection that's not primarily concerned with inclusion and legitimacy. There are such spaces invoked by Aguhar, Gringpo and *But Some of Us Are Brave*."[46] I agree. This chapter is a search for a minoritarian mode of self-care that is unreliant on the sort of sovereign, "legitimate," model minoritist subjectivity that is so shored up under neoliberalism. That search shares Alidio's hope for connectivity as it sifts through her poetic rendering of Aguhar's life and death.

The poem in question—which can be found in Alidio's 2016 collection, *after projects the resound*—begins with its title and continues beyond it.

> All the Pinays are straight, all the queers are Pinoy, but some of us
> hold our femme gaze straight into the cosmos
> behold a supernova of fat negation
> know Mark Aguhar as the real babaylan
> have mothers young enough to be our sons never to reach 26[47]

The poem places Aguhar above us, in the cosmos, as a supernova—less an entity than a cosmic event, a stellar explosion of galactic proportions. The phrase "fat negation" describes both the large scale of her disaffirmative performance and the negative experiences she too often endured as a consequence of her fat embodiment. And those who behold these aspects of the artist do so through what Alidio terms their "femme gaze," which should be understood as opposing the objectifying scopic eroticisms identified with the male gaze by the likes of Laura Mulvey or John Berger. The function of the femme gaze can be gleaned from Alidio's implication, at the end of this first stanza, that Aguhar can be seen at the same time as a mother and as a son. By marking Aguhar as a mother, Alidio upholds Aguhar as an anchoring source of caring attachment and performance that others depend on for sustenance. Notably, Alidio care-fully stretches her view of Aguhar's gender trans-temporally, while eschewing the violence of misgenderment.[48] This syntactical maneuver effectively affirms the femme gaze as a gaze that glimpses the other simultaneously as one who cares (maternal) and as one who is cared for (childlike). The femme gaze, as it appears in Alidio's poem, names a mode of perception through which the feminine and feminized are structurally predisposed to a more comprehensive view of caring relationality.

There is also something femme in Alidio's characterization of Aguhar as "the real babaylan." According to Grace Nono, the *babaylan* is best understood as a Native "ritual specialist" of the Filipino past and present.[49] They are those "whose services as helpers and curers are crucial to the survival of whole communities, especially those underserved by public institutions."[50] Throughout history, the figure of the *babaylan* has been characterized in a number of ways. Spanish colonizers cast Native ritual specialist women as witches. American colonizers dismissed them as superstitious. By contrast, many in the Philippines and the diaspora have positioned the *babaylan* as a proto-feminist figure, "powerful women during the precolonial times when gender relationships were egalitarian."⁵¹ Still others have claimed the *babaylan* for queer and trans purposes, positioning the figure as proof of preferable gendered power relations, prior to colonization, in which those now considered trans played pivotal roles as ritual leaders. The citation of the *babaylan* in Alidio's poem falls most in line with this last discourse, reclaiming Aguhar from the Christlike quality of her own "Litanies" for a genealogy more native to the Philippines. In placing Aguhar in this lineage, Alidio refuses to relegate the *babaylan* to the precolonial past and asks her reader instead to rethink in a new light the caring rituals Aguhar and others enacted on and through Tumblr.

It is in this light that we should read the poem's formal resonances with Aguhar's "Litanies to My Heavenly Brown Body," and by extension, the poem's formal resonances with the performance of revolting self-care.

Blessed be

our ugly grief
our helpless beauty
this very moment of utterance incarnate in an absent brown body⁵²

Though the phrase "blessed be" appears only once in the poem, the reader might be motivated by its right alignment on the page and the precedent set by Aguhar's "Litanies" to imagine the phrase at the fore of each of the lines that follow (i.e., "blessed be our ugly grief," "blessed be our helpless beauty"). Read in such a way, this portion of the poem becomes a mournful prayer to Aguhar, a kind of communication between life and afterlife. It seems to draw on her sacred and spiritual energies for affective assurance. But the first-person plural pronoun in these lines might also give the critical reader pause. Who is invoked by the use of "our," by "us"? Filipinas? Queer Filipinas? All those who identified with Aguhar? All those who continue to mourn her loss still today?

Even as the poem invites these inquiries, it resists attempts to locate stable answers to them. Consider the stanza that immediately follows:

I will never not

want to be violent with you (dare you to say
this isn't love, queen)
pray for
her resurrection every easter⁵³

If we imagine that the "I" of this statement stands in for Alidio, we might then assume that the "you" of the statement stands in for Aguhar, making the statement a straightforward expression of loving solidarity with Aguhar in instances of critically flippant revolt. But this reading is unsettled by the following line wherein the "her" that Alidio prays will be resurrected seems also to stand in for Aguhar, formerly the "you" of the poem. (The word "easter," we should notice, remains happily and irreverently lowercase, a slight jab from a queer, decolonial Filipina ethos to the most holy of Catholic holidays.) This fact invites an alternative reading of the prior lines: though the "I" continues to stand in for Alidio, the "you" now seems to the stand in for Aguhar's aggressor. In this alternative reading, the statement now suggests that Alidio's violent resistance against he who harms Aguhar can be understood as an expression of love directed at Aguhar. Because it is anchored by a comma, the poem's only punctuation, the parenthetical seems to remain stably addressed to Aguhar. Both the speaking subject of the poem and the subject to whom the poem is addressed, as these lines demonstrate, resist self-certain individuation and transparent recognition.

The uncertainty of subject/object designations and distinctions within Alidio's poem generatively complicates the project of revolting self-care as I have thus far theorized it. If we read Alidio's poem as a formal inhabitation of Aguhar's "Litanies," and if Aguhar's "Litanies" is a formal expression of virtual separatism, then Alidio's divergence from and disruption of this form can teach us something important about the relationship between what I am calling virtual separatism and the performance of revolting self-care. The poem's blurring of subject and object suggests that the virtual separatism made manifest through revolting self-care does not reify or rely on stable notions of proprietary, individuated selfhood. The self frays at its edges, becomes porous and plural in the poem. The poem presents a model of subjectivity that allows for the interpenetrable transit of others. Against the fantasy of a self-contained subjectivity compliant with neoliberal individualism, Alidio's poem can be read as a rendering of the interpermeable subjectivities formed within the sphere of Aguhar's virtual separatism.

With due deference to the untamable multiplicity of meanings and readings that Alidio has crafted into her poem, I read the model of interpermeable subjectivity made manifest in Alidio's queer Pinay poetics through the Filipino concept of *kapwa*. Virgilio Enriquez defines *kapwa* as a kind of "unity of the 'self' and 'others,'" "an extended sense of identity."[54] And casting the concept in gendered terms as a specifically Filipina structure of sociality and subjectivity, Neferti Tadiar calls *kapwa* a "weak" form of subjectivity in the sense that it is "inextricable from a sense of others." The danger here, Tadiar tells us, is that the hegemonic view of *kapwa* as an inexhaustible orientation toward others—a view buttressed by fantasies of bodily individuation—is part of what makes possible the profound exploitation of the Filipina within affective and postindustrial production. But Tadiar nonetheless invites us to conceive of *kapwa* "as the creative persistence of and reinvention of psychic structures which were replaced or destroyed by the modern subjectification processes carried out in colonial and capitalist spheres of production."⁵⁵

Alidio's final stanza performatively indulges in the fellow-being of *kapwa* through a ludic reenvisioning of part one of Aguhar's "Litanies to My Heavenly Brown Body." In all caps and in full, the section reads:

LOL YOUR PINAY SELF

LOL YOUR SUBCONSCIOUS DECOLONIAL INDIGENEITY

LOL RECOVERY AS AN ESCAPE HATCH FROM REAL NEGOTIATIONS

LOL CARING THAT WHITE PEOPLE THINK OUR BODIES ARE CHEAP

LOL THINKING THAT ONLY WHITE PEOPLE THINK OUR BODIES ARE CHEAP

LOL THINKING WHITE POETS MATTER AT ALL

LOL FRETTING OVER OUR FAILED TOKENIZATION

LOL AGENCY AND THE COURAGE TO SPEAK

LOL CENTERING OURSELVES IN THE NARRATIVE

LOL PRETTY TRAUMA POETRY AT OUR NATION'S CAPITAL

LOL RESPECTABILITY POLITICS

LOL SLUT SHAMING

LOL LANGUAGE SHAMING

LOL MOTHER TONGUE

LOL THE MOTHERLAND

LOL PRECOLONIAL PARADISE FOLK TALES

LOL UTOPIA UNTOUCHED BY QUEER PINAY RUIN ACROSS TIME & SPACE

LOL YOUR LOLA [grandmother]

LOL YOUR HIYA [shame]

LOL YOUR WALANG HIYA [shamelessness]

LOL OUR TENDER EMOTIONALITY⁵⁶

Those familiar with Aguhar's original piece will likely impute the force of a "fuck you" onto the "LOL" that begins each line of this section of the poem, which formally mirrors the disaffirmation of Aguhar's litanies. And yet, the LOL has no easy relationship to either identification or counteridentification. While lines like "LOL RESPECTABILITY POLITICS," "LOL SLUT SHAMING," and "LOL LANGUAGE SHAMING" seem clearly to enact a kind of dismissal, they might also pursue a kind of recognition between Alidio, Aguhar, and like-minded readers. Other lines are more obvious in their embrace of an ambivalence produced, in part, by Alidio's embrace of *kapwa* as both a sociosubjective and a poetic form. For these lines, possessive pronouns signify multiply. When

Alidio writes, "LOL YOUR PINAY SELF / LOL YOUR SUBCONSCIOUS DE-COLONIAL INDIGENEITY," she seems at first to be addressing Aguhar from across the dividing line between life and death. If, however, the poem amounts to a technology of revolting self-care, then the second person pronoun might refer to Alidio herself. Or else, it might just as easily refer to a presumed Filipina reader. The simultaneous invocation of each of these interlocutors (Aguhar, self, others) amounts to a poetic inhabitation of *kapwa*—the interpermeability and inextricability of self and other—even as it puts forward a critical (even skeptical?) metacommentary on notions of selfhood and subconscious decoloniality. This intervention appears again, as during the "blessed be" portion of the poem, when Alidio describes the perception of "OUR BODIES" as cheap or mocks the multicultural impulse of Filipino America that mourns "OUR FAILED TOKE-NIZATION." She invokes a contested first-person plurality, and the reader is left to decide who Alidio means to include in her collectivity.

Filtering Aguhar through Alidio not only foregrounds the Filipina facets of Aguhar's abject aesthetics of existence but also establishes that revolting self-care is not premised on the individuated selfhood that founds individualist fantasies of sovereignty, rationality, and property—fantasies that themselves found systemic neglect, abandonment, and disavowal. If I have theorized virtual separatism as a trans and queer feminist of color formation, I have not done so in order to reify identitarian community. The trans and queer, the femme and feminine, the Filipina and the fat, the other abandoned others—these are the subjects of Aguhar's virtual separatism because their interconnected experience of neglect and need inclines them toward the creative capacities of mutual aid and mutual defense that found the minoritarian ethico-politics of racial care advanced in this book. Drawing on the philosopher Jean-Luc Nancy, Wendy Chun has argued that certain performances of online self-exposure "relay their singular stories in a form that seems to deny singularity."[57] Considered as performances of this sort, Aguhar's visual art, selfies, text posts, and litanies are revealed as "a reaching toward community, which stems from both what seems to be held in common but also what can never be: the singular experience of abuse and vulnerability."[58]

What matters here is what, following Nancy, we might call the "singular plural" status of subjectivity within what I have been calling virtual separatism.[59] Each subject of Aguhar's virtual separatism is singular and irreducible, and so too are their struggles. But each is also plural insofar as their gathering around Aguhar makes them one singularity among many. By holding singularity and plurality, "I" and "we," in a single frame, we remain within the sociosubjective structure of *kapwa*. And we also reinforce something essential about racial care.

Especially in its minoritarian iterations, racial care must always simultaneously mind the singular needs of a singular subject alongside that subject's situation within more expansive constellations of social relation. The singular and the plural are irreducible to one another, but they are also inextricable from one another. Self-care and collective care cannot be easily disarticulated from one another. Thus, as Alidio's poem suggests, virtual separatism is not a utopia "untouched by queer pinay ruin across space and time"; instead, it is a contested, permeable, intersubjective gathering produced in and by that ruin. Filtered through the Pinay prism of *kapwa*, the Foucauldian formulation of "the care of the self for others" can no longer be read in the usual way as a statement of temporal or ontological priority in which one cares for the self in order to better care for others. It should be read instead as an assertion of temporal and ontological singular-plural simultaneity: the care of the self *as* a care for others; the care for others *as* the care for the self.

Remember Death

I am not sure if Eve Sedgwick had a subject like Aguhar in mind when she wrote, in 1994, of lesbian and gay studies' preoccupation with the suicides of queer youths.[60] Nevertheless, Aguhar's loss, *pace* Sedgwick, is both queer and now, both trans and brown. And we can count her loss among a number of femme losses in the second decade of the twenty-first century, a period of time that Leah Lakshmi Piepzna-Samarasinha has called "the femme suicide years."[61] Some might seek recourse to Aguhar's psychic interiority for an explanation of her suicide. Such persons would likely cite the depression and grief that flooded the end of her life, a tide that rose in the afterlife of her sister's suicide about a year prior to her own. There is also a reading that would recuperate her death for the project of revolting self-care. This reading would insist that Aguhar's death despite self-care is a critique of the wretched world in which we live, a critique that testifies to the urgency of revolting self-care's proliferation as a tactic expressive and generative of separatist structures of feeling capable of connecting minoritarian life back to itself. One reader of an earlier draft of this chapter articulated this approach to understanding Aguhar's self-annihilation in this way: "[Practices of survival] exist in revolt against conditions that make them necessary, conditions in which failure is often likely, if not inevitable. The failure to survive does not negate the practice, it is its reason for deployment."

I worry about equating suicide with a "failure to survive." This way of reading self-annihilation damns an unjust world that is certainly worthy of damnation, but it also risks robbing Aguhar of agency and autonomy in her final act. It risks, as a result, the reproduction of what Alexandre Baril teaches us to call "suicidism," the specific form of oppression faced by suicidal people for being suicidal.[62] What if suicide for Aguhar, or for someone like her, was something nearer to success? I would ask whether we can bear the question long enough to answer it, but some of us never have that choice. I didn't the winter I lost my friend Cris, another unprecedented queer and trans creature, under similar circumstances. What if we were to understand suicide not as a failure but as a line of flight directed away from an impoverished present? What if this is what we should take away from the encounter between Aguhar and a follower, posted to her blog years prior to her death, in which the follower comments, "I believe I can fly," and Aguhar captions the comment, "my suicide note"? Maybe. But, those of us who have survived the suicide of another know that the reasons for their self-annihilation are ultimately and painfully unknowable. When a loved one chooses to leave life behind, those of us left behind with it have only to grieve and to reconcile the impossibility of explanation with the incompossibility of explanations. "Incompossible": a word I borrow from Tavia Nyong'o who uses it as a way to keep queer of color realities that could have been, that perhaps should have been, within our reach.[63]

In the end, it seems only fitting to return to an instruction from the Call Out Queen herself, one found in the epigraph that began this chapter, "The Axes": "Remember death." Dylan Rodriguez, in *Suspended Apocalypse*, impels us to remember the "essential relation of death" that dwells in the chasm between the "Filipino" and the "American," the latter term soaked in the blood of the former because of an ongoing project of white supremacist genocide.[64] Elsewhere, Eric Stanley has argued that queer life amounts only to a kind of "near life" or "death-in-waiting" emptied out by a feeling of nonexistence.[65] Together, these arguments suggest that to remember death as queer and trans Filipino Americans is to remember that we exist, laugh, and love, to the extent that we do, in the shadow of death and under the weight of irresolvable antagonism. To remember death, therefore, is not only to remember that death is inevitable for all of us. It is also to remember that, especially for some of us, death is both now and then, it is as slow as it is fast and frequent, it is the defining immanence of our abjection. To be revolting is also to be depressive, decaying, degenerating, decomposing, dying. To the extent that we forget death, whether Aguhar's or any other, we become complicit in the production of death.

This leaves us with little choice. Our task is to embrace the militant melancholia that Muñoz describes when he reminds us to "bring our dead with us to the various battles we must wage in their names."⁶⁶ This, too, is racial care. And so, I conclude my analysis of Aguhar with just one more of the Call Out Queen's lines of inquiry and instruction, words to live by, to die by: "Will you remember me when I'm gone? Will you remember me for coining the term 'butch pageantry'? This is all I ask of you, my children. Go forth and proselytize."

2

The Racialized Holding Environment

In Julia Cho's play *Office Hour*, a Korean American adjunct instructor of creative writing named Gina is tasked with tutoring a Korean American student named Dennis. Dennis, Gina's colleagues tell her, is a "troubled" young man, and as soon as he appears on stage, audiences of *Office Hour* can see why.[1] He sits in Gina's office, directly across from her, hiding behind sunglasses and beneath a black hoodie. The writing he produces for her class is teeming with baleful violence and sadistic sex. He almost entirely refuses to speak. Gina does her best to get through to him, but she is visibly anxious. Because she sees what everyone else in the theater is seeing: Dennis is the living embodiment of a school shooter, and of one school shooter in particular.

Seung-Hui Cho was twenty-three years old when he opened fire on the campus of Virginia Tech. The date was April 16, 2007. The weather that morning was cold. With two semiautomatic handguns, a 9 mm Glock 19 and a .22-caliber Walther P22, Cho murdered thirty-two people—some while they were saving lives. He also injured twenty-three others—some as they fled to escape death. He then killed himself. It was, at the time, the deadliest shooting executed by a single gunman in the history of the United States.

Before he became a killer, though, Seung-Hui Cho was a lot like *Office Hour*'s Dennis. He was a young Asian man who was also a problem for his professors. As an undergraduate student of creative writing, Cho produced work that was excessively violent, filled with murderous fantasy, frightening to his peers and teachers. His behavior in school was intimidating, mean, and menacing—especially in relation to women. This was so much the case that Nikki Giovanni, in the fall of 2005, had Cho removed from her class upon learning that a number of her students had stopped attending for fear of him. Giovanni insisted that she would sooner resign than work with Cho again, and so the chair of the department, Lucinda Roy, took on the unwanted task of tutoring him in the tense privacy of her office.

In her book *No Right to Remain Silent*, Roy provides intimate details of the meetings she held with Cho prior to the massacre he carried out. The book outlines how she tried to aid Cho as a student of creative writing. Roy describes how she attempted to make the "atmosphere" of those meetings as "comfortable" as she could to "ease the tension in the room."[2] Some strategies to this end included giving Cho "plenty of time to respond" to her questions;[3] asking him to take off his sunglasses "in a way that would allow him to refuse if he wanted to";[4] asking about his family and friends; cowriting with him; offering him a copy of her own novel as a token of good faith; and, importantly, stressing that he seek counseling services.

These are performances of care-full pedagogy, and I lift them up here to highlight the holding environment they attempt to make for Cho out of Roy's office. I borrow the concept of the "holding environment" from the British psychoanalyst D. W. Winnicott who uses the phrase to describe the affective and adaptive architecture assembled for the infant by the mother through a good-enough performance of care.[5] In Winnicott's original theorization, the holding environment is that which enables the infant's uninterrupted development by providing ample nourishment and by shielding the infant from injury. But I theorize the holding environment's possibility within academic space—and, later in this chapter, within theatrical space—from the belief that the concept is a mobile one. Winnicott locates the holding environment not only in the familial space, between the mother and the infant, but also in the therapeutic space, in the care and protection provided by the psychoanalyst for the analysand.

While Roy's efforts to establish a holding environment for Cho are admirable, they are also ultimately and unfortunately limited. In a chapter titled "Translating Race," Roy suggests that "cultural assumptions" held by Cho's teachers and classmates "could have had both an obvious and a subtle role to play in how Cho was treated."[6] She admits that even she might have been reluctant to cultivate a relationship with him had they not "shared an immigrant's heritage."[7] The rest of Roy's remarks on this issue are worth quoting at length:

> Because there were things he had experienced that I had experienced myself, it was possible to begin to speak across our differences. Difficult as it was to try to communicate with him, it was made a little easier by the fact that we both knew what it was like to be identified in purely racial terms by people who were unsympathetic to your racial heritage. But I am reluctant to suggest that I understood him more than others, or that I had a clear sense of who he was.[8]

The limitations of Roy's holding environment are evident in her qualifying language: they were beginning to speak across difference; things were made a little easier by the similarities. By the end of the passage Roy remains uncertain that she understood Cho at all. And still, Roy's sense that an approximate experience of racialization could enhance her ability to engage in a good-enough performance of care for this student matters a great deal.

It is this hypothesis that takes center stage in *Office Hour*, a play that was itself inspired by its playwright's experience of racial and ethnic proximity to the shooter. "I could feel a familiarity with [Seung-Hui Cho] that was very uncomfortable," Julia Cho told the *Los Angeles Times*, highlighting the fact of their shared last names.[9] Writing *Office Hour* was Cho's way of responding to this discomfort. The play premiered at South Coast Repertory in Costa Mesa, California, in April 2016. It has since been produced across the United States, including at the Long Wharf Theater in New Haven, Connecticut; at the Berkeley Repertory Theatre in California; at Artswest Playhouse and Gallery in Seattle; and at the Public Theater in New York City, where I saw it performed twice in 2017. I argue throughout this book that Asian Americans inhabit an unsustainably neglected situation on the field of racial care, one that they can and have altered through recourse to minoritarian aesthetics. Through a close reading of Cho's play, and Dennis and Gina's relationship specifically, this chapter advances this claim in two ways: first, by shifting away from my first chapter's focus on self-care toward a focus on dyadic racial care; and, second, by positioning *Office Hour* as a case study through which to observe the gendered distribution of racial care and neglect in the institutional context of higher education.

I pursue both these ends by seizing the opportunity given in *Office Hour* to observe how the unique insight provided by the shared experience of approximate racialization can result in a racialized holding environment when put into performance within both the space-time of the academic office hour and that of the theater. One way to understand the racialized holding environment is as a protective and nourishing force field conjured by the performance and provision of good-enough racial care.[10] Though such structures might take majoritarian turns (think fraternity houses, locker rooms, and board rooms), I am interested here in a racialized holding environment that is also a minoritarian holding environment insofar as it provides sustenance specific to the needs of those suffering under systemic oppression—Cho and Dennis, in this case. These holding environments, whether academic or theatrical, are space-times in which the racialized abject is made to feel held by another, an object, or, indeed, the world. If, as Judith Butler has written, the abject occupies "those 'unlivable' zones of social life which are nevertheless densely populated by those who do not enjoy the status of the subject, but whose living under the sign of the 'unlivable' is required to circumscribe the domain of the subject," then the racialized holding environment names that fleeting fortress of livability within the unlivable life of abjection.[11] It is a provisional bastion in which the one cared-for may, as Karen Shimakawa has suggested, "feel 'held' in the sense of being supported, contextualized (and therefore recognized and constituted as a subject)."[12] Racialized holding environments are those energetic fields, generated by caring labor, that are invoked and induced whenever we are asked to "hold space" for the specificities of experience and emotion that emanate from students of color.[13] And I offer the racialized holding environment, in part, as a model, a starting point from which to begin to imagine similar (though nonidentical), intersectional architectures built for queer and trans students, disabled students, and other Others in need. Indeed, in their minoritarian iterations, racialized holding environments constellate the caring coordinates of performative worldmaking.

But racialized holding environments also come at a cost, and *Office Hour* makes this cost legible by taking it to its extremes. Because Roy (in real life) and Gina (in Cho's play) are architects of the racialized holding environment, they are also trapped by its scripts, held captive within the maternal and therapeutic functions that are essential to Winnicott's framework.[14] The women are not just tasked with teaching creative writing; they are tasked with the gendered labor of providing racial care. Such labor, unrecognized and unremunerated, is constantly being performed by women of color and other multiply marginalized faculty in the semiprivate spaces of the neoliberal university. Sometimes such labor is chosen. A faculty member sees a familiar form of suffering in a student and, out of something like a sense of duty, takes them into the racialized holding environment. But in other instances, faculty are left with no choice but to bring students into their offices, manage their students' racial feelings, and bear their students' masculinist or even their murderous leanings. This was Roy's circumstance. She had little choice but to tutor Cho when other faculty cast him out. It was her charge as department chair, an outcome of her location in the institutional structure.

What happens when multiply marginalized faculty members find themselves caught impossibly between these two positions: wanting to care for their students and wishing that they did not have to? This chapter offers one answer to this question over four sections. The first section offers a close reading of *Office Hour*'s opening scene, which lays bare the gendered dynamics through which the responsibility to provide Dennis with racial care is disavowed and then displaced onto Gina *because she is Korean American*. The following section examines the racialized holding environment at its limit by highlighting how the racial care Gina tries to provide for Dennis is complicated by issues of gender, sexuality, and disability that echo those associated with Seung-Hui Cho. The chapter's third section expands this book's theorization of anti-Asian neglect with a reading of the play's conclusion, which finds both Gina and Dennis moving through an affective experience that I describe as Asian American loneliness. And the chapter concludes by shifting from a diegetic analysis of *Office Hour* to a speculative analysis of the play's potential, and the potential of ethnic theater more broadly, to act formally as a racialized holding environment for minoritarian audience members.

My primary aim in all this is to establish a fundamental contradiction in the concept of racial care, one that is made evident in and through the social form of the racialized holding environment: even as racialized subjects may perform racial care in the service of anti-violence and life-sustainment, the requirement to perform such labor at all is itself a life-draining reiteration of racial violence. In arguing this point, however, I make no claims as to whether the racialized holding environment and the performance of racial care can address the problem of the American school shooter more broadly. This concern is beyond the scope of this chapter. In *Office Hour*, the fictional Dennis evokes, but does not represent, the actual Seung-Hui Cho who is himself a poor stand-in for the archetypical white male mass shooter who is so often driven by masculinist and ethno-nationalist ideologies.[15] I focus on *Office Hour* not because it offers the racialized holding environment as the solution we so desperately need for the problem of mass murderous violence but because in staging the racialized holding environment in relation to such a volatile expression of racialized masculinity we are better able to observe the problem of racial care intersectionally and at its limit. Roy's interaction with Cho and Gina's interaction with Dennis: these are both limit cases for racial care and the racialized holding environment. They force us to ask what these concepts can offer in the face of dormant murderousness, when every misstep might be another step closer to a mass shooting. By raising the stakes on racial care in this way, *Office Hour* makes viscerally evident the practice's potential costs, benefits, and dangers.

Displacement, Disavowal, Identification

Office Hour opens with a warning. Two of Gina's colleagues—Genevieve and David—have asked Gina to tea to caution her about Dennis, who they feel fits the profile of "a classic shooter."[16] For much of the conversation, they rehearse their frustrations with Dennis and narrate the work they have done to address both his concerns and their concerns about him. Genevieve exchanged emails with Dennis, attempted to connect with him verbally, begged a more senior colleague to remove Dennis from her class, and attempted to direct the young man to student health services before ultimately quarantining him off from his classmates until the semester's end.[17] David's story, though, is anything but a tale of prolonged pedagogical and administrative effort. He gripes about the inconveniently timed visits Dennis made to his office hours. He refers to Dennis at various points over the course of his narration as "really fucked up," a "little prick," and a "bastard."[18] He is cruel.

But despite how differently Genevieve and David deal with Dennis, they seem to share a belief that Gina's Asianness makes her better equipped for the task. Shortly after confessing to questioning Dennis's English language skills, Genevieve makes a proposal: "Well... maybe *you* could try talking to him," she suggests to Gina, "maybe you could get through to him a little."[19] When Gina demurs, insisting that she is not a therapist, Genevieve persists, "But you guys must have stuff in common—not psychologically but, you know, a background."[20] There is little doubt that this seemingly premeditated request functions as an insidious, if sincerely hopeful, displacement of gendered racial care and pedagogical labor from Genevieve and David onto Gina. After this conversation concludes, Gina is forced to care for and about Dennis.[21] But what exactly lies behind and beneath this displacement? What are its causes and consequences? Which forces, exactly, force Gina to care?

There are institutional and economic forces at work here. Gina explains at one point that she is an adjunct at the university and her job security is endangered if enrollment in her course falls below fifteen, a number threatened by Dennis's sometimes-frightening behavior. Her livelihood literally depends on her ability to be dependable in relation to Dennis. And even if we choose to assume that Genevieve and David share in Gina's situation of neoliberal precarity (their levels of job security are never mentioned in Cho's script), the differential ways in which the three professors each deal with Dennis reveal race, gender, and the academic class inequality of adjunctification as vectors of vulnerability to coercion and obligation.[22]

The first to receive Dennis in all his complication, Genevieve, a Black woman, seems to have done everything possible for the young man given institutional constraints and her own necessarily limited capacities for care and labor. There is ample evidence to suggest that Genevieve, at some significant cost to herself, has judiciously navigated the balancing act of tending to Dennis at the same time as she tended to her other students. Though Genevieve is not explicitly marked as Black in the script, she has been cast as such in every major production of the play thus far. This recurrent decision is perhaps meant to associate the character with Nikki Giovanni, the Virginia Tech professor who famously passed Seung-Hui Cho into the care of Lucinda Roy after reaching the limit of her own capacities to teach him.[23] David has similarly always been cast as a white man despite not being explicitly scripted as such; he is a white man whose concerns are self-centered and whose attitude is one of careless disregard for his student. This ubiquitous casting choice seems consciously to position white maleness as a guardrail that protects David from the overextension suffered by Genevieve.

As a result, the transfer of labor that occurs between Genevieve and Gina must be distinguished from the one that occurs between David and Gina. The former transfer can be considered a displacement. This displacement should not be viewed as a matter of misguided intention but as an unfortunate and unintentional consequence of the racialized and gendered impositions forced upon Black women in the US academy and elsewhere. By contrast, the transfer of labor from David to Gina is more correctly understood as a disavowal, one intentionally enacted by David to rid himself of responsibility for and to Dennis. In other, metaphorical words: whereas Genevieve reluctantly passed Dennis after her class, David happily failed him.

But this distinction between Genevieve's displacement and David's disavowal, though a necessary one, does not yet account for the invocations of Asian racialization that are scattered throughout *Office Hour*'s opening scene. It is possible to read good intentions into Genevieve's insinuation that Gina, given her Korean American background, is somehow uniquely positioned to get through to Dennis. As a Black woman, Genevieve likely shares a felt experience of the value in intraracial connection and care. Despite this, though, at least two problematics persist. First, Genevieve makes the request that Gina deal with Dennis on David's behalf as well as her own, a fact that undermines a recuperative reading of her remark by rendering her complicit in David's disavowal. Second, against the backdrop of the opening scene's various orientalist enunciations, Genevieve and David's implicit enlistment of Gina's Korean American ethnicity as a reason that she should care for Dennis appears less like an altruistic attempt to usher Dennis into an ideal educational context than it does like an act of racialized conscription that shields and sustains anti-Asian ignorances, insensitivities, and neglect while placing further strain on an Asian American woman and adjunct instructor in the process. The moment finds Genevieve and David guilty of participating in and, therefore, perpetuating the excruciating unspectacular violence that characterizes anti-Asian sociality in the United States.

Yet even as the obligation to take responsibility for Dennis is thrust upon Gina as a result of structural precarity, displacement, and disavowal, Gina rises to the occasion, motivated by a certain degree of racial and ethnic recognition. She seems almost to advocate for Dennis in his absence. Gina: "He doesn't seem that bad; I mean, he's quiet but ... They just turned in their first assignment. I guess I'll see."[24] At another point, when David proclaims, "It's not normal to not talk ever. It's not normal to be that isolated. It's not normal to be that sad," Gina responds, "It isn't? I mean. Isn't it?"[25] Lines like these suggest that Gina may be driven to engage with Dennis by her "projective identification" with him.[26] The lines locate the substance of Gina's connection to Dennis in what she sees of herself in him: a lonely and neglected Asian American, a struggling writer, and so forth. If this identification yields in Gina a caring attachment to and a sense of caring responsibility for Dennis, it does so as a consequence of a fact made evident in this opening scene: if Gina does not adapt to the needs of this student by making her office a holding environment for the outcast Korean American writer, then no one else will. She cannot but work at the collision point between the burden of care and the burden of representation. Unsupported by those around her in this work, whatever holding environment Gina is able to provisionally establish for Dennis in and as her office hours can only be psychically, structurally, and inevitably fragile and fallible.

Race, Masculinity, Murder

After its first scene *Office Hour* proceeds in a pattern that is both predictable and not. The general structure of that pattern is as follows: first, Gina attempts a performance of pedagogical care founded in a racialized projective identification; second, a momentary opening almost takes hold between Gina and Dennis; third, that opening closes and catastrophe strikes: a shot is fired and/or a life is lost; and, finally, there is a blackout, the scene restarts, and the play continues.

Many of these moments highlight how Dennis's expressions of racialized aggression are inextricably bound to his heterosexual masculinity. They also make even more legible the labor required to produce and sustain the racialized holding environment by demonstrating how well-intentioned racial care is sometimes fumbled or fails in the face of certain gendered and sexual dynamics.

As a first example, consider a moment early in the play that finds Gina attempting to relate to Dennis by opening up about her father. She tells Dennis that her father was an immigrant who lacked power. "He might've had a little if he'd stayed in his own country," Gina speculates, but at his job in the United States "he knew if he wasn't likeable, wasn't agreeable, they would get rid of him."[27] So Gina's father would spend his workdays doing the emotional labor he needed to do to fit in and get by. "Anyone who doesn't have the power knows that dance," Gina tells Dennis.[28] It is a dance done under duress, to the point of exhaustion. And doing such a dance at work, day in and day out, meant that her father would not speak when he returned home at night. He would instead stay silent. While Gina concedes that this silence might be read as a sign of depression, she also casts her father's silence as an attention-seeking strategy that sought control over others by forcing them to talk, wonder, and worry about him.

Gina lays these familial details out like a bridge between herself and Dennis. Her hope seems to be that sharing the story of her father might open some space to discuss Dennis's own performance of silence, a performance that echoes the silence for which Seung-Hui Cho would be scrutinized in the aftermath of the Virginia Tech massacre. Accounts of Cho following the shooting often emphasized the diagnosis of selective mutism that he received in high school. Selective mutism is marked by a challenge with verbal communication. But, as Margaret Price points out, the language with which many in the media and government responded to the shooting would wrongly cast Cho's "difficulty with speech" as a personal "failure" and not as a failure of the institution to provide ample supportive infrastructure.[29] Worse, Cho's mental illness was often cast as "*willful* deviance *resulting in* murderous violence."[30] For Price, characterizations like these reinforce a societal tendency to scapegoat mental illness as the cause of mass shootings. This is harmful because it individualizes violence, obscuring violence's roots in the toxic soils of neglect and abandonment, inequality and injustice.

Office Hour rejects this view and offers instead a way to read selective mutism in relation to issues of race and gender, workplace and family. Gina frames her father's silence not through a logic of medical diagnosis, but as a masculinist will to power in the face of what David Eng has called "racial castration," the psychosocial process through which Asian men are feminized, desexualized, and thus disempowered in the United States.[31] This tells us something about Gina's racialized holding environment: it is calibrated to respond to the (passive-) aggression that erupts when a man's masculinity bleeds from racial wounds. Later in the play Gina reveals that she once feared her father might abuse her mother, a moment that marks his strategic silence not only as a reaction to gendered anti-Asian racism in the workplace but also as a warning sign for gender-based violence in the home. One implication of this is that Dennis's strategic silence might be viewed similarly, as a warning sign for future violence. But by aligning her father's story up against Dennis's, Gina shows her student that he can trust her not to confuse his response to structural injustice for individual pathology. This is Gina clearing a path for racial care, which in this instance would require both she and Dennis to work through racial wounds, gendered anxieties, and how each shows up in the performance of everyday life. But just as something starts to open between Gina and Dennis that opening quickly collapses. Dennis suddenly throws himself from Gina's office window, there is a blackout, and the play restarts from before the suicide. Like the others in this section of the play, this death is a reminder: this is racial care at its limit.

When the play resumes, it does so with another scene that has something to teach us about the way gender and sexuality complicate and therefore constitute the workings of the racialized holding environment. Dennis admits to Gina that he is a virgin and complains that he has never been touched by a girl. "They look at me with ... revulsion," he mourns. Gina responds by asking Dennis if he has ever been touched by someone who isn't family. She moves toward him, drawn in by his vulnerability. She hugs him. But then Dennis kisses her. Gina shoves him away. They exchange horrified looks. The moment sends Dennis to the other side of the room where he "curls up into a ball as if trying to disappear."[32] Gina apologizes and what follows happens in the fallout of this misaligned moment.

As a strategy to get him to open back up, to speak about himself, Gina initiates a role-play. Using a pencil as a phone, she adjusts her voice to sound older, assumes a Korean accent, and begins to act as Dennis's mother calling to check in on her son and his career prospects as a writer. This act and the interactions that immediately follow provoke from Dennis the most lucid explanation for his behavior offered in the play: "The way I am is a rational response to the situation I'm in," he says, "Do you get that?" Dennis tells Gina about the horrible way he was treated as a child by other children. He describes living a life in which he existed as a problem for other people, a problem to be solved through therapeutic methods that never seemed to work. He has hateful things to say about those around him, "the skulls grinning on the streets; the death heads driving their cars; the morons; the idiots; the unenlightened; the oblivious."[33]

This sort of language is the closest the play comes to evoking the manifesto that Seung-Hui Cho sent to MSNBC on the day of his attack. In much more violent and vicious terms, Cho writes in the second person to an unnamed collection of "Hedonists," "Sadists," and "Terrorists." He is writing to the world, to his peers, to his eventual targets because, as he puts it, these people have "ravenously raped [his] soul." They have "fuck[ed] the living shit out of [him]." In Cho's manifesto he imagines himself, in an existential way, as a rape victim. Racially castrated, he is another Asian man in the United States forcibly relegated to a bottom position, both sexually and socially. In *Office Hour*, Dennis does not speak with the same unvarnished vitriol as Cho, but he does deal with a similar racial and gendered reality. Consequently, his lines in this scene expose the same anti-Asian psychosocial structures to which Cho seemed to respond with his manifesto and massacre. "Look at me," Dennis tells Gina, "*Look*. I didn't ask to be born this way, but here I am. I was born to be hated. I was born to be kicked. That's my function. Society needs people like me just as much as it needs the leaders, the celebrities, the admired."[34]

What Dennis describes in this passage is what it feels like to occupy the position of the Asian American abject within the dynamic that Shimakawa calls "national abjection."[35] Neither subject nor object, though productive of subjectivity in others, Dennis feels that he is socially dead. He even refers to himself as an untouchable "rotting corpse," the classic figure of abjection offered by the French philosopher Julia Kristeva.[36] So when Dennis argues that his behavior is a rational response to the situation that he is in, he does so to insist that his suffering is best understood as a byproduct of entrenched psychosocial structures rooted in racial, gendered, and geopolitical injustice. By allowing Dennis to make this point, the play again refuses the ableist scapegoating of "mental illness" that too often functions to individualize violence while obfuscating its other social causes. In *Office Hour*, Dennis is not deranged by cognitive impairment but by gendered racial violence, the desire for self-defense, and possibly the desire for anti-racist revenge. But again, just as Dennis, having spoken his truth, begins to soften into trust and vulnerability, catastrophe strikes. Gina discovers a collection of guns in Dennis's backpack, grabs one for herself, and then, out of fear, shoots him dead before another blackout restarts the play from the moment immediately preceding that shooting.[37] This blackout again reminds the audience to imagine, simultaneously, the good and bad outcomes of Gina's performance of care-full pedagogy. In this way, both *Office Hour*'s dramatic structure and its thematic content render the racialized holding environment as a form of racial care whose failure poses potentially catastrophic consequences.

This is nowhere more evident than in a scene near the end of the play wherein the holding environment of the office hour collapses under the pressure of white masculine encroachment. At a moment when Gina and Dennis seem on the cusp of a breakthrough, David—again, Gina's white male colleague—enters the scene uninvited. He is immediately antagonistic and condescending: calling Dennis "buddy," assuming the worst of him, goading him, and mocking his disabilities.[38] David gripes to Gina that complaints have been lodged against him, accusing him of racism and abuse of students. Not only does he dismiss these complaints as "a joke," but—in violent and hateful terms—he accuses Dennis of making them:

> I fucking know it's you. Chickenshit. You hate my guts, don't you? You'd like to string me up, torture me, hack me to bits the way your fucked-up protagonists do. Live out your little fantasies. Well, fuck you. You're a waste. And put your glasses back on, freak. No one wants to see your ugly fucking face.[39]

I read David's vitriolic enunciations as an onslaught of racial impingement—impingement being Winnicott's name for that which forces a failure in the holding environment to shield the subject from the assaults and insufficiencies of the outside world.[40] We might view racial impingement—whether in the form that Gina experiences, as the captivity of caring pedagogical labor, or in the form that Dennis experiences, as the blatant blitz of white masculinity—as a relentless interruption to minoritarian existence, a specific genre of microaggression, and a significant source of psychosocial attrition. Racial impingement is cause for racial care. It is and installs a kind of white noise in the psyche that cannot but disintegrate the subject by droning on and drowning out the possibilities and complexities of that subject's geopolitical histories, creative presents, or liberatory futures.

Indeed, it is David's white noise—static sounded by the certainty he feels about his own invulnerability—that seems to shatter whatever semblance of a racialized holding environment Gina and Dennis have built between themselves. For just as David's tirade tempers, just before he exits the room, Dennis, enraged and emboldened, pulls out a gun and shoots David, then Gina, and then himself; and then there is another blackout. But the play does not reset. Instead, a sequence of violent endings follows, endings that vary depending on the production. Here is The Public's staging: David shoots Dennis. Blackout. Lights up. Gina shoots herself in the head. Blackout. Lights up. Dennis aims a machine gun out the window of the office and opens fire. Blackout. Lights up. All three characters hide in the dark from another shooter who lurks outside the office. Blackout. Lights up. All three lie dead. Prerecorded gunshots sonically assault the audience in surround sound for what feels like too long a time. Blackout. Lights up.

And with this illumination, the play is reset and the audience is returned to a stand-off between David and Dennis. However, rather than allowing David to denigrate Dennis as she did in the first iteration of the scene, this time Gina lodges her body physically between her student and his harasser. She refutes David's unfounded allegations and implores him to stop bullying Dennis. "You intimidate him. He doesn't feel safe around you," Gina explains, rightly identifying the source of insecurity in the room before asking that source to see himself out.[41] Taken together, these scenes lay bare the vulnerability of the racialized holding environment and its inhabitants to the whims and warmongering of white masculine insolence. It also reveals the profound performative force carried by nurturant, protective, and feminine sacrifice—both personal and professional—in the construction and fortification of the racialized holding environment. Put another way, the promise of this moment is also its gender trouble: the forms of racial care that come at the greatest cost to women and femmes of color can also be those that promise the greatest reward for other minoritarian subjects.

Asian American Loneliness

At the beginning of *Office Hour*'s conclusion, Dennis stands alone on a dark stage. Finally, he has written something with the potential to connect to others. He reads:

It's four a.m.

It's four a.m. and I am eating a donut.

It's four a.m. and I am eating a donut and thinking about something I heard once about the Great Pacific Garbage Patch. It is hundreds of miles long. It consists of billions of pieces of plastic. There is no one cause. The pieces have come from everywhere. Some are big, some are small. It is a place of death. No fish, no animal survives there. The Patch is big and getting bigger every day. But it is so far away. We know it is there but we don't see it. And because we can't see it, we don't think about it. So it just sits there. Getting bigger day by day by day.[42]

The first lines of Dennis's monologue, in echoing prompts offered to him by Gina earlier in the play ("it's four a.m.," references to a donut shop), evidence a scaffolding constructed by her pedagogical labor. What follows next builds upon the accretive foundation of Gina's care-full teaching to provide a model through which to understand racialized violence. Here, the Great Pacific Garbage Patch serves as an ecologically oriented metaphor for anti–Asian American impingements, both micro and macro. To position the Great Pacific Garbage Patch as a metaphor for Asian American affective suffering resulting from impingement is to position racial impingement as pollution, as that which can accumulate within and around transpacific life and, in accumulating, threaten that life. When Julia Cho, through Dennis, characterizes the Great Pacific Garbage Patch as a "place of death"—as a necropolitical zone cultivated by constant, collective negligence—she makes this explicit.[43] From this perspective, Genevieve's and David's earlier uncertainties around Dennis's mastery of English as well as their invocations of chi-sucking appear, as they should, as little more than toxic waste. We might read Dennis's (and by extension, Seung-Hui Cho's) violent writings, including the text of this final monologue, as the excess and exhaust of racial impingement, that internalized toxicity that must be expelled and expressed for attrition to be alleviated, for life to be livable. We might also read this singular moment of creative expression from Dennis as a direct result of his time within the racialized holding environment.

If Dennis's final monologue clarifies the consequence of racial care, white noise, and negligence, then the play's final scene gestures toward the (im)possibility of racialized remediation. The lights come up on Gina bent over beneath a tree outside of her office. When Genevieve, her colleague, approaches her to ask what she is doing, Gina responds, "picking up some litter."[44] Indeed, Gina is bent to gather pages of Dennis's writing from the ground, pages that she threw in frustration from her office window earlier in the play. The moment is, in part, an optimistic one. Gina's act of collection is an act of care for Dennis, the "litter" evidence of and metaphor for the racial impingement he has been made to suffer throughout the play and throughout his life. About Dennis, Gina hopefully remarks: "Maybe he'll be okay."[45] But Genevieve—unsatisfied at Gina's seemingly unfounded optimism—presses on, asking whether Gina spoke to Dennis and, if so, what resulted. When Gina demurs Genevieve persists, and Gina responds in an impatient tone of voice:

GENEVIEVE: But you have to do something.

GINA: You too.

GENEVIEVE: Me?

GINA: Figure it out.[46]

This exchange expresses a certain struggle and structure of feelings found by the playwright in Gina, Dennis, and by extension in Seung-Hui Cho: namely, anti-Asian neglect and its affective companion, Asian American loneliness. Genevieve, in her insistence that Gina in particular must do something for Dennis, doubles down on the displacement of the gendered and racialized caring and pedagogical labor she effected earlier in the narrative. Gina's rebuff and redirection of Genevieve asserts that this student's needs must be met by everyone, at all levels, at all times. The exchange, in other words, resurfaces the complicated interracial relations with which the play began.

The pernicious power of Asian American loneliness is evident in the sense that nearly no area of Asian American life seems to escape its affective saturation. Asian American loneliness is a racialized condition of debility that indexes both a structural reality of racialized social isolation and a psychic and affective condition comorbid with other (deracinated) conditions more legible within the logic of medical diagnosis.[47] Asian American loneliness might be given in and as the isolation that characterizes the Asian immigrant experience and its often concomitant linguistic and performatic alienation. Or else and in other contexts, Asian American loneliness might be the mood of the model minority—the subject whose supposed success delegitimizes claims to suffering and solidarity that might be made to the dominant culture or its other dominated others. When experienced in this latter mode especially, the unbearability of Asian American loneliness for the (assimilative) Asian American subject often leads to the splintering of interracial coalition, insofar as this particular structure of ugly feelings frequently yields anti-Black performances of what Jared Sexton has called "people of color blindness."[48] And, indeed, this is one way to read the interaction that transpires between Gina and Genevieve in this late scene.

Gina no doubt has a right to her anger inasmuch as it emerges out of an experience of Asian American loneliness rooted in burden, isolation, and attrition. But one could argue that Gina misdirects her anger at Genevieve. She forgets that Genevieve had already done her due diligence with Dennis. She also forgets that Genevieve, as a Black woman, is likely also overwhelmed by the twinned burdens of care and representation. In other words, Gina's misdirected anger demonstrates that for all that Asian American loneliness might drain from Asian American life, it can lead to exacerbated anti-Black burden as well. By making this dynamic legible, *Office Hour* reminds its audience that the problem of the Asian American outcast is not the problem of Asian Americans alone and, therefore, cannot be left only to other, lone Asian American outcast(s) to solve. The project of ensuring the livability of Asian American life—whether in its academic instantiation in and as the interdisciplinary field of Asian American (theater and performance) studies or in its myriad activist manifestations nationwide—is too often misrecognized as the province of Asian Americans alone, and of Asian American women in particular. This must not and cannot be. For, as both *Office Hour* and Virginia Tech attest, Asian American loneliness, the condition of being neglected, abandoned, burdened, and alone—a lone adjunct made to martyr herself or a lone gunman driven to murder others—may risk the possibility of total annihilation, Asian American and otherwise.[49]

The Theatrical Holding Environment

After Gina exits the stage thinking she has gathered all of Dennis's writing from the ground, a stray page falls from a tree. Genevieve picks it up and, puzzled, reads:

This is the story.

The story is the story.

It tells itself to itself.

It tells itself to itself.

It tells itself to itself.

Again and again and again.[50]

Though within the world of the play these final lines are written by Dennis, my own interpretive impulse is not to read them as such. The insights into "the story" of Asian American abjection and loneliness that such a reading might yield have already been outlined here and elsewhere. My preferred analysis of the play's final lines approaches them from another angle: as meta-theatricality. From this vantage point, "the story" referenced in this passage must be that of *Office Hour*: a Korean American adjunct instructor forced to teach and to care for her troubled and potentially violent Korean American student. It is the story of Gina's office hours, the story of a racialized holding environment. Accepting this, the reiterated line, "it tells itself to itself," signals the inextricability of the story, the storyteller(s), and the audience, the inextricability of *Office Hour* and of those in the theater. Both are "itself," "the story."

Implied here, on the one hand, is the somewhat banal fact that the issues and imbalanced power relations depicted in and by *Office Hour* belong equally to the world of its audience as to the world of the play. "The story" reiterated in and as

Office Hour is here a stand-in for any number of ineffective and isolated political narratives and movements: the reiterative and ungenerative handwringing that happens in the aftermath of mass shootings in the United States; the echo chamber known as the political project of Asian Americanism; or the ongoing and too-often infelicitous efforts to save the planet from neoliberal racial capitalism. The lines obliquely imply that its audience must take responsibility for, if not action to solve, the problems posed by the play, even as the lines also belie a tired pessimism in relation to their own effort. The lines invite, for instance, a white and/or male audience member to identify with David and to notice that Dennis's destructiveness depends on David's, even as the lines seem also to doubt the penetrability of white male self-regard.

On the other hand, to the extent that "the story" of Gina's office hours can be said to be the story of *Office Hour* and to the extent that "the story" (of Gina's office hours) must be understood as identical to and inextricable from the storyteller ("*it* tells," the theater-maker[s]) and audience ("to *itself*," the theatergoers), the play's final lines propose a certain formal equivalence between the space-time of academic office hours and the space-time of the theatrical encounter. If "the story is the story," then it follows that the space-time of academic office hours and the space-time of theatrical encounter might both be understood as potential racialized holding environments. To position the theater, theoretically, as a racialized holding environment is to make the theater legible as a carefully controlled architecture of event and affect. Doing so enables us to utilize the holding environment as a fresh frame through which to analyze theater-making and theater-going, a frame more or less pertinent to divergent theatrical forms and genres.

Some readers may find *Office Hour* to be an unlikely play around which to mount an argument about the theater's potential to function as a holding environment. How can a play designed to induce so much discomfort be called a site of care? Wouldn't an analysis of, say, Julia Cho's *Aubergine* better support my claims? That play, after all, foregrounds the racialized care performed by a son for his dying Korean father and does so without all the gunfire.

But the gunfire, in some ways, better illustrates the point. In arguing that the theatrical encounter of ethnic theater can operate as a racialized holding environment, I am not suggesting that that holding environment must constantly feel comforting in its uninterrupted care-fullness. Rather, when operative, the theatrical holding environment can be accidentally undone (cue the cellphone ring) or else aesthetically altered in order to adjust the experiences and, possibly, the subjectivities of its inhabitants. *Office Hour* displays its awareness of this fact each time a shot is fired on stage, but especially in the unsettling onslaught of surround-sound gunfire that characterizes the play's climactic moment. This moment impinges upon the theatrical holding environment in order, it seems, to jolt or shock those within it into other modes of subjectivity more vigilant in relation to gun violence and the gendered, racialized, and ableist violences that subtend it. That the presence of the play's gunfire is signaled to audience members in advance of their entrance into the theater (a literal trigger warning) only supports the claim that *Office Hour*'s gunfire is at once a potential impingement and a conscious aesthetic strategy.

Considering the theater as a racialized holding environment in this way positions the theater's feminine side as efficacious insofar as it elevates the qualities it shares with the Winnicottian mother.[51] According to Winnicott, the holding environment is "reliable in a way that implies the mother's empathy."[52] Winnicott locates this empathy (a feeling-with) in the identification (a feeling-like) of the mother with the infant. This empathic identification yields a crucial performatic element of the holding environment: "a live adaptation to the infant's needs."[53] This capacity for live adaptation rhymes with a central theme of care ethics identified in the work of Daniel Engster and Maurice Hamington: "responsiveness to the other."[54] This possibility for real-time, live adaptation and responsiveness distinguishes the theatrical response to Seung-Hui Cho and his massacre from those responses communicated by way of the televisual. And while we can also note that the theater's most beloved (if often exploitative) cliché, "the show must go on," is testament to its reliability and real-time adaptability, the more crucial point regarding the racialized holding environment is found in the play of racial empathy and identification, in the sustaining slippage of feeling-with and feeling-like other racialized others.[55]

To that end, it is instructive to frame the production of an Asian American play as a racialized "transformational object." For Christopher Bollas, "transformational object" names an object that, similar to the Winnicottian mother, promises an aesthetic, affective, and existential experience of "enviro-somatic caring, identified with metamorphoses of the self."[56] Bollas tells us that "symbolic equivalents" to the mother-as-originary-transformational-object take many forms (deities, ideologies, commodities, artworks).[57] What he does not say but what we must acknowledge is that the specific materiality of those symbolic equivalents draws upon and inflects back upon the specific materiality of the subject that seeks them. In turn, the care and transformation promised and provided (if, indeed, it is provided) by the transformational object are similarly shaped by that specific materiality. Succinctly, the racialized transformational object of ethnic theater emanates two conjoined promises to the racialized subjects that experience it as such. First, there is the affective relief of identitarian representation (feeling-likeness, however incongruently), which Dorinne Kondo might prefer to call "the promise of public existence."[58] And second, there is the possibility of empathic recognition (feeling-withness, however distantly).

This fusion of feeling-with and feeling-like—a fusion that, as I have demonstrated above, is given in the play's final lines—might for racialized subjects approximate that uncanny and fleeting feeling of fusion that Winnicott and Bollas each believe originates in the holding environment of primary maternal relation, a provisional antidote for Asian American loneliness, if there ever was one. But the promise does not end there. Like the mother for the infant, the therapist for the patient, or the teacher for the student, *Office Hour*'s embrace of its Asian American audience, while always care-full, may at times feel more complicated than comforting. This is especially true when that care is expressed and extended in and as an externalizing and processing of snarled psychic stuff: (dis)identifications with murderers and the maternal, hateful resentment at the same, and the experience of being coercively cast within ethnically assigned roles and obligations. All this is to say: if the affective architecture of a given Asian American theatrical production constitutes a racialized holding environment, this is not because it always feels good. Sometimes it feels like a confrontation with something one has yet to process; but it is a confrontation constructed, at least, by trained artists in a carefully controlled context.

There is, finally, something to add about the interpersonal proximity promised by the theatrical racialized holding environment. Shimakawa has written that the proximity between the abject Asian American body on stage and the non–Asian American audience member might yield a generative racial discomfort in the latter as a function of the processes of abjection and critical mimesis. This potential is no doubt put to use in Julia Cho's play to disrupt the presumption that the racialized holding environment of commercial theater is one calibrated to whiteness. But the proximities of similarly suffering racialized bodies—onstage and off, intimate and not—endemic to the theatrical racialized holding environment might also serve as a source of solace. By requiring one to sit alone in the company of others and in relation to the transformational object, a stand-in for the mother, the theater provides an occasion to be alone together in a way that is less alienating than it is enabling. For Winnicott, the infant develops "the capacity to be alone"—that is, the ability to relax into the belief in a dependable environment—by spending time "alone in the presence of someone."[59] Attending Asian American theater, then, might combat the hard reality of Asian American loneliness—even and especially if one is a lone Asian American audience member in a sea of white theater patrons—by cultivating a similar capacity to soften into something like the sense that someone like you stands with you, to care for you and to fight beside you, on stage and in the melee of the social. As Summer Kim Lee has argued, rather than amounting to yet another instance of Asian American loneliness, attending a show alone as an Asian American subject can amount to a performance of "staying in, of turning and keeping oneself inward" and away from the demands of the social as an act of self-care.[60] Moreover, following Winnicott's formulations, I suggest that the racialized holding environment of ethnic theater—with its interpersonal proximities and circulating affects, with its demand that we disconnect from constant communications and cultivate the capacity to be alone, with its real-time adaptations and care-full gendered and racial attunements—might yield an alternative space-time within which (inter)subjectivity can be (re)formed, made more supple, and more sensitive.

My next chapter addresses another example of Asian American theater with an analysis of the Generic Ensemble Company's experimental musical, *The Mikado: Reclaimed*, a deconstruction of the eponymous Gilbert and Sullivan opera. Set in a dystopian near-future wherein Asians are again interned in the United States, this time for carrying a dormant virus that threatens white life, *The Mikado: Reclaimed* provides an opportunity to address an issue immanent to what it means to be held in and by the world: if the holding environment is a form of care conjured through performance to sustain the subject's life, what are we to make of holding patterns, pens, and cells—environments instantiated in the name of care for certain populations that simultaneously function to drain other populations of life?

At the end of *Office Hour*, everyone is alive. This fact demonstrates that (at least in the playwright's eyes) the racialized holding environment has the potential to deter or delay violence and premature death. This is not nothing, but it is also not much. At best, the racialized holding environment—whether given in the form of the office hour or the theatrical encounter—functions as a good-enough interval, an eye in the storm in which to be and just breathe and through which to see that the storm is not all that there is. At worst, the racialized holding environment often comes at immeasurable cost to those responsible for its upkeep, women of color especially and most frequently. That Gina dies multiple (false?) deaths in Julia Cho's play attests to this fact. The truth: the racialized holding environment too often takes life from one and gives it to another. But you have to do something. Again and again and again.

3

Racial Emotional Labor

Near the end of his classic work of minoritarian performance theory, *Disidentifications: Queers of Color and the Performance of Politics*, José Esteban Muñoz writes the following: "Minoritarian subjects do not always dance because they are happy; sometimes they dance because their feet are being shot at."[1] He is writing about what he calls "the burden of liveness," a term that aims to emphasize how people of color, women, queer and trans people, and other oppressed groups are often made to perform in particular ways for majoritarian audiences—or else.[2] Think of Black slaves being forced, under threat of violence, to perform for the pleasure and profit of white plantation owners. Or simply recall the many historical instances in which actors of color, to secure stable work on stages and screens, have had to shrink themselves to fit into small roles characterized by shallow racial caricature. To have one's performance prescribed by normative mandates and elite interests: this is what it is to face the burden of liveness. "Performance, from the positionality of the minoritarian subject," writes Muñoz, "is often nothing short of forced labor."³ This chapter takes this observation seriously, advancing our understanding of the burden of liveness by outlining some of the labors that multiply marginalized Asian Americans are often forced by social and structural circumstances to perform for majoritarian audiences. My aim is first to illustrate just how much of this forced labor can be construed as racial care, and then to show that it is possible to alter such coercive relations of racial care for the better through performance.

The burden of liveness is everywhere evident in the history of Asian America, and it is most obviously made manifest in performances of patriotism. After Pearl Harbor, Japanese Americans were forced to evidence their loyal attachments to the United States in any number of ways. Dorothea Lange's famous photo of a Japanese American-owned storefront baring the words "I Am An American" comes to mind. We can also recall Joshua Chambers-Letson's descriptions of Japanese and Japanese American school children reciting the Pledge of Allegiance from inside the concentration camps in which they were incarcerated at the time.⁴ Following September 11, Sikh men wore star-spangled banner-styled turbans, presumably to avoid violent animus. And on April 1, 2020, in response to the rise in anti-Asian violence that accompanied the coronavirus pandemic, former democratic presidential candidate and eventual New York City mayoral candidate Andrew Yang wrote the following in the *Washington Post*: "We Asian Americans need to embrace our American-ness in ways we never have before. We should show without a shadow of a doubt that we are Americans who will do our part for our country in this time of need."⁵

Insofar as each of these assimilative performances of patriotism amounts to an earnest attempt to avoid the violence that would follow from failing to perform in this way, each should be seen as exemplary of the burden of liveness. And these performances should also be understood as attempts at navigating what Summer Kim Lee calls the "burden of relatability" suffered by Asian American subjects who are forced "not only to be legible and transparent but also accessibly and accommodatingly so."⁶ Lee's concern is with "the psychic burdens and affective labors of sociality that slip into compulsory sociability," within which Asian American queers and other minoritarian subjects are expected not only to be social in order to be properly political but also to make themselves relatable to others—some who seek to support their well-being and some who, passively or actively, do not.⁷ If thinking with the burden of liveness helps me to emphasize the ways in which minoritarian subjects are made to perform in ahistorical or self-sacrificing ways for majoritarian audiences, thinking with the burden of relatability helps me situate those performances, those forced labors, within an entangled web of ordinary social relations.

This chapter is centrally concerned with one kind of forced labor that shadows multiply marginalized Asian American subjects across psychosocial life. Drawing on Arlie Hochschild's theory of "emotional labor" as well as on that theory's underpinnings in the work of Erving Goffman, my task here is to advance a theory of *racial emotional labor*. I argue that racial emotional labor can be understood as a form of racial care that multiply marginalized Asian American subjects have historically been made to perform, at their own expense, in relation both to whites and the nation-state. According to Hochschild, emotional labor "requires one to induce or suppress feeling in order to sustain the outward countenance that produces the proper state of mind in others."[8] By extension, then, racial emotional labor refers to the labor through which racially minoritized subjects adjust their self-presentation in order to induce in others certain feelings. In framing racial emotional labor as a form of racial care, my aim is to expose the relational and affective dynamics through which multiply marginalized Asian American subjects are coerced, in both ordinary and exceptional circumstances, into providing a certain kind of racialized care to their oppressors as a way to spare themselves and others around them from violence.

This sort of coercion is rooted in what Xine Yao has called "the emotional respectability required by the politics of recognition."[9] In order to be recognized as human, Yao argues, people of color must express their feelings in a way that white society deems acceptable or sympathetic. "To be unsympathetically unresponsive to the emotional demands of whiteness means foreclosing recognition as worthy of sympathy."[10] Yao's response to this unjust situation is to advance a performative politics of "disaffection" or "unfeeling," one that signals a certain "skepticism and reluctance to signify the appropriate expressions of affect that are socially legible as human, which can rise to the refusal to care and sympathize as part of the expected cues of deference that maintain and structure biopolitical hierarchies of oppression." Yao's argument is compelling, and when she asks, "Can a calculus of uncaring allow for us to better care for ourselves and others?," one must answer in the affirmative.[11] When people of color are not beholden to the emotional mandates that organize white sociality, they are better able to express, perform, and relate to others in ways that suit their own needs, desires, and movements. And yet, disaffection is not always a viable strategy. Sometimes to perform disaffection is too dangerous a risk to take. For this reason, this chapter focuses less on acts of refusal in the face of white social and emotional scripts than on situations in which such refusals are deemed too costly. These situations find Asian Americans navigating the burdens of liveness and relatability, which are each inextricable from the hegemonic emotional protocols that Yao opposes. These situations thus require a rethinking of such burdens through the lens of racial emotional labor.

This rethinking, however, must also be a reckoning with the definitional ambivalence that emotional labor has taken on in relation to questions of care. In her original theorization of the concept, Hochschild places her emphasis on emotional labor performed by flight attendants in the context of gendered service work. Flight attendants are made to smile, to speak amiably, and to perform positive affect in order to produce a satisfactory emotional experience in airline passengers. They are made to manage their emotions and the impressions they make on others. But, Hochschild asks, what effect does this kind of labor relation have on the flight attendant's experience of her own feelings and embodied expressive capacities? The question gestures to what is at stake in Hochschild's theory of emotional labor. When feeling and the expression of feeling are conscripted and managed by company policy for profit, the worker can become painfully alienated from herself.

This framework for understanding emotional labor contrasts with another, more colloquial understanding of the term exemplified in Leah Lakshmi Piepzna-Samarasinha's essay "A Modest Proposal for a Fair Trade Emotional Labor Economy."[12] In this essay Piepzna-Samarasinha writes about emotional labor as emotional support, which she deems a kind of care work whose ethics are characterized by a combination of consent, reciprocity, rest, and gratitude. Some critics bemoan what they consider the supposed misuse of "emotional labor" presented by Piepzna-Samarasinha.[13] For these critics, the conflation of emotional labor and emotional support dilutes Hochschild's original theorization and its focus on emotion work that is also paid work. My main concern in what follows is with racial emotional labor performed as part of paid employment, namely that which is exhibited by racially alienated actors in the theatrical workplace both while in character and not. In attending to these workplace performances of racial emotional labor, however, I also demonstrate that emotional labor–as–emotional support always entails at least some aspects of emotional labor as Hochschild theorizes it. If one is working to comfort and care for a friend who has experienced racial violence, one must also always work to produce a countenance that supports such aims. The reverse, I would argue, is true as well: emotional labor–as–emotion management can function as a performance of emotional support. Sometimes it is precisely by suppressing one's feelings of racial suffering, by *not* expressing them, that we provide implicit emotional support to majoritarian subjects whose psychic stability would be threatened by exposure to racial reality. By defending these claims, I demonstrate that the concept of racial emotional labor and the theory of racial care that this book aims to advance more broadly require a capacious rather than a restrictive approach to the concept of emotional labor.

To this end, this chapter analyzes two theatrical productions. The first, which I will discuss by describing my own experience as an ensemble member in it, is a production of W. S. Gilbert and Arthur Sullivan's opera *The Mikado*. The second is a radical adaptation of Gilbert and Sullivan's opera devised and performed by the Generic Ensemble Company (GenEnCo), a performance ensemble—formerly based in Austin, Texas—with an entirely Asian American cast of performers. That production, directed by GenEnCo's founder kt shorb and aptly titled *The Mikado: Reclaimed*, dissembles Gilbert and Sullivan's opera and puts it back together anew, in service to an anti-racist political project. *The Mikado: Reclaimed* imagines a near future in which Asian Americans are once again discarded into concentration camps, this time for carrying a deadly virus that threatens white American life. Notably, *The Mikado: Reclaimed* was first performed in 2016, more than three years prior to the emergence of COVID-19. And unlike the performances of patriotism described above, the racial emotional labor that appears in the stories I tell about *The Mikado* and *The Mikado: Reclaimed* are less about assimilation than they are about the obligation, often experienced by multiply marginalized Asian Americans, to either endure or enact racial-gendered violence, frequently in the form of auto-orientalization, in order to avoid the further escalation of that violence.

The first half of this chapter is dedicated to identifying and describing a form of racial care in racial emotional labor that does at least as much work to constrain and drain multiply marginalized Asian American life as it does to sustain it. In the second half of the chapter, I take up another form of care, one developed precisely to alleviate—or at least to redistribute—the burdens of liveness, relatability, and racial care. I offer a close reading of the rehearsal practices employed by GenEnCo to theorize what I call the *minoritarian team*, a social form with the potential to lighten, however ephemerally and incompletely, the workload of emotional labor, racial and otherwise. I also analyze the queer forms of racial care that the characters of *The Mikado: Reclaimed* perform for one another within the concentration camps in which they have been violently quarantined.

The Mikado

Undyingly popular since its London premiere in 1885, *The Mikado* by Gilbert and Sullivan is perhaps the most overtly racist relic of the musical theater canon to still receive regular productions. It is known for its unabashed employment of yellowface performance, and it is usually cast, as a matter of course, with white actors who don kimonos, wave fans, carry samurai swords, shade themselves with parasols, paint their faces white, and reshape their eyes to appear absurdly

East Asian. Such racial mimicry and abhorrent appropriation is the aesthetic milieu of the fictional and fantastical town of Titipu in which the piece is set, a land populated by characters with such egregiously exotic names as Nanki-Poo, Yum-Yum, Pooh-Bah, and Ko-Ko—a land that far too many have come to associate with and internalize as Japan. As Josephine Lee notes in her book-length study of the opera's historical legacy, "*The Mikado* in particular defies charges that it is a racist work. Though its characterizations, settings, and story clearly misrepresent Japan in ways that can be seen as patronizing and insulting, at the same time it is a comic opera that disclaims the seriousness of these representations."[14] Lovers of *The Mikado* often argue that the musical is only tenuously tied to Japan insofar as its original intent was to lampoon Victorian Britain by displacing British absurdities onto an exotic elsewhere for critique. My own view is this: to the extent that *The Mikado* has long been a source of orientalist fervor for the masses—a phenomenon especially exacerbated in the United States due to a failure by the opera's creators to maintain copyright there—it has also been a source of immense suffering for Asian Americans and for Japanese Americans in particular.

This is why I am almost ashamed to admit that during the summer of 2010, I spent several weeks as an ensemble member in a production of *The Mikado*. I was an undergraduate in need of money at the time, so when my school announced the opera as the main-stage musical of its summer season, I decided to audition. I did not know much about the show other than that it was Asian and vaguely racist. Or racist and vaguely Asian. And I knew that students cast in the show would receive a stipend and free on-campus housing. As an aspiring theater major at an almost entirely white institution, I thought: easy money. I thought: It would be racist *not* to cast me, an Asian American actor, in this production.

I thought wrong. Once rehearsals began, it was not long before I was made to move in orientalizing ways: with short steps, cow-towing, unfurling fans, and so forth. Just as swiftly, I was instructed to sing in nauseating, nasal tones that caricatured tonal languages. I remember a dressing room full of white castmates in yellowface who would say things like "Do my eyes look slanty enough?" and "Me look so pretty!" But they would say these things in a too-familiar accent: "Do my eyes rook sranty enough?" "Me rook so pletty!" In response to this orientalist onslaught, I found myself able to do little other than muscle forth some mild laughter. This is also what I did when the production's director, a former professor of mine, spotted me onstage and shouted from the audience: "James McMaster, you are the king of the ensemble!" It was bad racial care: an attempt to address my Asianness that took its cue from Gilbert and Sullivan's attempt to address Japan's. I laughed, standing before him in my kimono, eyebrows altered to exaggerate whatever Asiatic facial features I already have.[15]

My laughter in this instance was neither inaction nor acquiescence but a performance of racial emotional labor. For Hochschild, emotional labor can come in two forms: "surface acting" and "deep acting." Whereas in "deep acting" a social performer is actually attempting to *feel* otherwise about a given social exchange, in "surface acting" the social performer is only "acting as if he had the feeling." Were I deep acting when my director made his racist remark, I would be trying to conjure the real feeling that what he had said was good-humored and good-hearted. But I was surface acting. I was adjusting my comportment to comply with what Hochschild calls "the feeling rules" that govern everyday social life and interracial interaction.[16] When one is gifted with a compliment, for example, the normative feeling rules dictate that one should receive that compliment with an outward display of grace or gratitude. When one is told a joke, one is expected to respond to that joke with a smile, laughter, or some other evidence of good humor. But when a compliment or joke carries with it objectionable racial connotations, these rules of emotional exchange, though often experienced as race-neutral guidelines for maintaining smooth social relations, suddenly become secret sites of racial subordination.

To put this point another way, racial emotional labor is the other side of what Robin DiAngelo, writing in a social psychological register, famously calls "white fragility."[17] Where white people are concerned, DiAngelo writes, "the smallest amount of racial stress is intolerable."[18] To be forced to confront one's complicity with white supremacy is, for many white people, to have one's identity as a good, moral, and well-intentioned person called into question. It is potentially to have one's sense of self shattered. This experience of psychic instability often leads white people to engage certain "defensive responses," which for DiAngelo include affective responses "such as anger, fear, and guilt" and actions that range from antisocial withdrawal to outright racial violence enacted to secure "white racial control."[19]

It is possible, and in many ways worthwhile, to meditate on the generosity that subjects of color exercise each day in the amount of care taken to tiptoe around the psychic and affective crises that fragile white subjects are at risk of experiencing if their implicit racism is made explicit. When one considers the affective suffering that befalls white subjects as a consequence of white fragility, emotional labor can come to appear as a form of racial care. Racial emotional labor is often undertaken to induce in the unwitting white person, the racially subordinating subject, more pleasurable, sustaining, sustainable, or even merely endurable feelings. On occasion, this affective work is performed voluntarily, out of what may feel like an ethical impulse to keep an other, even an oppressive other, psychically intact and otherwise unhurt. But this is how white racial control continues: fueled perversely by the kind of care performed by racialized others, whether racially conscious or not.

Most racial emotional labor is not performed out of generosity. It is instead the embodied consequence of an almost infrared sociopolitical infrastructure of racial coercion. When I laughed at my director's joke, for example, I was attempting to act in accordance with that infrastructure. My sense was that such a performance, too often characteristic of the superior-subordinate workplace relationship, was required of me in the moment. The performance of laughter in response to ordinary racial and gendered microaggression in the workplace can be a mode of surface acting mastered by the marginalized to convince offensive interlocutors, ignorant to their own intrusive expressions, that no offense has been taken.

In these circumstances, as Eve Sedgwick teaches us, "it is the interlocutor who has or pretends to have the *less* broadly knowledgeable understanding of interpretive practice who will define the terms of the situation."[20] In my case, my director's (feigned?) racial ignorance meant that in order to avoid open conflict I had little choice but to protect him from the impression that an Asian person might consider his actions, and him by extension, and his production by further extension, racist. I was forced to protect my director, to care for him in a way, to remain relatable in his eyes. I protected him to protect myself from the violent consequences that are often incurred when a "subordinate," professional or racial, shatters a "superior's" sense of self or situation. Had I chosen in that moment to speak out, I would have been at risk of making myself an enemy of the entire production—not just of my director but of the cast and crew as well. I might have become the racial problem by exposing the racial problem. In Goffman's words, I was trying "to put the superior at ease by simulating the kind of world the superior is thought to take for granted."[21]

And so, we start to see how racial emotional labor can be understood as a burden of racial care. I was caring for my director and castmates by sparing them the fallout of their own white fragility, and I was caring for myself in the same way, by avoiding the violence that might befall me were I to trip a wire of the white psyche. My personal well-being as well as the continuity of my employment each required me to remain in relation to the people around me, racist or not, through a good-enough performance of racial emotional labor. And this performance was also, I argue, a performance of social reproduction. According to the socialist feminist Nancy Fraser, social reproduction "is about the creation and maintenance of social bonds."[22] Some of those social bonds are intergenerational, exemplified and reinforced in childcare and eldercare. But others run horizontally: among friends, members of a community, or even a workplace. "Simultaneously affective and material," Fraser writes, social reproduction "supplies the 'social glue' that underpins social cooperation."[23] And this is why racial emotional labor must be understood as a genre of social reproductive labor.[24] One of racial emotional labor's primary functions is given in the task of "sustaining connection" between differently racialized subjects.[25]

The performance of racial emotional labor is care work, which is to say socially reproductive emotional support, to the extent that it functions to reproduce the psychic stability of the white subject. It is also socially reproductive, by extension, insofar as it sustains the social bonds that allow whites and non-whites to remain in productive proximity to one another both in private life and in workplaces, theatrical rehearsal rooms among them, within a white supremacist society. The problem, of course, is that these social bonds are maintained only as a consequence of the coerced surface acting of the non-white subject. By sustaining these social connections, the non-white subject also sustains the relational hierarchies that define those connections. In other words, when non-white subjects, through the performance of racial emotional labor, work to reproduce the psychic coherence of the white subject, they are also reproducing what might simply be called white sociality itself by allowing the fantasy of white racial innocence to remain unnamed and untouched. In this way, the Asian American subject is recruited into performatively sustaining their own racially oppressive social situation.

This insight has significant implications for how we must then think about the racial emotional labor exerted, for instance, by Asian American actors performing in anti-Asian theatrical productions. Hochschild notably borrows the concepts of surface acting and deep acting from the preeminent theater practitioner Konstantin Stanislavsky. In doing so, Hochschild acknowledges that emotional labor is performed not only in everyday life but also whenever the curtain rises on theatrical performance. All stage acting is emotional labor. For the Asian American actor performing *The Mikado*'s musical numbers, this means a certain double duty. The racial emotional labor the Asian American actor performs for the benefit of their non-Asian director, castmates, and other coworkers is extended in and as the racial emotional labor that that actor must perform for the benefit of the production's mostly white audiences. Both performances of emotional labor reinforce the fantasy of white racial innocence at the expense of Asian American well-being. And both are also performed under surveillance, which is to say under the watchful eyes of white fragility.

These may seem like minor points given how rarely Asian American actors are cast in *The Mikado*. But the problem extends far beyond Gilbert and Sullivan.

Much of what is available in the larger musical theater canon for Asian American actors requires a similar tolerance for yellowface and a similarly self-defacing performance. We can think here of *The King and I* and *Thoroughly Modern Millie*. And we can also think of *Miss Saigon*, perhaps the most obvious example, which has been taken to task countless times not just for the historic use of yellowface in its original Broadway production but also for the numerous misogynist tropes it contains: a vision of Vietnam as a sexual playground for the US military and of Asian women as self-sacrificing martyrs.

The Mikado: Reclaimed, GenEnCo's radical adaptation of Gilbert and Sullivan's opera, represents an alternative to these mainstream productions. It critically deploys yellowface against itself and in so doing seeks to make explicit the notion that *The Mikado* requires an escalated performance of emotional labor. And whereas my experience in *The Mikado* has enabled me to demonstrate how the performance of racial emotional labor can function to uphold racist social relations on an interpersonal scale, *The Mikado: Reclaimed* provides occasion to consider the performance of racial emotional labor on the scale of the nation-state.

The Mikado: Reclaimed

The Mikado: Reclaimed premiered at the Vortex Theater in Austin, Texas, in February 2016.[26] It was devised, produced, and performed by the Generic Ensemble Company (GenEnCo), an experimental theater troupe whose mission involves making "the invisible visible through bold, socially relevant, body-centered theatre." On their website, GenEnCo writes: "We view marginal bodies, experiences, and subject positions as central to the form and content of creating work. As such we strive to promote, foster, and engage performance, writing and ideas of/with people of color, queers, gender queers, women, working class people, immigrants and youth."[27] The company was established in 2009 by artistic director, kt shorb, and it is shorb's training in the repertoires of Viewpoints, Suzuki, and the Theatre of the Oppressed that has historically determined the company's devising process. My perspective on that process and much of the argument that unfolds in what follows has been shaped by my time as a GenEnCo member at large. I earned this title between 2013 and 2014 by performing in the ensemble's workshop and fully staged productions of *What's Goin' On?*, a radical adaptation of Brecht's *The Good Person of Setzuan* that sought to take Brecht to task for his orientalism and his treatment of sex work.

GenEnCo productions tend not to place much emphasis on narrative, which makes it difficult to provide a synopsis for *The Mikado: Reclaimed*. Like other examples of what Hans-Thies Lehmann has called "postdramatic theater," the "progression of a story" is not what is most central to GenEnCo's adaptation.[28] This is partly a function of the company's desire to disassemble Gilbert and Sullivan's opera and to use its raw materials to make something capable of standing in opposition to its primary source. It is also because *The Mikado: Reclaimed* takes place in a concentration camp. The events of the production unfold, therefore, less in accordance with an Aristotelian plot structure than with the sort of stultifying regularity and repetition evocative of everyday incarcerated life.

What matters more to GenEnCo's adaptation than the sequence or accumulation of events, are the racist rules that govern them. In the world of *The Mikado: Reclaimed*, the prisoners are constantly surveilled by an unseen warden. They are also not allowed to speak to one another, except sparingly in non-English languages—and not all prisoners share the same ethno-linguistic skills. If the prisoners do speak in English, or if they step out of line in any other way, they are punished for it. They are electrocuted by glowing devices that have been implanted into their arms. As a consequence, what audiences witness over the seventy-five-minute run of GenEnCo's devised musical adaptation occurs mostly in silence or alongside musical accompaniment. The prisoners interact with one another through eye contact and gesture. But they also find ways to communicate with one another while rehearsing material from *The Mikado*, which they are always allowed to sing, and which they are periodically forced to perform on camera for a national audience. The adaptation's first few scenes are exemplary.

Upon entering the theater, audience members are confronted with a thrust stage on which seven performers, six women and one man, have scattered themselves across a number of wooden bunks.[29] "Block 5613" is written on the floor of the playing space indicating that what spectators can see represents only a small subsection of a larger carceral complex. The scene is eerily silent as the prisoners occupy themselves with isolated tasks: reading, daydreaming, fiddling with small objects. At this point, audience members have gleaned from the program that what they are seeing is an anti-Asian concentration camp set in the near future. The racial makeup of the entirely Asian American cast evokes the historical precedent of Japanese wartime incarceration.[30] The grayscale aesthetic the cast inhabits does, too: their faces (painted white) and their clothes (tattered and black) echo the black-and-white archival images taken by the likes of Dorothea Lange and Ansel Adams of life inside the camps.

This static scene ends when a voice is heard over a loudspeaker: "Places in two... clear the set please." The prisoners immediately begin to engage in vocal and physical warm-up exercises, as if preparing for a performance of their own. "To sit in solemn silence on a dull dark dock, in a pestilential prison with a lifelong lock..." The lines lead the incarcerated characters offstage. Seconds pass. A gong sounds. The scene shifts. The prisoners, now also performers in the world of the play, return to the stage smiling in a single file line, taking tiny shuffle steps. They are holding fans between their hands, which are pressed together and upward as if in polite prayer. Underneath it all plays the musical prelude to "Miya Sama," a song from *The Mikado*. On cue, the performers sing the lyrics in Japanese and in the most nasal tones. Their choreography consists of fan snapping, fan waving, cow-towing, a pantomiming of martial arts poses, more shuffle stepping, and more forced smiling. At the song's conclusion, the voice again: "Cut. Thank you." And with that, the performers scatter back to their bunks, letting go of their smiles and returning to the separation of their quotidian activity.

Audience members can infer that the prisoners' performance of "Miya Sama" is broadcast to a national audience from a screen hanging over the back of the stage that reads "The CDC Presents: Virus Times Live." The Centers for Disease Control and Prevention's role in producing this performance is explained soon after this opening sequence, when the sole male prisoner sings a lyrically altered version of "I've Got a Little List" from Gilbert and Sullivan's original opera. In *The Mikado*, this song is sung by a character named Koko, a lowly tailor who becomes the Lord High Executioner of Titipu. It is a paradigmatic musical theater list song containing categories of candidates to be executed at the behest of the Japanese emperor, the mikado. Generally, the candidates for execution include "society offenders who might well be underground and who never would be missed." Specifically, some candidates he includes seem rather arbitrary (e.g., those with "irritating laughs," and "all funny fellows, comic men, and clowns of private life"), while others deal in denigrating connotations like the "lady novelist" and "the lady from the provinces who dresses like a guy."

GenEnCo, far from indulging in the insidious gendered antagonism of Gilbert and Sullivan's version, uses its list song to explain the circumstances of the prisoners at the center of its production. It does so by identifying those responsible for the prisoners' incarceration, their surveillance, and their periodic punishment.

> There's the center for disease control, who sounded the alarm.
> Epidemiologists, I've got them on the list.
> And the cheap and chippy chippers who installed these in our arms
> Nanotechnologists, I've got them on the list ...
> They're all okay with bloodshed 'cause our blood's a different kind.
> They call us carriers ...

These lyrics reveal to the audience for the first time that the Asian Americans at the center of *The Mikado: Reclaimed* find themselves incarcerated because they have been identified as immune carriers of a disease that threatens white American life. Their holding pens are not merely concentration camps but quarantine centers as well.

These lyrics haunted me at the start of the COVID-19 pandemic, as did the larger set of circumstances depicted in GenEnCo's adaptation. Having seen *The Mikado: Reclaimed* when it was first produced, prior even to the ascendance of Donald Trump's first white nationalist regime, it was difficult for my mind not to race through the kinds of questions raised by the painfully prescient production. What would become of Asians in the United States given the Chinese origins of the novel coronavirus? Would we be forced to quarantine together? Would I, a Filipino, be counted among that "we," given how Asians in the United States were coming under attack indiscriminately as the virus spread through the country? Undoubtedly, *The Mikado: Reclaimed* assumed new relevance in the post-COVID world, and twice in 2020, once in March by the Vortex and once in May by HowlRound, the production was rebroadcast online and made available to a wider national audience. It was an early gesture in what would become a broad move to reimagine theater as the US social distanced and sheltered in place.

If *The Mikado: Reclaimed* can be called prescient, though, it is only because it is so responsive to the persistent way in which the Asian body has historically been constructed as a contaminant, contagion, and overall threat to the national body of the United States. When Chinese immigrants arrived at Angel Island in the early twentieth century, they were routinely subject to intrusive and mandatory medical examinations conducted by white, English-speaking public health officers. "These medical examinations," writes Nayan Shah in his book, *Contagious Divides: Epidemics and Race in San Francisco's Chinatown*, "were part of an emerging worldwide network of quarantine and health inspection that served as the 'imperial defense' against the potential invasion of epidemic diseases into metropolitan ports in North America and Europe," a defense that contributed to the construction of Chinese and other Asian immigrants as vectors of disease.[31] Moreover, in 1876, San Francisco's city health officer Dr. John Meares charged Chinese immigrants with contaminating the city with smallpox. The immigrants were deemed behaviorally predisposed to depravity and, by extension, to infectiousness. The reports produced by the San Francisco Board of Health and the Public Health Department at the time described Chinatown as a "plague spot" and a "cesspool." This transformed the neighborhood into, as Shah puts it, "the material manifestation of the alien within the modern American city."[32] This construction of Chinatown would be reinforced a quarter-century later, in 1900, when a single, suspected case of bubonic plague in the neighborhood led to the removal of all whites from the area and an unprecedented forced quarantine of all Chinese residents.

In this instance, San Francisco's Chinatown became what Karen Shimakawa might have us call a "[spatialization] of abjection," a physical space interior to the borders of the United States in which Asian Americans were, forcefully and paradoxically, constructed as alien to the nation-state.³³ Anticipating the quarantine camps at the center of *The Mikado: Reclaimed*, Shimakawa's theorization of the spatialization of abjection is especially insightful in explaining Japanese internment. As Shimakawa puts it, the anti-Japanese concentration camp

> represents a crisis in the process of abjection in that it spectacularly demonstrates the ways in which Japanese Americans had to be forcibly removed from the inside to the symbolic 'outside' in order to maintain the integrity of the construction of 'U.S. American,' while at the same time registering their always-already position on the inside.³⁴

GenEnCo's production combines the historical case of San Francisco's Chinatown with that of anti-Japanese concentration camps during World War II. What results is a quarantine camp that Achille Mbembe might call "necropolitical" because it is a "zone where the violence of the state of exception is deemed to operate in the service of 'civilization.'"³⁵ From behind the alibi of public health, the camp serves to keep the white inhabitants of the nation-state safe by keeping Asians, imagined as infectious, isolated and encaged.

The camp also serves an important ideological purpose for US nationalism, a purpose pursued through performance. The early lines of GenEnCo's list song reveal the company's reason for adapting *The Mikado* and its racist tropes. Again, I quote the song's lyrics at length:

> There's the nosy shits who listen in on everything we say
> but we've discovered singing keeps the punishment at bay.
> The telecast producers who can really spin a tale
> Who know that this is nothing more than an oriental jail.
> And when it's time for broadcasts, "look they're happy," they insist.
> They'd none of them be missed, they'd none of them be missed . . .

These lyrics inform GenEnCo's audience members that the performance of "Miya Sama" is broadcast across the United States to its non-Asian and non-incarcerated population. The lyrics also imply that the purpose of that broadcast is to quell, in advance, any dissent that principled members of that population might aim at the state, the state of exception, or the state of things by functioning as proof of ongoing Asian American life (or something like it) inside the camps. And "Miya Sama" is not the only song that serves this purpose. Later in the play, a trio (one man, two women) are forced to broadcast another classic from *The Mikado*, "Three Little Maids." The smiles are again too wide, the fans again flutter too eagerly, and the only male performer is forced to indulge in the "racial castration" concomitant with his Asian racialization, to borrow a framework from David Eng.[36]

The prisoners' performance of "Three Little Maids," like the performance of "Miya Sama" before it, returns us to the performance of racial emotional labor, which is this time enacted at significantly greater intensity and on a more expansive social scale. For the period during which performers are forced to inhabit material from *The Mikado*, they are forced to sustain an outward countenance that meets the demands put forth by the content of the songs in question. They are forced to suppress certain feelings in order to produce in others the impression that they are engaging in auto-orientalizing song and dance of their own volition, perhaps even for pleasure. The point of this performance, from the perspective of *The Mikado: Reclaimed*'s unseen captors, is to sustain a whole range of ethno-nationalist fantasies, including the fantasy that racial quarantine camps are necessary for the protection of the national body in pandemic times; the fantasy that the Asians kept in those camps are well taken care of; and the array of orientalist fantasies that any performance of *The Mikado*'s musical numbers functions to fortify. By reproducing social fantasies such as these, the prisoners' performances of "Miya Sama" and "Three Little Maids" accomplish on a national scale what my own performance of racial emotional labor, described earlier in this chapter, accomplished on an interpersonal scale. They induce in their audience an agreeable affective experience, one that leaves the overall fantasy of racial, and now also national, innocence untouched. With its renditions of *The Mikado*'s musical numbers, GenEnCo at once offers up a metaphor for racial emotional labor taken to its extreme and a rendering of the scalar spectrum on which various performances of racial emotional labor might be located.

As is often the case with racial emotional labor and with the burden of liveness more generally, the prisoners of *The Mikado: Reclaimed* are forced to perform their song and dance under threat of violent racial retribution. A moment just prior to the performance of "I've Got a Little List" illustrates this point. Having acted without enthusiasm through much of the play's early events, a member of block 5613 chooses suddenly to speak aloud. She bemoans the unsustainability of her situation. "The young ones don't even remember what it means to be free," she cries, "but, before the suffering gets me, I'm going to feel it on my lips if not my body." As she bellows these lines and others like them, her fellow detainees attempt to stop her, shushing and shoving their hands over her mouth. She refuses to stay silent.

Refusal is often invoked within critical theory as a performance of passive resistance. Sometimes a performance of refusal is politically motivated, as in the oft-invoked example of work stoppages. Other times it is not, as when Melville's Bartleby simply prefers not to. Entering into this theoretical scene with minoritarian subjects in mind, Lilian Mengesha and Lakshmi Padmanabhan have astutely articulated "refusal" as implicitly political "non-engagement, inaction, and bodily incapacitation."[37] But through her fearless speech, *The Mikado: Reclaimed*'s outspoken prisoner demonstrates that engagement, action, and an expression of capacity can also amount to a performance of refusal if what one refuses is the majoritarian mandate that forces the minoritarian subject to remain unengaged, inactive, and incapacitated. Such a performance of refusal discloses, too, that the burden of liveness can be felt as much in the inactivity of constrained comportment as in the activity of outward-facing output. The sobering reality, of course, is that refusing what is required of one by a racially overdetermined social situation, especially when under surveillance, can have severe consequences for its performer.

In this instance, the speaking prisoner's speech-activity provokes a violent response from camp officials: she and all the other inmates are electrocuted by the devices implanted in their arms as punishment for her transgressions. Then, in a blackout, she disappears from the block and reappears on the screen that hovers over the back of the stage. The prisoners and the play's audience members watch together in horror as the screen shows her being beaten to death, her bloodied face a warning to the other prisoners. With these consequences in mind we might say that the performance of racial emotional labor can also be construed as a performance of care for other minoritarian subjects, where care is understood as a passive kind of protection. As Joan Tronto argues: "Protection is an element of care insofar as it prevents, and tries to mitigate against, harm."[38] If to shatter white racial fantasy while in the company of other racially minoritized people is so often to put those people at risk for retaliation, then to sustain white racial fantasy can also be, indirectly and unfortunately, to extend care by protecting oneself and others from that same risk.

The Minoritarian Team

I have argued thus far that subjects of color are often forced, under threat of violence, to care for white subjects by sustaining, through the work of impression and emotion management, the white subject's fragile psychic stability vis-à-vis fantasies of racial and national innocence. With this reality in mind, what remains of this chapter analyzes the rehearsal practices of both the Generic Ensemble Company and the characters played by the company's members in *The Mikado: Reclaimed*. In a practice-based research article on the production, shorb writes that "depicting resistance to carceral violence narratively onstage also cultivated a culture of care in the rehearsal room."[39] As they tell it, the ensemble behind the piece "sought a space of healing and repair" through which to process experiences of racial harm in a way that might eventually connect with an audience.[40] For shorb, the primary performative mechanism for bringing about healing and repair was "reappropriation," which they define as "a process whereby a community whose cultural legacy has been defaced through harmful misinterpretation takes an object of that misinterpretation and transmutes it into something that furthers an identitarian strategic project."[41] With this aspect of GenEnCo's process accounted for by its artistic director, I turn my own focus toward the ensemble's more mundane rehearsal practices in order to put forth forms of care through which the burden of racial emotional labor might be alleviated, or at least suspended, for multiply marginalized Asian American subjects and other oppressed people.

Every Generic Ensemble Company rehearsal begins the same way: the ensemble participates in a "check-in." The cast and crew sit in a circle on the floor of a rehearsal room and shorb introduces the ritual. One after another, moving around the circle, each member of the ensemble says their name, their gender pronouns, and a comment about their physical and emotional state and needs. After all the ensemble members have been introduced, shorb leads the ensemble through what they term "the sit," a brief period of meditation during which one is to attend to one's breathing, to one's own feelings, and to the affects and energies that circulate the room.

After about a minute of meditation the check-in is over, and shorb begins to lay out a set of community agreements in accordance with which the company will devise its new work. "We are giving gifts," shorb professes. The implication is that no one is forced to participate in GenEnCo's production. Thus one's actions during this time and in this space are all gifts born of generosity. Such generosity is meant to allow the ensemble members to take risks, to become intimate, and to commit the whole of themselves to the devising process. Other key ground rules include "move up, move back," a call for each ensemble member to be aware of how much space they take up with their voices, bodies, and points of view; "ouch and oops," a method for acknowledging microaggression and foregrounding accountability to one another; and, finally, a plea for each member of the ensemble to take care of themselves, a proto-Foucauldian reminder that caring for the self translates to care for the ensemble. GenEnCo's rehearsal rituals and regulations provide an antidote to the various burdens outlined thus far in this chapter. The check-in and community agreements, instituted by shorb, a gender nonconforming Japanese American, model a methodology for collectively establishing a set of social proprieties that are fitted less to the demands of fragile white psyches than to the needs of Asian Americans multiply marginalized by gender, sexuality, (dis)ability, and other categories of otherness. The collective process of pronoun clarification, for example—what some, including Dean Spade, have called "the pronoun go-round"—establishes a social protocol within which trans, nonbinary, and gender nonconforming persons can speak themselves into (semi-)public alignment with agreed-upon gendered proprieties rather than against them.[42]

The third protocol of GenEnCo's check-in, the statement of personal circumstances, operates according to a similar logic. It may provide an opportunity, for example, for an ensemble member to alert the others to an extant injury that will affect their ability to participate in certain physical activities. In instances such as this, the statement of circumstances amounts to a statement of access needs aimed at securing social and material accommodation for disability. The space made for the statement of circumstances might also allow an ensemble member to alert the others to an ongoing inability to arrive at rehearsals on time because they are navigating self-care/childcare/eldercare difficulties or because their car is out of commission and they cannot yet afford the repairs. Or else, the space might enable ensemble members to alert one another to the severity of their attrition in the face of recent anti-Asian aggressions. By naming racial harms they may have suffered, ensemble members not only mark potentially unmarked racial dynamics, thus enabling the entrance of those dynamics into conversation for critique. They also establish, by way of counterexample, acceptable protocols for interracial intimacy, availing themselves of the possibility of good-enough racially attuned care. While I cannot speak to the kinds of concerns and conditions that were raised during the rehearsal process of *The Mikado: Reclaimed*, the above examples approximate the kinds of conditions that were spoken into the space during the devising of *What's Goin' On?*, the project on which I worked with GenEnCo. These examples cast the check-in as a form of care that allows minoritarian subjects to establish social and emotional protocols, both openly and collectively, so that they might more comfortably engage in the work of theater making.

Another way to articulate this claim would be to say that the check-in reveals why the language of inclusion so often touted in the era of multiculturalist white supremacy is inadequate as a framework for addressing the social struggle and affective suffering of multiply marginalized Asian American subjects. "Inclusion" inserts new subjects into social situations organized according to the pre-established protocols of white civility. So inserted, such subjects must nimbly navigate those protocols, which may exist in antagonistic or ignorant relation to them. This can be individually draining and interpersonally dangerous. What is needed, sociopolitically, is the total redefinition of given social situations. The check-in aspires to allow for this by enabling minoritarian subjects to collaboratively establish, from the onset of an ongoing social encounter, new protocols that prioritize the equitable distribution of racial emotional labor. And the community agreements amount to a number of mechanisms meant to ensure the collective upkeep of those protocols. "Ouch, oops," for instance, empowers ensemble members to say "ouch" if they wish to mark speech-acts and behaviors that have hurt them, whether intentionally or not. The agreement then requires the harm-doer to respond accountably by saying "oops," at which point the person impacted is given the opportunity to set the terms for how that harm will be addressed or not.

To be sure, the execution of "ouch, oops" is rarely completed without ample awkwardness or apprehension. The technologies offered in the check-in and the community agreements—time consuming as they are—are best practices and parameters, not magic spells. And they are care practices and parameters put to good use not only by shorb and her ensemble but also by multiply marginalized Asian Americans across the country in other contexts. While living in New York City between 2014 and 2019, I observed that check-in processes have served as recurring rituals among a number of activist organizations including NQAPIA (National Queer Asian Pacific Islander Alliance) and the New York City-based GAPIMNY (formerly Gay Asian Pacific Islander Men of New York)—Empowering Queer and Trans Asian Pacific Islanders. Also based in New York City, the Yellowjackets Collective (YJC)—a beacon of Asian American feminism, queerness, and interracial solidarity—has famously made good use of community guidelines. YJC's guidelines have included aspirational bans on toxic masculinity, anti-Blackness, and calling the police as well as requests for others to "center queer femmes/womxn of color," to "be open to being checked," to "be financially honest," and to practice "enthusiastic consent."

In each of these cases, the check-in and the community agreements are ultimately about the cultivation of a form of care that might be called the *minoritarian team*. For Goffman, a team is "a set of individuals whose intimate cooperation is required if a given projected definition of a situation is to be maintained. A team is a grouping, but it is a grouping not in relation to a social structure or social organization but rather in relation to an interaction or series of interactions in which the relevant definition of the situation is maintained."[43] This means that members of the same theater troupe or community organization do not constitute a team simply as a consequence of coming together. Rather, a team coheres through a collective commitment to fostering a shared situational definition, which is to say a shared understanding of and orientation toward the social proprieties, performative norms, and feeling rules that a given gathering will require of each of its participants. Teammates "tend to be related to one another by bonds of reciprocal dependence," as when actors rely on one another to maintain the believability of a scene, "and reciprocal familiarity," or what Goffman calls an "intimacy without warmth," as when a costume assistant supports an actor in a quick change.[44] The check-in and community agreements are designed precisely to induce interdependence and familiarity among its participants by rendering personal circumstances as caring responsibilities to be shared among the group.

Most situations are defined according to the mandates of whiteness, meaning the feeling rules governing those situations serve to shield the white psyche from confrontations with its own culpability for unspectacular racial violence. But where the minoritarian team is concerned, the projection of a collective anti-capitalist, anti-racist, feminist, queer, crip, and trans definition of a situation becomes everyone's duty to uphold. This is what it means to center minoritarian subjectivity in a given situation, what it means to perform caring attachment collectively. If a participant voices concern about a knee injury, it becomes the responsibility of a team of performers not only to adjust staging and choreography to accommodate that disability but to actuate a shame-free atmosphere in which such accommodations are not earned by the injured teammate but provided for them as a matter of course and, if at all possible, in advance of their asking for it. And if a team requires rehearsal, this work can occur backstage between different groupings of teammates; two forgetful teammates may find themselves asking one another "what are X's pronouns again?" (in X's absence) as a way to maintain X's gendered projection of themselves into a situation and, by extension, the collective projection of the situation as a home for trans and gender nonconforming persons. A situation whose inhabitants are all members of the same anti-racist team—and they may all be of different racial identifications—is a situation defined against interpersonal racism and designed to alleviate the burden of racial emotional labor.[45] A minoritarian situation is one in which everyone is on the same team, allowing for aliveness to an occasion without the burden of liveness, racialized relation without the burden of relatability.

Queer Racial Care and Its Absence

In circumstances such as those depicted in *The Mikado: Reclaimed*, it may not be possible to intentionally restructure social protocols so that they become more suited to minoritarian well-being. I conclude this chapter, then, by returning to GenEnCo's musical adaptation to inventory the queer forms of racial care engaged by its prisoner-performers as they seek to sustain themselves through and beyond the violence of mandated, auto-orientalizing racial emotional labor.

About two-thirds into the musical, the prisoners perform another song from *The Mikado*, "Here's a Howdy Doo." This time, however, the performers do not perform in service to the nation but for their own purposes. "Here's a Howdy Doo" begins as a collective attempt to raise the spirits of a female detainee who is especially ravaged by the conditions of her incarceration. Throughout *The Mikado: Reclaimed*, at irregular intervals, a bell rings and this detainee dresses herself in a skirt and leaves the block. We know from the list song's lyrics that she leaves the block to be raped by a warden who is more than twice her age in exchange for the mitigation of violence against her fellow detainees. It is an element of GenEnCo's theatrical deconstruction that evokes a long, transnational history within which, as Vivian Huang puts it, Asian women "have been conscripted to give and grant (sexual, emotional) access" to the men of xenophobia and empire.[46] Aware of their fellow detainee's sacrifice, the other prisoners, during "Here's a Howdy Doo," dance and twirl around her; they smile with sincerity; they pantomime; they play with one another and in playing with one another they expand the field of possible behaviors and relations that are available under their highly controlled and surveilled circumstances.

Central to this performance is a romantic relation between the abused female inmate and another female inmate. In Gilbert and Sullivan's opera, "Here's a Howdy Do" is sung by two presumably heterosexual characters, Nanki-Poo and Yum-Yum, who have fallen in love and are considering marriage. But Nanki-Poo is soon to be executed and Yum-Yum, if she were to marry him, would have to be executed as well. In the context of *The Mikado: Reclaimed*, the song carries a similar connotation: in the dystopian near future of GenEnCo's creation, the two incarcerated women risk death with their unsanctioned queer romance. In *The Mikado: Reclaimed*, then, "Here's a Howdy Doo" aligns with a long legacy of what Muñoz calls queer "ephemera."[47] Muñoz teaches us that evidence of queer life has often been difficult to come by because queers have aspired to "encrypted sociality."[48] They have intentionally covered their tracks to avoid being followed by aggressively phobic forces. As a result, queerness, like performance, is frequently a phenomenon known only ephemerally. "Here's a Howdy Doo" offers a queer performance of racial care insofar as it enables queer connection among suffering Asian inmates without revealing itself as evidence of that connection to antagonistic authorities.

Here GenEnCo and the speculative world the company brings into being reveal two contributions that musical theater can make to the culture war over racial care. First, musical theatrical rehearsal can institute, or support the institution of, alternate realities within which queer of color worldmaking can be made more possible. Released from more serious surveillance and scrutiny as well as from the expectations of reality and realism, even the most violent artifacts of the musical theater repertoire become opportunities to inhabit sociality differently. *The Mikado: Reclaimed* is proof of this. Second, the aesthetic project of queer worldmaking, even and especially in the most exceptionally violent circumstances, can itself be understood as a performance of racial care insofar as it makes space for the expression of queer attachments and relations whose suppression within oppressive regimes of situational obligation often leave queer subjects of color in malnourished isolation, untethered to the world.

This brings me, finally, to a moment in GenEnCo's musical adaptation that comes shortly after "Here's a Howdy Doo." The two incarcerated women at the center of that song stand before one another, holding hands as one of their fellow inmates officiates their wedding with a rendition of "Tit Willow," a meek ballad from *The Mikado*. Another inmate wraps them in a symbolic white cloth. The others of the block bear witness. The song continues even after the wedding concludes, and during the singing of its last verse another romance sparks. The singer lets the song carry her toward a flirtation with another female inmate who accepts her advances. Each couple ends up sharing a bed as night falls on the incarcerated collective.

While they sleep, another of the women incarcerated in this block sings "Alone and Yet Alive" as a soliloquy. In Gilbert and Sullivan's original opera, the song is sung by a character named Katisha, a caricature of ugliness and undesirability. Unsurprisingly, then, in *The Mikado: Reclaimed*, the song signals a sadness over its singer's singled isolation as well as a certain amount of jealousy resulting from the fact that none of the block's other women desire her. The singer exits the stage after singing the line, "may not a cheated maiden die." The line signals that the singer's jealousy of the two queer couplings has merged with an instinct for self-preservation—she may not want to be punished, electrocuted, by the warden for an unsanctioned intimacy between women to which she was never afforded access.

In the morning, a bell rings, beckoning one of the newlyweds to the warden's quarters where he will rape her as he has so many times before. Many of the other inmates reluctantly implore her to go—if she does not, they will all be electrocuted by the implants in their arms. She refuses to go, they are electrocuted, and her spouse is pulled into the warden's office by her arm implant. On the screen that hovers above the back of the stage, audience members and inmates watch together as she is beaten bloody. She returns to the stage only to die and be laid to rest in her bed, covered by the white sheet beneath which she was earlier wed. Her wife mourns her by singing *The Mikado*'s "The sun whose rays are all ablaze." And then the concentration camp's disembodied voice again: "Clear the set please," an indication that they are being made to perform, once again, to appease a national audience. The inmates move only to hang a large cloth concealing their friends' corpse. Like the undead that they are, they gather their props for performance only to lay them at the foot of the stage. They start saying their goodbyes to one another, exchanging silent hugs and wiping streaming tears. "Places for 'Wedding Day.' Stand by for live telecast transmission in 5, 4, 3..." But when the broadcast begins the performers do not sing. They do not dance. They only drop the sheet that conceals the corpse of their friend, exposing what they are forced to endure to the rest of the nation. There is an immediate blackout, and the sound of a mass murderous electrocution. All the inmates are dead. End of play.

The musical's conclusion knots together a number of thematic threads from both *The Mikado: Reclaimed* and *Racial Care*. According to shorb, the "collective death" that occurs at the end of the play "was chosen by the ensemble deliberately to address issues of (il)legibility of Asian Americans and anti-Asian racism in the context of Austin, Texas in 2016."[49] It was, in other words, a creative decision dedicated to challenging regional anti-Asian neglect by showing how such neglect can lead to loneliness, which can lead to antisocial violence. In GenEnCo's production the instigator of that violence is the Katisha figure, a queer woman kept from intimate care. Elsewhere in this book, the perpetrator of that violence is Dennis, the stand-in for Seung-Hui Cho, in Julia Cho's *Office Hour*. The events also evidence aesthetic performance's potential to instantiate more sustainable psychosocial circumstances. It can facilitate mourning. It can shield illicit, queer intimacy from antagonistic observers, allowing suffering racialized subjects access to nonnormative caring relations. And, in addition, the conclusion to *The Mikado: Reclaimed* reminds us that the refusal to endure continuous violence can manifest as a refusal to live, one that resonates in some ways with Mark Aguhar's untimely departure. The multiply marginalized Asian Americans of GenEnCo's concentration camp are murdered, but their loss can also be construed as a mass suicide. It is a set of suicides that is also a solidarity statement about the ways that ethno-nationalist expectations around racial emotional labor, whether performed on the national scale or on the scale of an ordinary social situation, can be fatal. And so, this book's body count continues to rise. These deaths demonstrate that more potent performances of racial care have yet to be uncovered. They show us that something about our frame of reference is lacking or too narrow. We are missing something. My last chapter will turn to dehumanist innovations in critical theory in an attempt to articulate what that something is.

4

Dehumanist Care

Let me begin this last chapter of *Racial Care* by remembering some of the people we lost on our way here. Countless have been killed by state neglect amid surges of COVID-19. Others have been taken by the blows of anti-Asian street violence. We lost Mark Aguhar to suicide; she was only twenty-four. And Seung-Hui Cho, at twenty-three, murdered thirty-two people before committing suicide himself. At different points in Julia Cho's *Office Hour*, Dennis and Gina, the student and teacher at the center of the play, each end their own lives. At other points, they murder one another. Two of those incarcerated in *The Mikado: Reclaimed*'s fictional concentration camp are also murdered—beaten to death by an unseen warden, a racist and a rapist. The others in that production die, too, executed en masse—or maybe they commit mass political suicide. Across these pages I have attributed these deaths, in one way or another, to the ordinary attrition suffered by Asian American subjects in the early twenty-first century as a result of the enduring neglect and antagonism (anti-Asian, anti-woman, anti-queer, anti-trans, etc.) that continues to structure their experience of psychosocial life. I have offered some conceptual tools for assessing how racial care is unevenly distributed across several distinct but interrelated scales: the self, the dyad, and the collective. I have also put forth a range of aesthetic and performative strategies through which Asian Americans have managed to contest their position on the field of racial care.

And still, I have often wondered while writing this book why premature death remains such a persistent problem for Asian American subjects despite every effort to allay its inevitability. On the one hand, the answer is obvious. No amount of racial care can forever beat back the violences of state-sanctioned slow death under socioeconomic crisis ordinariness. On the other hand, I struggle to shake the feeling that there is more that we can study, understand, rehearse, and perform in the way of care that might help make life more livable for multiply marginalized Asian Americans especially. It is this unshakable feeling that has motivated the writing of the chapter you are now reading, which seeks to widen the theoretical frame that I have established thus far. If my third chapter attended at length to the scale of collective racial care amid national crisis, this chapter widens its focus from the interpersonal, the racial, and the national to the ecological, the diasporic, and the decolonial. To make this move is not to abandon racial care as an analytic but instead to open its uses outward toward inextricably related concerns that must be addressed if Asian American well-being is ever to be approached, attained, or sustained.

To this end, this chapter turns to the aesthetic and poetic work of Jess X. Snow, one of queer Asian diasporic movement culture's brightest stars. Snow is a nonbinary filmmaker, poet, muralist, children's book illustrator, and visual artist. Their work has been supported by institutions ranging from the Tribeca Film Institute to the Smithsonian Asian Pacific American Center. Their poetry has earned them a Pushcart Prize nomination; their films have been screened all over the world; and their murals and political illustrations have appeared on walls across the settler colonial United States, at countless protests, and in mainstream publications like the *Los Angeles Times* and the *New York Times Magazine*. Whenever I am called upon to describe Snow's art practice, the first adjective that comes to mind is "radical." Their body of work advances, with visionary clarity, a queer feminist of color politics rooted in decolonial, migrant justice, climate justice, anti-capitalist and abolitionist social movements. Consider, for example, that one of Snow's illustrations appears on the cover of A. Naomi Paik's, *Bans, Walls, Raids, and Sanctuary*, a book that calls for an abolitionist sanctuary movement capable of challenging the long history of anti-migrant violence in the United States.[1] Snow's cover image extends Paik's argument in an aesthetic register, depicting a human family of three (two adults, one child) running above, in front of, and below a flock of birds. The birds are diverse; they come in many shapes, sizes, and colors. By placing these birds and these humans within the same aesthetic frame, Snow casts migration as a natural tendency that both species share, and this framing in turn denaturalizes the border regimes that restrict, police, and punish human movement.

In this instance and across their work, Snow's political vision is expressed in and as the human's entanglement with the nonhuman and the environment. Snow's oeuvre is filled with flourishing flora and untamed animals, with vast blue skies and wide-open fields. And humans are often enmeshed in all of it. Take, for example, a mural Snow completed in 2021 on Mosco St. in Manhattan's Chinatown in collaboration with the W.O.W. Project and with support from the NYU Asian/Pacific/American Institute. Against a red backdrop, the mural depicts a young Asian person holding a red envelope. Nearby, two Asian elders hold each other in a desperately needed embrace. The mural's main text, "IN THE FUTURE OUR ASIAN COMMUNITY IS SAFE," is an anticipatory answer to the escalation of postpandemic anti-Asian violence.[2] And across the image, migratory birds mingle with plant life native to Lenapehoking territory. An accompanying land acknowledgment stresses: "OUR VISION OF SAFETY FOR CHINATOWN COMMUNITIES IS INTERCONNECTED WITH INDIGENOUS FLOURISHING AND SELF DETERMINATION." The statement marks the artist's awareness of the fact that Chinatown sits on stolen Native land. It signals an aspiration for Asian-Indigenous solidarity that is common across Snow's body of work, an aspiration rooted in an awareness of the incommensurability that exists between Asian and Native Americanness under settler colonialism. As Snow writes in the artist statement accompanying the piece, the mural is meant to be an "interactive portal" brought to life in collaboration with augmented reality artist Wiena Lin through which passers-by will be invited to imagine a world of simultaneous Asian safety and Indigenous sovereignty, a world in which humans and nonhumans are entangled with one another in a complex web of what we might call dehumanist caring relations.

Through close readings of Snow's filmic, poetic, and visual artwork, this chapter advances a theory of *dehumanist care* capable of attending to the caring relations that connect Asian diasporic, Indigenous, and nonhuman worlds. I draw the concept of *dehumanism* from Julietta Singh, who coined the term precisely to bring processes of dehumanization, the decolonial, and the nonhuman into a single analytic frame.[3] Dehumanism opposes mastery—the mastery of the colonizer over the colonized as well as the mastery of the human over nonhuman others and the environment. On ethical and political grounds, it also opposes human exceptionalism and settler notions of sovereignty. Dehumanism requires human subjects to cede the high ground of ontological hierarchy so that they may cultivate mutually supportive relational bonds not just with one another but with nonhuman others as well. This is what it means to forge "dehumanist solidarity," which Singh argues is "inherently queer" insofar as such solidarity transgresses the normative bounds of acceptable intimacy.[4] When we honor the imperative of dehumanist solidarity, we push the human subject to engage in a process of becoming dispossessed—dispossessed not of Indigenous claims to land but of the masterful, human, settler desire to rule over it and others.[5]

With these insights in mind, the *care* of dehumanist care must be reimagined as Maria Puig de la Bellacasa helps us to imagine it: not as something launched, however relationally, from the sovereign ground of human intentionality alone but instead as "a force distributed across a multiplicity of agencies and materials."[6] In this view, care is no longer reduceable to something given and received between subjects and objects. It is instead something that circulates among humans, animals, plants, and other nonhuman entities. In pursuing mutually sustaining dehumanist solidarities, it is essential to remember that multiply marginalized Asian diasporic and Indigenous subjects are all caught up in what Michelle Huang calls "ecologies of entanglement," those "networks of circulation that diffuse the boundaries of the human by foregrounding the relationships between us and the world with which we interact."[7] In studying the circulation of care across the threads of dehumanist entanglement woven throughout Snow's oeuvre, in tracking care's transit across relationships between dehumanized humans and the nonhuman, my aim here is to offer a more complete rendering of the various relations through which life is sustained despite the harsh realities of a barely habitable world. My mission is to answer the call, made by Mel Chen in the conclusion to *Animacies*, for "an ethics of care and sensitivity that extends far from humans' (or the Human's) own borders."[8]

Dehumanist care refers to the vast repertoire of caring activity that passes between the dehumanized human and the nonhuman in ways that align with a larger decolonial project. To adopt a dehumanist ethics of care is to adopt a way of living and tending to life whose ethical contours can be glimpsed in the works that I discuss in what follows. In each of this chapter's next two sections, I show how Snow, through aesthetic means, attempts to induce in those who encounter their work a collective attunement to the necessity of dehumanist caring relations. I first focus on the film *Afterearth*, cowritten by Snow and Kit Yan, which situates Asian diasporic, Native Hawaiian, and Native American subjects in relation to one another and the environment. Thinking across Asian American and Indigenous studies, I argue that *Afterearth* attempts to bring about an impulse of dehumanist reparation in its viewer. In making this move, I work to rescue Melanie Klein's psychoanalytic formulation of reparation from the colonial qualities that cultural studies scholars have identified in the concept. Then the following section of the chapter attends to a poem and an illustration that together render the death of a honey bee. There I describe the range of poetic and aesthetic strategies utilized by Snow to bring about what I call "dehumanist grief," an affective experience premised on the acknowledgment of nonhuman life as grievable life. At stake in my analysis is this: when we are able to feel the circulation of dehumanist care among Asian women, Indigenous women, the nonhuman, and the environment, we are better able to imagine and inhabit what Alexander Weheliye calls other "modalities of the human" that are defined less by possessive individualism than by an attunement to interdependence and entanglement.[9]

The chapter concludes by gesturing toward a utopian horizon for Asian Americanist care theory. Taking inspiration from Snow's poetic meditation on the death of the honey bee, I call this horizon "home," and I follow the figure of "home" throughout Snow's work in order to imagine what a just arrangement of caring relations might feel like for the multiply marginalized Asian diasporic subject. My argument, ultimately, is that such an arrangement must be imagined on a broad, planetary scale, because the specific racial care needs of multiply marginalized Asian American subjects will never be met completely if we fail to cultivate dehumanist caring relations across the imagined ontological divide that continues to separate the dehumanized human from nonhuman others and the environment.

Dehumanist Reparation

Created with support from the Smithsonian Asian Pacific American Center, *Afterearth* is an experimental documentary about thirteen minutes long. It unfolds over four vignettes, each associated with a specific element: fire, water, wind, and earth, in that order. With each vignette, the film's audience is given the opportunity to spend time with an Indigenous and/or Asian woman as she meditates with palpable reverence on the relationship between maternal care and the environment. The film also unfolds as an immersive experience, its action stretching across three channels. While the film's main events take place center-screen, the film's outer channels are often awash in lush landscapes. We are given glimpses of deep green leaves and tall grass, of a mountainside and the ocean waves that flirt with it, of the sky stretching its light blue the way a child might stretch first thing in the morning. All this is a reminder to the viewer: you are not just *on* Earth; you are immersed in it, of it, entangled with it.

Throughout 2018 and 2019, *Afterearth* screened at both national and international film festivals, many specifically catering to Asian diasporic audiences. And in April 2020, at the onset of the COVID-19 pandemic, the Smithsonian Asian Pacific American Center once again lifted *Afterearth* up and into the view of a larger public, this time as part of *Care Package: Poems, Medications, Films, and Other Cultural Nutrients for Times Like This*. As discussed in my introduction, *Care Package* was an online exhibit dedicated to making cultural works available as nourishment to Asian Americans in need of such affective sustenance. As a part of *Care Package*, *Afterearth* expanded its reach, albeit in adapted form as a single-channel viewing experience, for anyone to view online. As Vivian Huang and Summer Kim Lee suggest, both *Care Package* and *Afterearth* revealed "the vitalizing force of collaborative art practice as a form of care-taking and home-making in uncertain times," times that have been made uncertain not only by the crisis of COVID-19 but also by the ongoing, ordinary crises of climate change and settler colonial capitalism.[10]

Against such crises, the first scene of *Afterearth* aligns the film's approach to care with certain Indigenous insights and politics. The film opens on what appears to be the side of a volcano. There sits Hinaleimoana Kwai Kong Wong-Kalu, whose name indexes Chinese heritage on her father's side, and English, Portuguese, and Kanaka Maoli ancestry on her mother's side. She is wearing a skirt the color of molten lava, which is covered in a print of white flowers resembling the flower she wears in her hair. She is also barefoot as she sings a song she composed herself entitled "'Ku Ha'aheo E Ku'u Hawai'i," or "Stand Proud My Hawai'i," which she will later tell us was "made popular by the protectors of Mauna Kea," referring to the Native Hawaiians who in 2014 defended the mountain from the threat of desecration posed by the construction of the Thirty Meter Telescope. Some may recognize Wong-Kalu as the first transgender candidate for statewide office in Hawai'i, or as the subject of the 2014 documentary *Kumu Hina*. And those who do will not be surprised by her dedication to the project of sustaining and restoring Hawaiian culture. Wong-Kalu is a model of what Michi Saagig Nishnaabeg writer Leanne Betasamosake Simpson calls "Indigenous resurgence," which "in its most radical form, is nation building, not nation-state building, but nation building" rooted in a struggle for sovereignty, for land, and for a way of being in the world that prioritizes right, reciprocal relations with one another and the nonhuman environment.[11]

It is significant that *Afterearth* begins in the Hawaiian context and with a subject that straddles Indigeneity and Asian diaspora. The tendency since the 1970s, for both the state and activists, has been to collapse Asian Americans and Pacific Islanders into a single demographic category.[12] As a result, Native Hawaiians and other Indigenous Pacific peoples, politics, and epistemologies have historically been relegated to a subsumed or secondary position relative to those of the Asian diaspora (e.g., Asian/Pacific/American, AANHPI, APIDA). This has made it more difficult for Pacific Islanders to receive resources and services specifically tailored to their needs. By beginning with Wong-Kalu, *Afterearth* challenges the violence of conflation and subordination that produces such material disparity. Because of her mixed heritage, it is possible to read Wong-Kalu as a representative of both Indigeneity and Asian diaspora. But because she spends her part of the film advocating for Indigenous resurgence, it is most appropriate to read Indigeneity in the film as prior to Asianness. The film gives primacy of place to the place-based insights that define the Native Hawaiian ethic of "aloha 'āina—the onto-genealogical ethic of caring for land and water as cultural value, political strategy, and 'ike kūpuna (ancestral knowledge)."[13] This becomes the basis for the dehumanist ethic of care unfolded over the course of the film's other vignettes.

Moreover, by opening with a call for Indigenous resurgence, the film also signals an awareness of the critique of "Asian settler colonialism," which emerges at the nexus of Asian American studies, Native Hawaiian studies, and settler colonial studies. Should we conceive of Asian migrants as settlers, as Haunani Kay-Trask and Candace Fujikane have asked us to with respect to the Hawaiian context?[14] Are Asian migrants better understood as "arrivants," the term Jodi Byrd uses to name those who have been forced—by empire, for instance—to migrate into settler colonial contexts?[15] Or would it be more accurate to say, as Iyko Day does, that Asian North Americans are best understood as members of an "alien" labor force defined by its disposability and deportability?[16] *Afterearth* raises these questions but resists any desire for easy answers to them. What it offers instead is an oblique reminder not to collapse Indigeneity and Asianness into a single demographic category but to hold both pan-national and pan-ethnic categories in tense relation to one another. Asian Americanness cannot be thought outside of Asian settler colonialism and neither can Asian American racial care, which nearly always plays out on stolen land.[17]

This is partly why it is necessary to recast racial care in a dehumanist mold that is itself shaped by Indigenous insights and insights centered on gender and sexuality specifically. When Wong-Kalu finishes her song, the film shows us a photo of her and her mother, which she holds in her hands. She speaks: "A mother gives birth to a child. A child grows and reaches their capacity, and then must in turn care for the mother, care for the parent, as the child was once cared for in its upbringing." This line is followed by a story about the influence Wong-Kalu's grandmother had on the trajectory of her life. "I remember my maternal grandmother putting her hand over mine—my name at the time was

Colin—and she said, 'Colin, you have to study hard now. One day you're going to become a teacher.'" Together the passages highlight how the guidance Wong-Kalu received from her grandmother came to organize her life as a *māhū*. At the beginning of *Kumu Hina*, the 2014 documentary that uplifts Wong-Kalu's work and life, she tells us that the word *māhū*, which is closely aligned with transness, describes those Kanaka Maoli who have "embraced both the feminine and masculine traits that are embodied in each and every one of us."[18] In the same segment she also stresses that "*Māhū* were valued and respected as caretakers, healers, and teachers of ancient traditions" prior to the intervention of Christian missionaries and the growing influence of Western definitions of gender and sexuality in Hawai'i.

It is striking, then, that the story Wong-Kalu communicates in *Afterearth* is a story about the care she received both from the nuclear family form (from her mother) and from outside it (from her grandmother). It is a story about how this care came to organize a life lived as *māhū*, which is to say as a caretaker, an educator, and a steward of Indigenous resurgence. This first segment of *Afterearth* therefore foregrounds a form of care that extends beyond the colonial forms of regulated sexuality (of patriarchal nuclear family units) that J. Kēhaulani Kauanui tells us emerged in the Hawaiian context "both as a protective measure [against Western imperialism] and in the quest to secure sovereignty recognition of the kingdom" since the nineteenth century.[19] With this in mind, the claim of *Afterearth*'s opening vignette is clear: to do right by a decolonial vision for Hawai'i is to do away with heteropatriarchal arrangements of existence by pursuing, as Kauanui puts it, "decolonizing relations to land, gender, and sexuality" simultaneously.[20]

The film's closing vignette makes a similar point, though in a more explicitly Asian American context. It starts by situating gender within settler colonial capitalism. When we first see Kit Yan, he is standing in the middle of a meadow. Then, as images of deforestation flash before our eyes, we hear Yan in a voiceover posing a question that evokes his transness: "How can I feel at home in this body when my body is not at home in this world?" The overlay doubles down on what the audience has already learned from Wong-Kalu and others who share their decolonial project: the heteropatriarchal norms that make our world unhomely to trans life are born of the same settler colonial capitalist regime that perpetuates the destruction of the planet's life-forms for profit. Shortly after this, Yan's mother, Wan Ping Oshiro, appears in the film. We learn from Yan that he and his mother immigrated to Hawai'i from China just after he was born. We also learn that Oshiro is deeply intimate with the Earth and deeply knowledgeable about the resources it provides to sustain human and nonhuman life. We watch

Oshiro as she spends time among the trees as if they were old friends, kindly and with a smile on her face. We listen as she speaks of vegetables, of fruits, of birds, and of seeds.

Both Wong-Kalu and Yan are children tasked with taking up the care practices that have been passed down to them from their grandmother and mother, practices that Sara Ruddick might characterize as "preservative love" and "nurturance," which are about sustaining life and supporting growth, respectively.[21] Wong-Kalu gives us a decolonial return to maternal care by mothering the movement of Indigenous resurgence. This much is evident in the song she sings, which concludes with the lyric, "for my nation I give my all so that our legacy lives on." Yan, echoing Oshiro, offers a dehumanist appropriation of maternal care. He teaches us something of the entanglement of human life with nonhuman life when he says, "My mother taught me that food comes from the ground. She taught me that in order to eat you need seeds. And that, in order to have seeds, you have to have a history." This sentiment is then extended in yet another line spoken by Wong-Kalu in the closing moments of the film: "Does the land continue to give birth to generation after generation? It continues to provide for us. It continues to nurture us and shelter us. One day, when the mother becomes frail and like a child then it will be our children to take care of us. And thus the cycle of life." These words feel like the thesis statement of *Afterearth*. They open out into a capacious understanding of "mother" that includes not only the women we have seen throughout the film but Mother Earth as well. Wong-Kalu's statement frames the land as a mother (giving birth to human life, nurturing its growth) and also as a practitioner of preservative care (providing humans with resources, living space, and shelter). At the same time, Wong-Kalu's words speak to the fragility and dependency of the land and its elder generations. Her words highlight the need for reciprocity between mother and child, between Earth and its inhabitants.

In its closing moments, then, *Afterearth* puts forth a vision of what I call dehumanist reparation, the psychosocial process through which the human subject might realize its complicity with harm done to the Earth and, as a result of this realization, seek to repair the injury suffered by the environment and those native to it, human and nonhuman alike. In order to lay bare how this process unfolds, I recount and recalibrate the psychoanalyst Melanie Klein's work on "reparation" as well as the debates surrounding the concept within cultural studies scholarship. Klein's conceptualization of reparation focuses on a male infant who hungers for nourishment from his mother, whom he at first does not experience as a discrete, coherent person but rather as a part object, "a good breast."[22] When he is nourished by the breast, cared for by the mother, the infant experiences feelings of love and gratitude. But when the breast does not readily present itself in moments of hunger or need, the infant experiences feelings of aggression and hatred, which are acted out against the mother in phantasy. The catch, however, is that the infant's revenge phantasies eventually cause him to feel that the assault he imagined against the bad breast, experienced as a withholding of nourishment, was also an assault on the good breast, on which he depends for life. This negotiation between good breast and bad breast, loved object and hated object, ushers the infant into what Klein calls the depressive position. Eve Sedgwick characterizes the depressive position as an "anxiety-mitigating achievement that the infant or adult only sometimes, and often only briefly, succeeds in inhabiting."[23] It involves the mitigation of anxiety because it is characterized by the predominance of other feeling states such as guilt and despair for damage done. It is from within the depressive position that reparation, the process by which "we make good the injuries which we did in phantasy and for which we still unconsciously feel guilty," becomes possible.[24]

This is the originary Kleinian scene, but to adapt reparation for dehumanist purposes it is necessary to scale the concept up. The mother is the infant's first object of love and hatred, of reparation and aggression. But, as David Eng reminds us, Klein's theory of reparation also teaches us how loved objects and hated objects come to be designated as such. "As the infant's social circle enlarges love and hate are dislodged from the singular figure of the mother to be divided among *different* objects."[25] This first happens within the space of kinship, in relation to siblings. Then, once in school, it becomes socially acceptable for a child to decide that some of their classmates are worthy of love while the others are okay to hate. This process furthers as life continues, gradually including ever more distant others, until eventually the process of reparation starts to give way to abstraction, such that one begins to project love and hatred onto places, ideals, interests, and activities. The crucial example for this chapter emerges when "an idealized love for the 'mother'" transforms "into an idealized preservation of the 'motherland.'"[26] This is where Eng starts to expose the colonial thread sewn into the seams of Klein's theory. Klein writes:

> The child's early aggression stimulated the drive to restore and to make good, to put back into his mother the good things he has robbed her of in phantasy, and these wishes to make good merge into the later drive to explore, for by finding new land the explorer gives something to the world at large and to a number of people in particular. In his pursuit the explorer actually gives expression to both aggression and the drive to reparation. We know that in discovering a new country aggression is made use of in

> the struggle with the elements, and in overcoming difficulties of all kinds. But sometimes aggression is shown more openly; especially was this so in former times when ruthless cruelty against native populations was displayed by people who not only explored, but conquered and colonized. Some of the early phantasied attacks against the imaginary babies in the mother's body, and actual hatred against new-born brothers and sisters, were here expressed in reality by the attitude towards the natives. The wished-for restoration, however, found full expression in repopulating the country with people of their own nationality.[27]

For Eng, this passage proves that Klein's theory of reparation operates according to the logics that underpin projects of settler colonization. Just as the infant directs its aggression at the mother, Klein's imagined colonizer visits "ruthless cruelty" on Native peoples after arriving upon an unknown land. But rather than naming a process of providing love and care to these damaged Natives, Eng demonstrates that in this passage "reparation comes to name the psychic process of responding to European colonization and genocide of [I]ndigenous peoples by repopulating the New World with images of the self-same."[28] In other words, the colonizers are able to see only those who are similar to themselves as objects that are worthy of love and repair. Native peoples, in the colonizer's eyes, remain hated objects, subject to what Patrick Wolfe teaches us to call a "logic of elimination."[29]

It is tempting, given Eng's critique, to turn away from the reparation concept completely—at least if one is intending to take it up toward dehumanist or minoritarian ends. His point is well-taken: Klein's original formulation abides uncritically by a settler colonial logic. But my intention here is to rescue reparation both from itself and for care theory. By placing Indigenous insights and decolonial declarations at the center of its concerns, *Afterearth* asks us to reread Klein and, moreover, to revise Klein both on her own terms (i.e., reparatively) and on altered terms that unequivocally oppose settler colonial resolution. The film draws our attention to the love its subjects feel at once for both mother and motherland, and it highlights the care its subjects receive from both as well. In this way, *Afterearth* teaches its audience that reparation, reenvisioned for a dehumanist ethics of care, is a process, whether in phantasy or in performance, that seeks to make good the damage done to the land and those native to it, human and nonhuman. It does so not through a restoration of settler subjectivity or sovereignty but through a dehumanist release from these ways of being and a concomitant alignment with efforts aimed at environmental and Indigenous resurgence. Indeed, the film itself is an attempt to shift its viewers into a reparative position by inducing in them the realization that the planet humans have pillaged in the name of profit is not just, through destructive climate events, a source of suffering—the bad breast—but a fragile source of sustenance as well.[30]

Afterearth's middle vignettes illustrate this point. The figure at the center of the film's second vignette, Isabella "Isa" Borgeson, is a queer, multiracial Filipina American poet from Oakland, California, with a homeland in the Philippines, in Leyte.[31] The first thing Borgeson tells the audience of *Afterearth* is a story about her mother, whose relationship to the Pacific Ocean shifted dramatically in the afterlife of Typhoon Haiyan in 2013. A category five super typhoon, Haiyan was one of the strongest ever to make landfall in the Philippines. Many were left homeless by Haiyan, others went missing, and more than six thousand people were killed by the storm. If the ocean was once a site of healing for Borgeson's mother, it was now, in a post-Haiyan world, darkened by the shadow of death. Standing in a desert, and then at a shoreline, Borgeson spends most of her appearance in *Afterearth* performing a poem. Throughout it, she speaks as a mother might to a daughter. She describes felled debris beneath bare feet, homes being washed away, boats buried in the sand by the storm, the corpses of family members floating in the seas, and the weeping of mothers that followed it all.

Haiyan, the violent intensity of it, was in many ways the result of settler colonial capitalist conduct. It was worsened by climate change, and the filmic events that follow Borgeson's portion of *Afterearth* remind us of this. When we meet Kayla Briët, the figure at the center of the film's third sequence, she is standing amid an expanse of hilly lands, surrounded by musical instruments and singing. In a voiceover, she introduces herself as a twenty-year-old filmmaker and composer of Chinese, Dutch-Indonesian, and French descent on her mother's side and Prairie Band Potawatomi and Ojibwe on her father's. Briët relays to us some of what she has learned from her father about the Prairie Band tribe, the reverence they have for trees, the sun, and nonhuman kin. When we hear her singing voice, it is like the wind: sweet relief to a world of rising temperatures. And her singing accompanies a montage of moving images, each of which evokes the current climate crisis and its basis in human behavior: broken glass bottles at the bottom of the ocean, ice caps melting, wildfires, war wreckage, and rising waters, maybe the same waters that left Borgeson's motherland in ruins. It is a series of images that asks its audience to reckon with the role empire has played in bringing about the end of certain vulnerable worlds by making visual and material its effects. And beneath this montage, a single sung refrain, "wish we didn't need another world."

To read Borgeson and Briët's vignettes together reparatively is to acknowledge what is similar about the mother and the motherland both in Klein and in common understanding. Under heteropatriarchy, both mother and land are understood to house nearly unending natural resources. The infant understands its mother as endlessly giving until, suddenly, her nourishment is withheld, and this withholding is experienced as a persecution. The subject of climate change complicity—when he is not simply disregarding the damage he causes, confident that his wealth or privileged societal position will afford him safe retreat from the consequences of his crimes—relates to the planet in a similar way. He assumes that the world of which Briët sings is filled with an endless supply of natural resources to be extracted for human ends. He has no good explanation for why that world so often responds undesirably, devastatingly, to such extraction. He has only bad feelings, as with the bad breast, only an aggressive desire to empty the world of its resources even further. Such a response, of course, is possible only because of the centuries-long effort to secure settler colonial capitalist hegemony, an effort that requires the elimination of Indigenous peoples, practices, and knowledges. To recognize this is, again, to recognize that multiply marginalized Asian diasporic subjects who, like Borgeson, seek environmental reparation for flooded homelands must consider their struggle to be inextricably linked to movements for decolonization. It is to recognize that environmental reparation in (post)colonial contexts must not amount simply to a repopulation of the land with new settler subjects, whether white or Asian, because true reparation depends fundamentally on the success of movements for Indigenous resurgence and self-determination.

Borgeson's poem describes a mother reckoning with the wreckage of a motherland. When the poem's speaker worries that the young woman to whom she speaks "will only know ocean as flood," we should hear in her words a desire to sustain an attachment to water, the element after which Borgeson's portion of the film is named. Her poem will go on to offer the daughter it addresses "all the ocean cannot swallow," an offering that includes what it is to dance with "the ghosts of all our drowned cousins" and the memory of the young woman's *lola*, Tagalog for grandmother, "swimming in a holy ocean with her *barkada*." The word *barkada*, which refers to a group of dear friends, notably contains in itself a vestige of the Spanish word for ship, *barca*. And the word is spoken as Borgeson herself swims in the ocean holding what looks like a small boat. With this pun, both poetic and visual, Borgeson reclaims and resignifies the historical harms of Spanish colonization for anticolonial Filipino purposes.[32] "We come from mothers who learn to pray in water," she says, "when you sing to this ocean our ghosts will sing back." The line implies that by treating the ocean as something sacred, the queer diasporic subject can make contact with those they have loved and lost. To treat the environment with care is to extend care, too, to the mothers in the Philippines whose lives are threatened whenever waters rage well beyond the shoreline. Another way to put this would be to say that *Afterearth* presents its audience with a vision of reparation in which self-preservation and ethical possibility are not separable, as Eng has shown they are in Klein, but inextricable. Indeed, the film argues that for the multiply marginalized Asian American subject (and the loved ones on whom she depends for continued care) to adopt an ethics of dehumanist care in times of climate crisis is both to inhabit a reparative position in relation to the entangled ecosystems in which she is situated and to refuse the ordinary aggression exerted on the planet by those who never seem to question their complicity within what Naomi Klein calls "disaster capitalism."[33]

In *Afterearth*, ultimately, care is positioned as a common repertoire of reparative tactics through which queer and trans Indigenous and Asian diasporic subjects can begin to address the dehumanizing damage done to their communities by colonialism, capitalism, and the climate crisis. The film is a vital contribution for many reasons, but one of the most important is the work it does to attune its audiences, most frequently Asian American in composition, to the role care can play in the cultivation of what Michael J. Viola, Dean Saranillio, Juliana Hu Pegues, and Iyko Day term "solidarities of nonalignment" among dehumanized subjects. Such solidarities are rooted in the recognition that struggles for decolonial, anti-capitalist, and abolitionist alliance must be attentive to the incommensurability that exists among these categories. They must be "grounded in horizontality, humility, and an intense faith in the power of the subaltern to remake the world beyond the old patterns of colonial domination."[34] It is with this orientation that we must approach the mixed experiences of Wong-Kalu and Briët, through which the film reminds us that there are many in existence for whom the political projects of Indigenous resurgence and Asian American racial care unfold in tandem. By situating queer and trans Asian diasporic struggles against gender-based violence and climate catastrophe within the frames of settler colonialism and capitalism, the film orients queer and trans Asian diasporic eco-politics toward a reverence for Indigenous leadership and support for Indigenous resurgence. Through both verbal and visual means, the film imagines a nonaligned, dehumanist solidarity between multiply marginalized Indigenous and Asian diasporic people, and between each of these groups and the nonhuman world. It is this move that makes it a genius work of minoritarian care theory.

Dehumanist Grief

Honey bees, so often viewed in the popular imagination as a metric of environmental health, have experienced alarming rates of mortality in the last few decades. In the United States, honey bee colonies have suffered due to colony collapse disorder, which results in abandoned hives and mass death among honey bees. The causes of this remain somewhat mysterious, though experts believe that pesticides and pathogens are at least partly responsible, as are changes in environment and in the climate.[35] To be sure, that humans have played a significant role in undermining honey bee health is undeniable. And yet, humans rely on honey bees for their well-being. As pollinators, honey bees are essential to sustaining biodiversity. Crops and wildflowers depend on them for continuity, which means that humans, by extension, do too. This is why it is essential for human beings to better attend to the honey bee with dehumanist care, and this is what Snow's poetry and visual art help us to do.

Snow's treatment of the honey bee (or rather, her treatment of our treatment of the honey bee) takes two forms: a hand-drawn image of a honey bee's death among flowers titled, *Funeral for the Honey Bee*, and a poem that they have performed on offbeat stages in towns large and small titled "The Last Words of the Honey Bees." The two pieces seem to accompany one another, with the poem endowing the honey bee with human language in an effort to allow the sub-subaltern insect in the image to speak, to enter into the space of appearance by way of a certain personification. These are the honey bee's words:

> Honey, our hive is built and ruled
> by women. Honey, we were once *wild*.
> Honey, look at the flowers. We raised
> them into artichoke, pepper, squash,
> and apple for you, Honey. You found
> our hive and renamed it *colony*—or
> a factory of Yellow, Black, and Brown
> honey—we are the silent workers
> who bring home your dinner,
> whether or not our Honey comes home.[36]

In Snow's writing, the honey bee self-identifies as a woman and speaks within the conventional lexicon of social reproduction. She speaks of "raising" the flowers into fully grown fruits, and of managing dinner, even when her Honey does not come home. The poem, in other words, makes evident an affinity between the world-reproducing activity of the worker bee, an insect popularly understood as female, and the social reproductive labors of the human woman. The worker bee and human woman are allied in and entwined by the poem, a dehumanist solidarity at a distance. The honey bee and the woman of color saddled with the slog of social reproduction are mutually constituted by their shared burden and responsibility to sustain he who Sylvia Wynter tells us has come to figure as the Human itself: Man, bourgeois white masculinity in the abstract. The point of the poem in many ways is to charge the Human with negligent ingratitude and to cast the Human as a threat to the very continuity of the world.

It is telling, then, that the last words of the honey bee are addressed to an other, a "you" that the speaking, dying insect repeatedly calls, "Honey." Honey, in this context, is another name for Man, he who favors white monoculture to the wild flower, where wildness might be understood according to the terms Jack Halberstam has outlined: as a category critical of humanism, characterized by ungovernability and saturated with racialization.[37] Indeed, as Snow's poem makes clear, the Human is responsible for renaming the hive a "colony" and for reframing the hive as a factory. This citation of honey bee history dates to the early seventeenth century, when the honey bee was used by the ruling classes of England as a metaphor to motivate and justify the new world of settler colonial capitalism.[38] This fact raises two profound ironies. First, colony collapse disorder does not refer to decoloniality but to the consequence of anthropogenic negligence. Second, Snow names the Human "Honey" in order to signal that his very existence, like honey's, is produced by the victim of his negligent violence, the honey bee.

In light of these ironies, consider the poem's first explicit reference to colony collapse disorder:

> when this colony collapses into a pool
> of Yellow, Black and Brown honey,
> the women are always the first to go.[39]

The overt invocation of yellowness, blackness, and brownness produces an image of racialized entanglement and entangled raciality within the experience of anthropogenic catastrophe. The assertion that "women are always the first to go," in the poem's following line, returns race to gender in a relation of inextricability and references the swift suffering faced by feminized and racialized beings—whether worker bees or women of color—burdened with the reproduction of the world at the end of the world. Crucially, the poem's proclamation that women are the first to go also references the flight of the worker bee from the hive in situations of colony collapse, a departure flight that results in the abandonment of the queen bee and the death of her domicile. Snow's honey bee narrates this movement:

> I open my wings and my colony
> drops dead. I close my wings
> and every flower at my funeral begins to grieve.[40]

Here the poem invites us to turn to its partner image, *Funeral for the Honey Bee*, as an aperture through which to view the floral grief incited by the insect's final moments (see figure 4.1). In the top left corner of the illustration a sunflower bends under the profound weight of a profound loss. In the bottom right, another seems to bow its blossom, petals simply unable to stand. There is no grass in the image, no ground on which to find stability. Rather, a number of red flowers seem to float, to process in the illustration's central clearing. The flowers act as so many pallbearers to the bee: availing her to the attentive others in the scene, maintaining composure in the interest of maintaining the memory of a life and the lives that life made possible. This floral funerary performance in Snow's image can be glimpsed as a wilting, an emptying of nourishment from the body that exceeds the Freudian frameworks of mourning and melancholia, even in instances when those frameworks have been redesigned specifically to address what it is to experience racial and national loss.[41] At stake in this wilting is not, primarily, the situation of psychic interiority in the afterlife of loss but instead the ontological proximity of grieving to dying.

Put simply: grief is a kind of attrition. Grief is debilitating. To grieve is also to wilt is also to die. It is to be emptied of the stuff of life, to concede to a comportment of collapse in the absence of the sustenance formerly provided by the lively ones that we have lost. We wilt when we lose those on whom we have learned to rely to sustain our lives. When a star dies, the constellation of which it is a part will never be the same. Something similar happens within an ecology of entanglement, a dehumanist care web, when we lose a source of care within it. Anyone who has lost a parent—a life-giver and sustainer—knows this. We dehydrate; our dying and deterioration accelerate. We are nearer to our own death when we are nearer to the death of another, when we grieve. To quote Donna Haraway, "grief is a path to understanding entangled shared living and dying; human beings must grieve *with*."[42] Haraway's appeal for the human to "grieve with" the nonhuman presupposes a certain blockage of the human's ability or will to do so. It seems, in this way, to implicitly cite a Butlerian discourse of grievability.[43] We might say that the anthropocentric frame within which grievable life exists excludes the honey bee and that the death of the honey bee, either in the singular or the plural, fails to signify as a grievable death.

FIGURE 4.1. Jess X. Snow, *Funeral for the Honey Bee* (2014). Courtesy of the artist.

The potential of Snow's poem and illustration lies in their ability—by way of symbolism and affect—to jostle loose the obstruction that separates the nonhuman from grievability. Snow's poem entwines the lives and labors of worker bees and women of color. Her illustration reveals a resonance in how grief is made manifest in humans and flora. It teaches us something about what loss costs a care web. These moves are attempts to induce an attunement to the entanglement of humans, nonhumans, and the environment itself. They are attempts to induce dehumanist grief as a form of racial care.

And this is not all that Snow seeks to do in these works. The last lines of Snow's poem, though they head at first in dystopian directions, ultimately help us to glimpse an ethical and political horizon for care theory. She writes,

> Honey,
> do you see our queen?
> She is next. And then
> the Earth, and you,
> Honey. Every drop
> of my Yellow
> Black & Brown
> is falling into a field of white.[44]

Then, on the page and before the poem's final lines, there is a single hard return, an interval, a last breath before the honey bee speaks its last words: "Honey, / I'm home."[45] The line is a winking citation of the heteronormative division of domestic work; one man's respite is another woman's reproductive labor. At the same time, however, and in no uncertain terms, the passage as a whole describes the collapse of an entangled world and the subsumption of minoritarian difference into white supremacist homogeneity. The honey bee, we are to assume, passes with her proclamation of homecoming. But to where, or into what, does the insect pass? What are we to make of this homecoming? Is there life after death?

"Home"

Thus far, this chapter's dehumanist inquiry has implicitly followed Rachel C. Lee's call for an Asian Americanist critique that moves away from the ambition to consolidate "a political community of rights-bearing subjects" and toward a methodology that, hopefully, both asks and enacts how we might best "caretake entangled populations beyond the narrowly defined species-being to which Asian Americans have thought themselves to belong."[46] However, if Lee is attempting to guard against a seemingly compulsive will to liberal humanist wholeness within Asian Americanist critique by way of a revalorizing recourse to biological fragmentarity, mine is an attempt to restore that which appears in the world as a singularity to a wholeness that is larger than itself, a whole that might also be thought of as a *home*.

Home has historically been a vexed concept and context for queer Asian Americans especially. Eng has argued that *home*, the place of belonging par excellence, troubles both queer and Asian diasporic life. While queers are still often exiled from families of origin and sent into social ostracism and homelessness, Asian Americans—"suspended between departure and arrival," as Eng puts it—"remain permanently disenfranchised from home, relegated to a nostalgic sense of its loss or to an optative sense of its unattainability."[47] This is not, however, to say that queer Asian Americans are always and everywhere alienated from home. As Gayatri Gopinath argues, "the construction of 'queers' being 'like Asian Americans' in their alienation from 'home' needs to be rearticulated in light of the ways in which queer diasporic subjects—and queer female diasporic subjects in particular—inhabit and transform home space rather than simply existing in exilic relation to it."[48] Gopinath's critique highlights the roles that Asian diasporic women and femmes tend to play in the private sphere. It is a feminist intervention that aligns with how Snow's poem invokes the often-burdensome work of social reproduction. Taken together, Eng and Gopinath clarify something about the *home* concept: as a spatiotemporally discrete dwelling space constituted by exclusions and a disproportionate distribution of gendered and racialized labor, home can feel like an impossibility in relation to Asian Americanist, trans/queer, and feminist concerns. At the very least, it is a space and a feeling for which the multiply marginalized Asian American is always made to work.

However, I propose that Snow's art opens a window from which multiply marginalized Asian Americans might come to view the category of *home* with refreshed eyes. Here we can consider one last piece of Snow's creation, a brief work of animation from 2017 titled "Migration Is Natural."[49] The video, which is viewable on YouTube, is both voiced and illustrated by Snow. It tells the story of their family, their migration from China to "America," and the unbelonging with which Snow struggled there. The political function of the story is to challenge the givenness of border regimes, but it also reveals something of the reason Snow creates the work that they do. They describe the challenge of growing up "tripping over syllables of Chinese and English." "Stuttering, without homeland, and afraid to speak, I belonged to no country," Snow explains, "So I drew myself my own."

The country they describe is nothing like the settler colony whose coherence Snow aims to challenge by making migration seem like a natural thing and by making borders seem unnatural and constructed to constrain free movement. To the contrary, the country Snow imagines emerges out of aesthetic and poetic practice. It is less a nation-state than it is, in Snow's words, "a future that does not yet exist, where home is not a place bound by borders but a place where imagination thrives." The animation that accompanies this line finds a flock of birds migrating upward and into the stars. They are stand-ins for the migrant humans for whom Snow's art practice, to borrow a formulation from Harsha Walia, aspires toward "worldmaking as a process of homemaking."[50] Because in imagining a rich place called home, Snow tells us, "We remember the carbon of our body was birthed from stardust." That is, we remember that humans are inextricably entangled with the nonhuman world. We are all made from the same matter. This realization comes with its own kind of belonging, and the conclusion to Snow's animation illustrates as much: "Here, with no land left to push us off of, we create home amongst the stars. Here, shining whole and a hundred unseeable colors, we are a migrant constellation. We are home. We are home."

These final lines, on the one hand, remind us that the question of home cannot be disentangled from the question of land. They ask us to remember that many of those we call diasporic are also Indigenous peoples who have been forced from their homes, from their lands, through displacement and death. With this in mind, the question, "Where are you from?" must be met with an answer about place, one's people, one's past (we lived there) and one's present (we are from there, of there). On the other hand, because Snow places us impossibly in the sky among the stars, the conclusion to "Migration Is Natural" casts home in a way that resonates with how José Esteban Muñoz describes queerness in *Cruising Utopia*. From this vantage point, whether for the diasporic subject or the dying insect that has left its hive, home can be sensed ontologically as a horizontal ideality toward which we must strive.[51] With this utopian horizon of home in view it becomes meaningless to ask the abject, anti-Asian question, "Where are you from?" for home is a nonplace that we may never have been but that can be visited in fleeting, performative moments of aesthetic and affective excess and ecstasy. To arrive at this sort of home would be to arrive at a just curation of caring relations, inclusive of the here and the now, the then and the there, the living and the dead. This vision of home is one without borders, a place where you belong without question, where the caring attachments that anchor you to the world are felt and expressed.

Even as these two visions of home as land and horizon appear incommensurable, highlighting the tension between the people, politics, and fields evoked by the terms "Indigenous" and "Asian American," they advance a shared sense of stakes. In each case, the homeless, made so by empire, colonization, poverty, political instability, climate crisis, gentrification, transphobia, and homophobia are, like the honey bees, those who have the most to gain from a redistribution of care. In each case, home must be imagined beyond what Joan Tronto famously describes as a "caring democracy," which remains yoked to liberalism, capitalism, and the state. And indeed, the latter, utopian vision of home can only truly exist in the decolonized world demanded by the former, a world in which unprecedented social movements have brought about some communist distribution of power, resources, life-chances, and care—from each according to their means, to each according to their needs. Home, in short, is what I am writing for. It is what we are fighting for.

And if home in Snow's "The Last Words of the Honey Bees" marks a death, it does so only in order to imagine home as a release of the self into the entangled infinitude of life, an experience of interpermeability-cum-dispossession wherein all that is accumulated and proliferated is—as Fred Moten and Stefano Harney might have it—"unpayable debt."[52] I write this well aware of the warnings that care theorists sometimes issue against positioning care within a debt framework. Hil Malatino, for example, argues that "if we're serious about addressing the production of burnout, fatigue, exhaustion, debility, and disability within trans lives and communities, we cannot afford to internalize and operationalize a concept of care as debt."[53] His worry is that we do more harm than good when we refuse to relinquish the fantasy that care can be accounted for neatly within a logic of exchange. "The fantasy that care work—within and beyond the home—can be somehow equalized (a fantasy held dear by many feminists, myself included) ushers into the ostensible private sphere the same forms of neoliberal task tabulation that circulate (unjustly) in our waged labor lives."[54]

Malatino is right to caution us against the way neoliberal imperatives can creep into our intimate relations. But to recognize the debt incurred by the cared-for as an *unpayable* debt is to establish an ethics and politics of care that is unafraid to look past an exacting calculus of exchange in order to look toward the "home" that can be glimpsed, as a utopia, on the horizon. I recognize, as Harney does at the end of *The Undercommons*, that even the most loving revision of debt—the kind that shows up in phrases like "I owe everything to my mother, I owe everything to my mentor"—can fast become "oppressive and very moralistic."[55] And within Asian American studies, scholars such as erin Khuê Ninh and Mimi Thi Nguyen have made clear the damage that debt can do to Asian American subjects, families, and movements.[56] However, I remain convinced by Harney's suggestion that unpayable debt, which cannot be reduced "to an individualisation through the family or an individualisation through the wage laborer," can instead become "a principle of elaboration."⁵⁷

An elaboration of what? Olivia Michiko Gagnon, writing in direct response to the dehumanist project Singh assembles in her work, offers an answer to this question that brings us back to the stuff of Snow's poetic and aesthetic interventions as well as to the ecologies of entanglement that, by connecting human and nonhuman life, shape both in turn. Gagnon writes, "if encounters"—and I would specify, "caring encounters"—"with (human and nonhuman) others *are* the way that I become myself at all, then the unpayable debt that accrues between us is an ethical fact that can beautifully organize my life."⁵⁸ In other words, entanglement means: we owe each other everything. And we should live accordingly.

Each of the artists and activists in this chapter advances this claim through their work. In *Afterearth*, we see unpayable debt in the way the figures at the center of the film reckon with the reality that they owe everything to their mothers and motherlands. Call this a dehumanist reparative position. In Snow's study of the honey bee, unpayable debt inheres in a utopian vision of home as an ideality of care justice, of caring entanglement as its own sort of surplus value, and of dehumanist grief as a simultaneous process of wilting and watering in perpetuity. What I am suggesting—indeed, what I am attempting to perform in my own writing—is that stagings of our entangled ontology—whether filmic, as in *Afterearth*, or poetic and visual, as in Snow's renderings of the honey bee—participate in an ethico-political project with the potential to attune us all to the most fundamental infrastructure of social life: the uneven distribution of care and neglect that founds and structures the reproduction of our world in all its complexity. In doing so, I am taking a cue from Snow and the other artists assembled in this chapter, each of whom seems to believe that there is ethico-political value in making our entangled ontology not only legible but *felt* through aesthetic encounter.

In a beautiful engagement with the work of Inuk artist Tanya Tagaq, Gagnon asks and answers the question, "What does it mean to feel entangled?"⁵⁹ Gagnon suggests that feeling entangled is a way of feeling oneself inside history and inseparably from others, human and nonhuman, across time and space. And just as it matters that *Afterearth*'s address of Asian diasporic care needs begins on native Hawaiian land, it matters that Gagnon weaves her understanding of entanglement from Inuit lines of thought, because "Inuit conceptions of both temporality and the interconnectedness of all life open out onto an ethics of care and responsibility."⁶⁰ An ethic of this sort, adapted to meet the care needs of multiply marginalized Asian Americans, is about abandoning what Gagnon calls "the presentist discourse of neoliberal individualism"⁶¹ that underpins model minoritism by instead attuning to one's situation within ecologies of entanglement and asking questions about "co-implication, vulnerability, and intimacy," "indeterminacy and unknowing."[62] I see in this list of qualities a set of instructions for anyone who aspires to a dehumanist ethic of care. Like Singh, Gagnon is asking us to live in a way that relinquishes human exceptionalism and settler forms of sovereignty, which short-circuit the receptivity required for good care. Our task is to suspend our sense of ourselves as discrete subjects and autonomous actors, and to feel instead just how deeply we depend on one another for that fragile thing called life, how deeply we will need each other as we stumble toward that distant thing called home. It is with this orientation, this ethics and politics of dehumanist care, that we must continue.

Conclusion

RACIAL CARE: JUNE 2020

It was June 2020. George Floyd's name was everywhere: on the internet and on television, on protest signs and in the empty platitudes of liberal and conservative legislators alike. Those opposed to the project of Black liberation saw their cities overcome with "rioters," "looters," and "criminals" of all kinds. Those in favor found in the streets an antidote to the isolation they had experienced while attempting, in those first few months of the pandemic, to flatten the curve of coronavirus infections. They found sociality in struggle, togetherness in protest, magic in mutual aid, mutual defense, and multiracial coalition. They also found that the rumors were true: the cops proved to be all tear gas and rubber bullets, exactly as violent as radical organizers argued they were. People were changed by their experiences of direct action and confrontation. It was a moment pregnant with more political hope than I had ever before felt in the air: hope that the neoliberal order might fray or even fall; hope that an ideology of individualism might give way to an ethics of interdependence; hope that our collective political push might finally put an end to policing and prisons. The uprisings led even the most experienced organizers to wonder aloud, "abolition in our lifetimes?" And though our enemies would prove too powerful to topple just yet, this simple fact must not be forgotten: that summer, a Black-lead multiracial movement managed to mobilize the masses in pursuit of a radical restructuring of racial caring relations in the settler colonial United States.

The popular tendency is to imagine the 2020 uprisings as a set of spontaneous events spurred by yet another viral video of anti-Black police murder; but this is only somewhat true. Take, for example, the deep historical conditions that yielded the uprisings that occurred in the place where I lived at the time. Madison, Wisconsin, the capitol city of the most segregated state in the United States, sits on stolen land, which the Ho-Chunk nation has called Teejop (Four Lakes) since time immemorial.[1] In an 1832 treaty, the Ho-Chunk were forced to cede the land to the United States. And throughout the following decades, as the Ho-Chunk resisted federal and state government efforts to eliminate them from the territory, Black people began to migrate to Madison seeking economic opportunity and establishing communities that would grow over the next century. When Hmong refugees were resettled in Wisconsin throughout the 1970s and 1980s, uprooted by the US imperial war in Vietnam, they were often placed in tight proximity to these Black communities, which had been deeply disenfranchised by structural racism. It is out of this reality—this confluence of settler colonial, anti-Black, and imperialist factors—that the community organization at the center of this concluding chapter would emerge.

Two decades prior to the 2020 uprisings, a Hmong refugee woman named Kabzuag Vaj founded the Asian Freedom Project with the intention of supporting Hmong women and youth in Wisconsin. In 2003, largely due to the proximity of Hmong and Black communities in Madison, the organization would change its name to Freedom Inc. as it grew its focus to include Southeast Asian and Black women, youths, and LGBTQIA+ people. Freedom Inc.'s mission: to end violence against these communities. Its frameworks for doing so: "gender justice, queer justice, Black and Southeast Asian liberation, anti-colonialism—which are rooted in radical Black queer feminisms, Hmong and Khmer feminisms."[2] For years, the nonprofit would help low- to no-income community members find housing; flee domestic violence; and navigate the healthcare, immigration, and criminal punishment systems. It would also offer culturally relevant programming to members: support groups, arts activities, youth camps, and the like. All these racial care efforts brought marginalized people into contact with one another, transforming strangers into community members, cultivating political consciousness and people power. Indeed, Freedom Inc.'s organizing efforts would prove essential to the movement that emerged in Madison following the murder of Michael Brown in 2014. The organization was also central to the uprisings that occurred in 2015 following the killing of Tony Robinson, a Black nineteen-year-old, by Madison police officer Matt Kenny. And when Derek Chauvin murdered George Floyd in front of the world, as members of the Ho-Chunk nation sent support to Minneapolis in an effort to protect Native institutions amid the uprisings without relying on the carceral settler state, Freedom Inc. led Madison's movement for racial justice in collaboration with the Party for Socialism and Liberation and Urban Triage, an organization dedicated to empowering Black youths.[3]

Fittingly, however, the face of Freedom Inc.'s leadership in that time was not primarily Vaj's but that of her former mentee turned co-executive director M. Adams. Both Black and queer, Adams was a national leader with the Movement for Black Lives at the time, an explicitly abolitionist and anti-capitalist coalition of Black organizations nationwide. And it was in coordination with the Movement for Black Lives that we in Madison advanced our four demands, each an intervention into the distribution of racial care on stolen land. "Free them all" called for the release of all prisoners in Dane County and elsewhere, noting the increased risk of COVID transmission among the incarcerated. "No cops in schools" sought to make educational institutions safer for Black students as well as for other marginalized students.[4] A call for Black "community control" over the police was rooted in an analysis of low-income Black communities as domestic colonies in the United States, an analysis that also importantly recognized "that the rights and histories of our Indigenous family must also be respected."[5] And our final demand, "defund the police," was fundamentally a matter of racial care because it insisted upon shifting funds from the anti-Black institution of policing toward the stuff of social reproduction. Defund the police, we argued, in order to re-fund education, health care, housing, cultural programming, community organizations, and other public goods. Against the view that uprisings appear almost out of nowhere, Freedom Inc.'s organizational history shows that uprisings in actuality emerge like sparks from the slow burn of continuous community organizing. In this case, that organizing was performed and made possible by an interracial coalition in which Asian Americans, specifically Hmong and Khmer women, youth, queers, and trans people, had long played an indispensable role.

What remains of this book is a meditation on Freedom Inc.'s coalitional performance of politics, one that returns me to the critical project at the heart of my writing: the cultivation of a radical ethics of racial care in the Asian American case. Thus far, I have emphasized the power of the aesthetic to induce shifts in the arrangement of racial caring relations, an arrangement that positions Asian

Americans as uniquely neglected subjects, as afterthoughts in the US political imagination. But as Freedom Inc.'s various activities illustrate, the aesthetic realm is not alone in its ability to alter racial caring relations. The work of political organizing also contains this capacity. Accordingly, and thinking across Asian American studies, critical refugee studies, and Black studies, my conclusion here aims to establish that art practice and movement work belong on a continuum of interventions that might be made within the ongoing culture war over racial care. The 2020 uprisings were nothing if not battles in that war. And so, I end *Racial Care* with a close reading of the racial choreography on display in the way that Freedom Inc. chose to fight those battles. My aim is to excavate the relational logics of multiracial coalition that defined the performance of racial care in the summer of 2020 and in the early twenty-first century more broadly.

To start, consider the role that Freedom Inc.'s Southeast Asian members played throughout the uprisings. When the group's Black members lead a mile-long march from the location of the city's Juneteenth celebration to the Dane County Courthouse, the group's Southeast Asian members, almost all of them women, walked along the outside of the march. They served as a protest security team by becoming a sort of perimeter, a shield for their Black comrades and others. Another action took the form of a car caravan. Demonstrators, myself included, met in the parking lot of Freedom Inc.'s offices and drove together to the city's outskirts where we confronted the president of the Madison school board at her home, demanding the removal of cops from schools. During this action, Southeast Asian members of Freedom Inc. positioned themselves at the rear of our automotive assembly. Sometimes they would hang out of windows, shouting instructions at the protesters driving in front of them. Other times, at intersections or when the caravan slowed, they would leap from their cars, direct traffic, and run interference with unfriendly cops.

Through these performative acts of protective racial care, Freedom Inc. presented an alternative to Tou Thao, the Hmong American cop who stood by for nine minutes and twenty-nine seconds while Derek Chauvin killed George Floyd in Minneapolis. Many commentators have positioned Thao as an exemplary representative of Asian American model minority complicity with anti-Blackness. But, as Ma Vang and Kit Myers argue, not only does this view obscure the material realities that would disqualify Hmong Americans from model minority status, including high rates of poverty (28.3 percent) and lower levels of educational achievement (46 percent with a high school education or less).[6] It also fails to attend to a certain continuity between the way Hmong soldiers were recruited by the United States as allies in its imperial war against communism in Vietnam and the way Thao was incorporated as a cog in the US machinery of anti-Black domestic warfare.[7] As Vang and Myers argue, Thao epitomizes how "anti-Blackness is embedded in Hmong soldiering and policing, showing how Hmong state allyship did not necessarily end with the conclusion of war" in Southeast Asia.[8]

Against this kind of complicity, Freedom Inc.'s Southeast Asian security team spent much of the uprisings modeling an ethics of racial care that refused alignment with US state violence. They did so by keeping their bodies between the agents of such violence and others who sought those agents' abolition. It was a defensive choreography of coalition, one that belied a certain high-stakes wager: that in the US context, Southeast Asians are less likely to face a frontal assault from the state than are their Black comrades. And this wager was also a racial care instruction: when they come for the most vulnerable, the rest of us must forge safety from the stuff of solidarity.

This was the same logic that subtended another especially salient scene of racial care that summer. On June 1, 2020, Freedom Inc. and its partner organizations led approximately two hundred protesters in an occupation of one of Madison's busiest intersections. For hours we disrupted traffic and, with it, our neighbors' sense of normalcy. The sun burned that day, and the pandemic raged. But organizers countered these conditions with care, distributing sunscreen, masks, hand sanitizer, water, pizza, and other snacks to those who were on their side. Cars were assembled into a barricade that protected demonstrators from oncoming traffic, and music blared from those cars' speakers. We danced in the street. It was joyful revolution, irresistible fun. And then, Black organizers from Urban Triage and Freedom Inc. took to their megaphones with instructions. They asked the white members of the crowd to form a perimeter around the rest of us. Whites in attendance were to stand in a circle, shoulder to shoulder, facing outward. They were to keep watch for cops and other would-be representatives of racial-colonial violence. They were to be our first line of defense. It was, in the words of Augusto Boal, the founder of the theater of the oppressed, a "rehearsal for the revolution."[9] If the safety of the others present at the action were suddenly to come under threat, then the white demonstrators who were less vulnerable to state violence would be instructed to enact what they had rehearsed. They would return to their marks in this perimeter and follow the example set for them by Freedom Inc.'s Southeast Asian security team. This, the organizers seemed to argue, was their care ethical duty as white comrades in the struggle against racial violence. And it was a duty that white comrades would need to perform, at great risk to themselves, later that day.

When our occupation finally concluded, organizers led us in a march toward the state capitol just a few blocks away. Almost immediately, though, white allies alerted Hmong members of Freedom Inc.'s security team to a dangerous situation: between our contingent and the capitol there was a white man roaming the streets, armed with a gun, motives unknown. The white allies had alerted the police to the man's presence, but the police had done nothing to address the threat he posed. Black leaders of the march responded to this news without surprise, asking protesters to take a knee just as we approached the street where we would encounter the threat in question. I remember the television of my mind switching back and forth between two channels. On one channel, a movie played in which the people, united, proceeded undefeated. But on the other channel played a horror movie, or a period piece, in which we were slaughtered. Bullets buried into bodies, bodies strewn across streets. And I could not have been alone in thinking this way. Why were we stopped except to prevent precisely this outcome? It was a paranoid fantasy that was also a rational racial fantasy, one that emerged from the shared sense that this white man with a gun might be so opposed to Black life and the solidarities supporting it that he would open fire on all of us in broad daylight. It was as if we all anticipated the events that would come to pass elsewhere in Wisconsin that August following the shooting of Jacob Blake by Kenosha police. Seventeen-year-old Kyle Rittenhouse would open fire on three pro-Black protesters while patrolling a Kenosha demonstration much like our own. All of his victims were white men. Only one survived. Rittenhouse now walks free, a poster boy for what Elisabeth Anker teaches us to call "ugly freedom."[10]

Imagine the thickness of the air, then, when organizers eventually called for white volunteers to stand between our assembly and the white man with a gun. They would have to perform the protective form of racial care that they had earlier rehearsed. The stakes were nothing less than life or death. And still, almost instantly, white comrades rose from the crowd and stepped into the line of fire. They built a racialized barrier with their bodies as an act of racial care. Their whiteness offered no guarantee of safety, but it did offer a more sustainable fantasy of it than did racial otherness. So there they stood, their risk allowing the march to proceed unscathed.

I raise this scene in order to lift up the performative pedagogy of racial care enacted within it. This collective act of mutual defense laid bare the logic of racial vulnerability that organized our pursuit of racial justice that summer. Whites, imagined as the least vulnerable to police and vigilante violence, were recruited as shields for the non-white people on their side, including members of the Freedom Inc. security team. In taking up the duties of racial care assigned to them by Black organizers, white protesters rehearsed their role in the struggle for just relations of racial care. Their instructions were these: follow Black leadership, be willing to risk, know what you have to offer, go where you are needed, learn from this.

Simultaneously, protesters who were neither Black nor white were encouraged to remain within the circle of racial care, receiving their own kind of ethical and political education. It is not difficult to imagine a scenario in which Black organizers, because of the disparities in vulnerability to state violence produced by anti-Blackness, would choose to enlist, say, Asian American protesters as additional shields in the face of impending racial violence. To do so would seem logical if, for example, one were to follow Frank Wilderson in thinking that Asian Americans operate as little more than "junior partners" to anti-Black civil society.[11] But in the given scene, Freedom Inc. eschewed this afropessimist frame. Being rooted at once in the liberation struggles of Black and Southeast Asian peoples, the organization could not but remain strategically, ethically, and politically attentive to the vulnerabilities produced by anti-Blackness and white supremacy both. It is this situated and relational attentiveness, the sort essential to care ethics, that finds expression in the protective performance of racial care that Black organizers enacted in defense of themselves and their non-Black comrades of color at this particular demonstration in Madison. What resulted was an opportunity for non-Black protesters to experience and internalize the reality that all racialized and colonized peoples benefit when Black liberation struggles tame white supremacy.

And yet, this welcome outcome of Freedom Inc.'s performance of racial care also warrants some suspicion. One might worry, for instance, that Freedom Inc.'s performance of racial shielding might run the risk of racial essentialism or something like it. What if one of the outer circle's white accomplices already had a criminal record? What if they were undocumented? What if the threat had opened fire? The assumption that whiteness confers to all its beneficiaries equal safety from state and vigilante violence cannot hold up under scrutiny, and it is therefore imperative to understand Freedom Inc.'s concentric circles as a kind of contact improvisation whose identitarian racial logics must always yield to the micro-adjustments required by a more precise analysis of power.

There is also a certain specter of saviorism that haunts the scenes I am describing. One wonders whether these white protesters might have risen in defense of others only or mostly to bring honor onto themselves. But even if saviorism were at play here, this misfortune is mitigated by the fact that the above performances of racial care were the result of what performance theorist André Lepecki might call Freedom Inc.'s "choreopolitical plan," which he asserts is the "minimum condition of sociality" out of which freedom might be felt and made manifest across diverse actors in performance.[12] That the sort of racial shielding enacted amid the uprisings is a planned form of racial care in this sense, a coordinated strategy defined by "the preexistence of a (soft) choreography," should teach us something about how to tend to others amid emergent circumstances of racial crisis.[13]

The lesson is well stated by Vaj in a podcast conversation recorded in June 2020 regarding the role Hmong community members and others must play in Black liberation struggles. "Don't ask people how you can show up for them. Already have those built relationships so that when it happens again—because it's going to happen again—you show up in a way that you know how."[14] Vaj's reminder is imperative: we are not acting ethically if our racial caring relations with communities other than our own emerge only in times of sudden and serious crisis. This sort of racial care, exceptional and short-term, too often gives way to the sort of saviorism that should be guarded against. "If you're showing up to protect Black people," Vaj tells me during a phone interview, "they don't need that. Whether you're playing security or whether you're in the streets: you're showing up for George Floyd because you're actually marching for your own life and for your own liberation."[15] What we need, according to Vaj, is to recognize that the struggles for Black and Southeast Asian liberation, indeed all minoritarian struggles for liberation, are inextricably linked. What we need is to make manifest a movement thick with trust and reciprocity, to sustain a minoritarian coalition of caregivers and receivers gathered together to keep one another alive and to end those systems that would end us first.

As I write this, nearly five years have passed since the uprisings. Sometimes those days feel like a distant memory; other times, they feel like yesterday. In either case, what is most palpable about the present moment is how impossible political improvement feels in the US context. Faced with a second Trump presidency, the country appears to be plunging full-bodied into the frigid waters of fascism. Corruption reigns and the crises taken up across the preceding pages of this book persist: the planet burns, unwellness is everywhere, and the state's assaults on minoritarian life continue to intensify. We are never not at war with one another. And all the while sea levels rise, military budgets rise, police budgets rise, prison populations rise, rents rise, prices rise, corporate profits rise, suicide rates rise, and so, too, do the body counts brought on by mass shootings. Perhaps this will change by the time you read these words. Perhaps it will not.

Whatever the case, it could not be clearer that we deserve better than the carceral, war-torn world that we have. As the uprisings argued in 2020, ours is a world that must be abolished so that something new and more nourishing might be built in its place. Abolition, as Ruth Wilson Gilmore reminds us, is not merely destruction, not merely flames engulfing a Minneapolis police sta-

tion; it is chiefly about "presence," the cultivation of sustained and sustaining webs of racial caring relation like those performed by Freedom Inc. and its allies in the streets.[16] Because of this, as Patricia Nguyen argues, it is useful to understand abolition as "durational performance."[17] It is something we must do with our bodies over time. "The object of abolition," write Stefano Harney and Fred Moten, is "not so much the abolition of prisons but the abolition of a society that could have prisons, that could have slavery, that could have the wage, and therefore not abolition as the elimination of anything but abolition as the founding of a new society."[18] This new society, I suspect, would glimmer with the knowledge that no one is disposable. It would embrace transformative justice approaches to handling harm. And with Indigenous sovereignty over the land restored, it would value above all else our ontological interdependence. Care in this future would be placed at the center of our shared political, economic, and psychosocial concerns. Attentiveness to arrangements of caring relation, to their ever-shifting microdynamics, would rise to the status of a sacred ethical ideal. And those now known as Asian Americans, at long last, would no longer live neglected lives. The future that Harney and Moten help us to imagine would necessarily be one in which the forces that produce anti-Asian neglect (white supremacy, anti-Blackness, settler colonialism, and neoliberal racial capitalism) would be rendered unrecognizable, if not utterly obsolete. "Abolition requires that we change one thing," Gilmore writes, "everything."[19]

But this, of course, will not come easily. And in the meantime, this ruthlessly mean time, we continue to wage the culture war over racial care. Because it is always worthwhile to soothe another's suffering. Because the race war rages on with or without our resistance. Though shared experiences teach us that racial care is often a life-stealing trap, a Sisyphean boulder to be pushed up a mountain as steep as our suffering is ceaseless, we persist. While Asian Americans yet occupy an unsustainably neglected situation on the field of racial care, through theory, art, organizing, and in our everyday lives we still struggle to shift racial caring relations in our favor. Like Kristina Wong, we build mutual aid efforts from good intentions and left political imperatives. We make plays from the praxis of Asian American feminism. Like Mark Aguhar, we perform self-care in public. We do so for ourselves and for other minoritarian subjects for whom survival is a task that requires inspiration. Like the character Gina does for Dennis in Julia Cho's *Office Hour*, we care for those in need when no one else will; we build for them holding environments in which to find racialized respite, relief, refuge. Like the members of the Generic Ensemble Company, we check in with one another. We attend to singularity, to specificity, and we rehearse the kinds of caring relations we wish we could take for granted. Like Jess X. Snow, we make art with the power to meet people where they are, to heal them there, and to shift them into unprecedented awareness of dehumanist caring relations.

And finally, like Freedom Inc. and the others who sought justice for George Floyd in pandemic times, we organize, we mobilize, we fail and fight on. We sweat, standing shoulder to shoulder, staring into the eyes of oncoming violence. We hold the line. We do not back down. We whisper and we shout.

You've got my back, I've got yours.

If they want to harm you, they will have to get through me.

I will be here, with you, when they come for us.

These are the promises prescribed to us by a radical ethics of racial care, an ethics rooted as much in relations of mutual defense as in the ontological reality of our interdependence with all life. Those of us who long for a just arrangement of racial caring relations can strive for nothing less than abolition; nothing less than decolonization; nothing less than the careful cultivation of a world, a home, that would actually be worthy of our living in it. To this end, we are called upon to think beyond the family, the settler state, neoliberal capitalism, and white supremacy; to think about race, gender, sexuality, disability, class, and other axes of difference as inextricable from one another; and to refuse unmarked and abstract renderings of caring relation, caregivers, and care receivers. I have endeavored to demonstrate that the aesthetic and social movements of multiply marginalized Asian America are crowded with forms of racial care whose often overlooked brilliance is given in how they manage to combat the negligence and violence of crisis ordinariness in the early twenty-first century. In the end, I offer *Racial Care* itself as a form of care. It is written against racialized care imbalance and psychosocial suffering; it is written for all those who care enough, actively and eternally, to keep lit the flames of multiply marginalized Asian American life. Racial care is what we must do for one another when the world wears us down to hold itself up. And so, at the end of the world, we begin again.

Notes

INTRODUCTION

1. Cathy Park Hong, "The Slur I Never Expected to Hear in 2020," *New York Times*, April 12, 2020.

2. Jeong, Russell, Aggie Yellow Horse, Tara Popovic, and Richard Lim, *Stop AAPI Hate National Report*, accessed November 13, 2024, https://stopaapihate.org/reports/.

3. *Care Package: Poems, Meditations, Films, and Other Cultural Nutrients for Times Like This*, Smithsonian Asian Pacific American Center, accessed March 25, 2021, https://apa.si.edu/care/.

4. B. Fisher and Tronto, "Toward a Feminist Theory of Caring."

5. It may seem that white subjects, because they sit atop the US racial hierarchy, would have no need for racial care. However, my definition of racial care refers to "racialized subjects" and not to "subjects of color." It refers to "suffering" rather than to "violence" or "racism." I have made these choices to keep white subjects as players on the stage of racial care. White fragility demands from subjects of color the kind of care one might exercise while walking on thin ice—this point is central to my third chapter. The white insistence on remaining unmarked obliges non-white subjects as well as white subjects with racial consciousness to engage in a preservative labor of racial care. If at times it seems that I theorize racial care without regard for the white reception of racial care, it is because I believe in the following proposition: the white anti-racist project is diminished to the extent that the white subject is unable to relinquish its "need" for racial care.

6. Glenn, "From Servitude to Service Work." In making this move toward the social, I follow the methodological example set by Martin Manalansan in his article "Queering the Chain of Care Paradigm."

7. Gilmore, *Golden Gulag*, 28.

8. Kondo, *Worldmaking*, 11.

9. While the most visible assaults on Asian American life following the emergence of COVID-19 have taken the form of physical assault, it is notable that this sort of violence represents only 13.7 percent of the incident reports tracked by the Stop AAPI Hate Project through June 2021. The more frequently reported forms of violence took the less

spectacular forms of "verbal harassment" (63.7 percent) and "shunning" (16.7 percent). This data reflects my view that because anti-Asian violence is often inflicted almost immaterially, racial care must be imagined and enacted accordingly.

10. K. Wong, "Wong Flew over the Cuckoo's Nest and Almost Dropped Dead," 113.

11. I should mark what K. Wong's decision, as a Chinese American woman, to take on in performance the character of a Cambodian American woman reveals about the risks of theorizing racial care in the Asian American case. On the one hand, the coalitional impulse of Asian American panethnicity might seem to some a license for Wong to shift between East and Southeast Asian identities in performance, intending to care for both. On the other, we should pause at Asian American panethnicity's tendency to run roughshod over Asian histories of imperial warfare and, by extension, over the tensions that still exist among Asian (American) peoples because of those histories.

12. K. Wong, "Wong Flew over the Cuckoo's Nest and Almost Dropped Dead," 113.

13. K. Wong, "Wong Flew over the Cuckoo's Nest and Almost Dropped Dead," 113.

14. K. Wong, "Wong Flew over the Cuckoo's Nest and Almost Dropped Dead," 112.

15. Raghuram, "Race and Feminist Care Ethics."

16. Hankivsky, "Rethinking Care Ethics," 256.

17. Hankivsky, "Rethinking Care Ethics," 259.

18. Even as I ascribe to an intersectional approach in this book, I am weary of the unintended work that intersectionality does within two mainstream schools of care theory: care ethics and social reproduction theory. In the introduction to her book *Black Feminism Reimagined*, Jennifer Nash writes, "If there is nothing more damning than the accusation of 'white feminism,' intersectionality stands as the field's primary corrective, its way of naming and labeling (even if not performing) a correct, ethical, and virtuous feminism" (15). The problem with this, Nash teaches us, is that "once the field has effectively reconfigured itself" by following the guidance of intersectionality "black feminism is imagined as no longer necessary or vital" (30) — as, I would argue, are other modes of minoritarian study. Intersectionality and the specific Black feminists associated with it (most frequently Kimberlé Crenshaw and Patricia Hill Collins), are now frequently positioned as a solution for care theory's shortcomings. They are recruited by the discourse to mark the outer limits of care theory's internal audit around minoritarian difference. Intersectionality becomes *the* methodology through which to analyze difference, while other analytics developed within minoritarian intellectual traditions such as Black studies, Asian American studies, and other critical ethnic studies and Indigenous studies formations remain under-cited, if not wholly untouched. It is true that some of this erasure might be explained by the observation that so much of care ethics thrives outside the US context, but this caveat alone cannot account for the deracinated sensibilities of the field at large. *Racial Care* aspires to a deeper engagement with minoritarian knowledges.

19. Malatino, *Side Affects*, 16.

20. Puar, *Right to Maim*.

21. For more relevant works on care at the intersection of Asian Americanist critique and disability thinking, see James Lee, *Pedagogies of Woundedness*; A. Wong, *Year of the Tiger*; Bolton, *Crip Colony*; Kim, *Care at the End of the World*; and M. Chen, *Animacies*.

22. Nishida, *Just Care*, 7.

23. On "minoritarian," see Muñoz, *Disidentification*; and Chambers-Letson, *After the Party*. On women of color feminism, see G. K. Hong, *The Ruptures of American Capital*. On queer of color critique, see Ferguson, *Aberrations in Black*. On trans of color critique, see J. N. Chen, *Trans Exploits*. On crip of color critique, see Kim, "Toward a Crip-of-Color Critique"; and Moshe, *Decarcerating Disability*.

24. Hobart and Kneese, "Radical Care," 2. See also Nadasen, *Care*.

25. See Spade, *Mutual Aid*; Lewis, *Full Surrogacy Now*; and Malatino, *Trans Care*.

26. See Lewis, *Abolish the Family*; O'Brien, *Family Abolition*; Page and Woodland, *Healing Justice Lineages*; and Kapadia, "Downward Redistribution of Breath."

27. The Chinese Exclusion Act of 1882 banned Chinese laborers from entering the United States and kept Chinese immigrants already in the country from becoming US citizens. The Angel Island Immigration Station in San Francisco operated from January 21, 1910, until November 5, 1940. Known to some as "the Ellis Island of the West," it became the most significant site at which immigration from China was processed during the era of Chinese exclusion. During the exclusion era, only existing US citizens and their immediate families were allowed entry into the country, as were those who fit the exempt categories of students, teachers, diplomats, merchants, and travelers.

28. The first march on Washington for gay and lesbian rights occurred in October 1979, on the same weekend as the National Conference of Third World Lesbians and Gays, which also took place in the nation's capital. These were landmark events in queer Asian American history and some of the earliest instances when Asian American gays and lesbians from across the country could cultivate consciousness and community at a national scale. Since then, numerous organizations dedicated to sustaining queer Asian American life have emerged in cities across the United States, including Trikone (Chicago), founded in 1986; GAPIMNY (New York City), founded in 1990; AQUA (Washington, DC), founded in 1997; and Lavender Phoenix (the California Bay Area), founded in 2004. Each is or was dedicated in some way to meeting the psychosocial care needs of queer Asian Americans. Support groups and social events have mitigated undesirability in the face of sexual racisms, fundraisers have met members' material needs, and collective advocacy efforts have worked to rescue people from incarceration. This queer and trans history should be seen as a legacy of 1968, for it could have come to pass only under the banner of "Asian American."

29. Here I have in mind political organizations like AAPI Women Lead, the Asian American Resource Workshop in Boston, and 18 Million Rising, which has specialized in digital organizing around Asian American issues since 2012. Relevant cultural organizations include but are not limited to the Asian American Writer's Workshop in New York City and the Smithsonian Asian Pacific American Center in Washington, DC.

30. See Tronto, *Caring Democracy*; The Care Collective, *Care Manifesto*; and Hamington and Flowers, *Care Ethics in the Age of Precarity*.

31. See Ferguson, *Reorder of Things*; G. K. Hong, *Death Beyond Disavowal*; and Melamed, *Represent and Destroy*.

32. Cohen, "Punks, Bulldaggers, and Welfare Queens."

33. Snyder and Mitchell, *Biopolitics of Disability*, 14.

34. Ninh, *Passing for Perfect*.

35. Rodriguez, *White Reconstruction*, 17.

36. Rodriguez, *White Reconstruction*, 7, 17.

37. Here I follow the claim that Mimi Khúc makes about the state of Asian American mental health and about model minority mental health in particular: we are all "differentially unwell," in need of differentiated kinds of care. See Khúc, *Dear Elia*, 5.

38. Berlant, *Cruel Optimism*, 10.

39. Culture wars are often dismissed as abstract distractions from more concrete class wars, but the culture war over racial care must be understood as an essential element of class struggle insofar as it is ultimately a battle over the means and norms of (psycho)social reproduction.

40. Lowe, *Immigrant Acts*, 22.

41. For more on reverse stigmatization see McMaster, "In Defense of Virtue Signaling."

42. Lowe, *Immigrant Acts*, 67.

43. Day, "Being or Nothingness," 102.

44. Sandra E. Garcia, "Where Did BIPOC Come From?," *New York Times*, June 17, 2020.

45. S. K. Lee, "Staying In," 34.

46. For another example of the Asian American as afterthought, consider the frequency with which the shorthand "Black and brown" was used during the Obama and Trump years by activists, educators, journalists, politicians, and others to mean something like "those racial minorities who bear the brunt of racial oppression." Where do Asian Americans fit within this phrase? To be sure, there are many Asians in the United States who are held within the category of Blackness, and many more are hailed by brownness: West, South, Southeast, and mixed-race Asians especially. These facts, no doubt, are part of what allows José Esteban Muñoz to assert that "Brownness" is "coexistent, affiliates, and intermeshes with" Asianness or "even a yellowness." For Muñoz, brownness is not reducible to Latin Americanness; it is nonidentitarian. And yet, it is notable that even Muñoz's conception of brownness does not (aspire to) include Asianness within its embrace in every instance. This is partially a sign of respect from Muñoz: recognition that Asianness and perhaps yellowness deserve their own treatment. But it also illustrates that "Black and brown," even imagined as maximally capacious, leaves Asians who are neither held nor hailed by either Blackness or brownness out of frame. Thus, when used as shorthand to refer to the most oppressed of racial subjects, the phrase belies an assumption that non-brown Asians are so comparably unaffected by racism as to be unworthy even of mention in certain racial justice–oriented conversations. All the time, the term fails to account for all Asian Americans. It is as if East Asians and others tied to yellowness are imagined to be so educationally and economically advantaged as to supersede the need for racial care. See Muñoz, *Sense of Brown*, 138.

47. In his book *Model Minority Masochism*, Takeo Rivera argues that "within the antiracist paradigm upon which Asian American studies and the Asian American movement were founded, we can characterize Blackness as occupying the position of racial superego, an Afro-Asian superego, the disciplinary apparatus of the Asian American psyche, counterposed to the id of assimilation and the fulfillment of the model minority." I would extend this claim to argue that the discourse around Asian settler colonialism suggests that

Indigeneity inhabits a similarly superegoic position within the Asian American psyche. It is this psychosocial reality that produces the ethico-political pressure in Asian American subjects to do right by minoritarian coalition. This pressure gives way to an Asian American performance of "moral masochism that necessitates self-interrogation, while simultaneously making its subjects intently and uncomfortably aware of their socialities." This moral masochism, in other words, returns Asian Americans to their always-present imperative of relationality. It opens onto an ethics of self and solidarity, an ethics of racial care that finds Asian Americans tending again to their own needs while also trying to stay in step with those who suffer more than they do. See Rivera, *Model Minority Masochism*, 49, 66.

48. This dynamic has lessened, to an extent, with the rise of Palestinian solidarity organizing after October 7, 2023. Although it is worth noting that at the time of this writing this solidarity movement is most often framed as an Asian American issue only by those already committed to the larger project of an Asian American left—despite the work Viet Thanh Nguyen and other Asian American political organizations have done to advance the observation that Palestine is in Asia.

49. Two points. First, my focus on areas in which Asian Americans are more likely to experience loneliness and isolation is not in any way meant to disregard Ninh's focus on the need for care experienced by those raised in Asian America's overachieving ethnic enclaves. And second, while Texas is among the five states most populated by Asian Americans, its size and political orientation render it a wholly different battleground than the other four, which are California, New York, New Jersey, and Washington. Abby Budiman and Neil G. Ruiz, "Key Facts About Asian Americans, a Diverse and Growing Population," *Pew Research Center*, April 29, 2021, https://www.pewresearch.org/short-reads/2021/04/29/key-facts-about-asian-americans/.

50. Russell Heimlich, "Most Asian Americans Describe Themselves by Country of Origin," *Pew Research Center*, June 21, 2012, https://www.pewresearch.org/short-reads/2012/06/21/most-asian-americans-describe-themselves-by-country-of-origin/.

51. Kang, *Loneliest Americans*, 15.

52. A. S. Fisher, "Introduction," 7.

53. Here I am gesturing toward the work Rhacel Salazar Parreñas has done on migrant Filipinas caught up in an international division of reproductive labor. See Parreñas, *Servants of Globalization*. I am also following Sami Schalk's framing of (dis)ability as "the overarching social system of bodily and mental norms that includes ability and disability." See Schalk, *Bodyminds Reimagined*.

54. For more on the call for More Life, a call derived from Tony Kushner's *Angels in America*, see Chambers-Letson, *After the Party*.

55. On "racial melancholia," see Eng and Han, *Racial Melancholia, Racial Dissociation*; and Cheng, *Melancholy of Race*. On "national abjection," see Shimakawa, *National Abjection*. On "racist love," see Bow, *Racist Love*. On "model minority masochism," see Rivera, *Model Minority Masochism*.

56. Mimi Khúc, *Open in Emergency*, accessed November 13, 2024, mimikhuc.com/projects/open-in-emergency. For more on *Open in Emergency*, see Khúc, *Dear Elia*.

57. Tronto, *Moral Boundaries*, 104. In her introduction to *Performing Care*, a volume

she coedited with James Thompson, Amanda Stuart Fisher takes up Tronto's claim that aesthetic work is not care work. Fisher notes that Tronto, in a footnote, has recently qualified her initial refusal to accept the act of making art as an act of taking care by citing dance therapy as a possible exception. Fisher's move is to suggest that socially engaged performance should also qualify as a mode of care. I agree with Fisher, but the forms of care I write about here exceed the bounds of both drama therapy and socially engaged performance to imagine how aesthetic forms not necessarily intended as works of care might nevertheless function as such. See A. S. Fisher, "Introduction," 7.

58. Sedgwick, *Touching Feeling*, 150–51. On the reparative impulse of minoritarian performance studies, see Chambers-Letson, "Reparative Feminisms"; Muñoz, *Sense of Brown*; Kondo, *Worldmaking*; Eng, "Colonial Object Relations"; and Nyong'o, "So Far Down."

59. For more on the queer figure of the aunty see Khubchandani, "Critical Aunty Studies."

60. Hong et al., "We Go Down Sewing," 11.

61. Jackson, *Social Works*, 34.

62. Chuh, *The Difference Aesthetics Makes*, 15.

63. For more on form, please see Levine, *Forms*; and Fawaz, *Queer Forms*.

64. Piepzna-Samarasinha, *Care Work*, 32.

65. Taylor, *Archive and the Repertoire*, 2.

66. See Jackson, *Social Works*; and A. S. Fisher and Thompson, *Performing Care*.

67. Hamington, "Care Ethics and Engaging Intersectional Difference," 83.

68. O'Brien, *Family Abolition*, 181.

69. Marx, "Critique of the Gotha Program," 531.

70. Grace Lee Boggs, interview by Amy Goodman, *Democracy Now*, September 17, 2009.

CHAPTER ONE. REVOLTING SELF-CARE

1. Here, I am invoking Audre Lorde's "A Litany for Survival," in *Collected Poems of Audre Lorde*.

2. McCracken et al., "You Must Be New Here," 3.

3. See Brown, "Neoliberalism and the End of Liberal Democracy."

4. See B. Loewe, "An End to Self Care," *Organizing Upgrade*, October 15, 2012, http://archive.organizingupgrade.com/index.php/blogs/b-loewe/item/729-end-to-self-care.

5. See Piepzna-Samarasinha, *Care Work*.

6. Lorde, *A Burst of Light*, 130.

7. Kim and Schalk, "Reclaiming the Radical Politics of Self-Care," 339.

8. Foucault, "Ethics of the Concern," 282.

9. Foucault, "Ethics of the Concern," 285.

10. When Foucault speaks of freedom, he means something distinct from but related to liberation, or the general overcoming of a calcified system of domination. As an example of the liberatory, Foucault cites the struggles of colonized peoples to overthrow their colonizers. Practices of freedom, by contrast, are the performatic modes by which one

navigates relations of power on all scales of social life. Foucault offers the negotiation of power within quotidian romantic relationships as an example, and we can consider any number of Aguhar's microinteractions on social media within this frame as well. With Elisabeth Anker, we might even say that Aguhar's performance of the care of the self engages in a practice of "ugly freedom" in the sense indicated by "The Axes." Her self-care is ugly because it is "unvalued"; because it challenges aesthetic hierarchies that privilege beauty; and because it "dwell[s] in the gulf between powerlessness and heroic expressions of untrammeled agency." Anker, *Ugly Freedoms*, 14.

11. Muñoz, *Disidentifications*, 143.

12. Tongson, *Relocations*, 23.

13. Pérez, "Proximity."

14. Nguyen, *A View from the Bottom*.

15. This claim is informed by the work of Caleb Luna. See Caleb Luna, "Romantic Love Is Killing Us: Who Takes Care of Us When We Are Single?," *The Body Is Not an Apology*, September 18, 2018, https://thebodyisnotanapology.com/magazine/romantic-love-is-killing-us/.

16. Berlant, *Cruel Optimism*.

17. Foucault, *Security, Territory, Population*, 194. It is true that Foucault prefers the term *counter-conduct* to revolts of conduct because "the word 'revolt' is both too precise and too strong to designate much more diffuse and subdued forms of resistance." However, I retain the language of revolt in order to retain the affective propulsion of the term's revolutionary connotations as well as for reasons related to abjection that become clear later in this chapter.

18. Foucault, *Security, Territory, Population*, 195.

19. Before "cancel culture" became the rallying cry of conservatives seeking to skirt responsibility for this or that harm done, debates about interpersonal violence, accountability, and social media revolved around the more modest category of "call-out culture." To call someone out is to confront them publicly for some harm they may have done. Someone has posted something racist online or they've committed sexual violence, and someone else, in an effort to hold them accountable for their transgression, challenges their behavior in the arena of social media. Proponents of call-out culture argue that social media–based call-outs are useful because they allow marginalized subjects to address harm and to seek accountability outside the unaccommodating channels provided by institutions and the state. And while conservative arguments against call-out and cancel culture amount to little more than spurious accusations of censorship and flimsy defenses of free speech, more compelling criticisms of call-out and cancel culture have emerged on the left among abolitionist thinkers. For example, adrienne maree brown has argued that call outs are too often used to shame those who have committed harm whether by mistake or on purpose. In this way, call outs too often reproduce carceral logics of disposability, doing damage to marginalized communities and cultures in the process. This fact has led thinkers like ngọc loan trần and Loretta Ross to propose "calling in" as an alternative, one that happens in private and with a softer touch. See a. m. brown, *We Will Not Cancel Us*. See also trần, "Calling IN."

20. Roy Pérez, "Mark Aguhar's Critical Flippancy," *Bully Bloggers* (blog), August 4,

2012, https://bullybloggers.wordpress.com/2012/08/04/mark-aguhars-critical-flippancy/.

21. Pérez, "Mark Aguhar's Critical Flippancy."
22. Foucault, *Government of the Self and Others*, 43.
23. Foucault, *Government of the Self and Others*, 52.
24. See Foucault, *Fearless Speech*, 16.
25. Garlough, *Desi Divas*, 12.
26. The parrhesiastes is importantly not tantamount to the pedagogue. Though she enables her listeners to better attune to themselves as ethico-political beings—to better know themselves—in parrhesia "the person who tells the truth throws the truth in the face of his interlocutor, a truth which is so violent, so abrupt and said in such a peremptory and definitive way that the person facing him can only fall silent, or choke with fury, or change to a different register." This is the shared affective logic and potential of call-out culture and parrhesia, and this is the convergence of the two in Aguhar. See Foucault, *Government of the Self and Others*, 54.

Furthermore, Foucault importantly distinguishes parrhesia from classic performance studies analytics such as John Searle's "speech act" and J. L. Austin's "performative." Parrhesia, for Foucault, is a "speech activity," the opposite of the performative utterance. Whereas a performative needs the support of context, status, and intention to come to fruition, parrhesia entails an irruptive enunciation of truth that opens a situation out into unknowability.

Against Austinian performativity, parrhesia more nearly aligns with Diana Taylor's notion of "the animative," an affective and animating designation that aggregates "potentially chaotic, anarchistic, and revolutionary" activity. See Diana Taylor, "Politics of Passion," *E-Misferica* 10, no. 2 (2013), https://hemi.nyu.edu/hemi/pt/e-misferica-102/taylor.

27. Ahmed, *Living a Feminist Life*, 57.
28. Wu, *Sticky Rice*, 1.
29. Aguhar, *Call Out Queen Zine*.
30. Aguhar, *Call Out Queen Zine*.
31. Aguhar, *Call Out Queen Zine*.
32. Foucault, "On the Genealogy of Ethics," 260.
33. Mia Mingus, "Moving Toward the Ugly: A Politic Beyond Desirability," *Leaving Evidence* (blog), August 22, 2011, https://leavingevidence.wordpress.com/2011/08/22/moving-toward-the-ugly-a-politic-beyond-desirability/.
34. Judith Butler, "What Is Critique? An Essay on Foucault's Virtue," *Transversal Texts*, May 2001, https://transversal.at/transversal/0806/butler/en.
35. This labor of attracting care to oneself precedes the phases of care that Joan Tronto has articulated for feminist care ethics. For Tronto, the first phase of care, "caring about," involves noticing the need for care in others. This, for Tronto, entails what Nancy Fraser has called a "politics of needs interpretation." Who decides what counts as a need for care and how? Aguhar shows us that before we seek to answer to this question, we must reckon with some others. Who has to work to have their needs for care recognized as such, and how do they perform that work? What does such work cost them? And how does the structure of our world burden some people with the work of attracting care

while allowing others to receive generous amounts of care passively, without ever realizing such work is necessary for the survival of others? See Tronto, *Caring Democracy*. See also Fraser, "Women, Welfare."

36. See Piepzna-Samarasinha, *Care Work*; and Nishida, *Just Care*.
37. Foucault, *Government of the Self and Others*, 43.
38. Dean, *Blog Theory*, 96.
39. Dean, *Blog Theory*, 4.
40. Dean, *Blog Theory*, 63.
41. Dean, *Blog Theory*, 63.
42. Dean, *Blog Theory*, 113.
43. Dean, *Blog Theory*, 102.
44. See Francisco-Menchavez, *Labor of Care*.
45. Kimberly Alidio, email message to author, May 19, 2017.
46. Kimberly Alidio, email message to author, May 19, 2017.
47. Alidio, *after projects the resound*, 66.
48. Alidio tells me that she agonized over the line "have mothers young enough to be our sons," because it can potentially be read as an act of misgendering. In republications of the poem, the phrase "our sons" is sometimes replaced by the word "transfemmes." See, for example, Alidio, "All the Pinays are straight, all the queers are Pinoy, but some of us," in *Q & A: Voices from Queer Asian North America*.
49. Nono, *Babaylan Sing Back*, 1.
50. Nono, *Babaylan Sing Back*, 1.
51. Nono, *Babaylan Sing Back*, 6.
52. Alidio, *after projects the resound*, 66.
53. Alidio, *after projects the resound*, 66.
54. Cited in Tadiar, *Things Fall Away*, 45–46.
55. Tadiar, *Things Fall Away*, 386.
56. Alidio, *after projects the resound*, 67.
57. Chun, *Updating to Remain the Same*, 162.
58. Chun, *Updating to Remain the Same*, 162.
59. See Nancy, *Being Singular Plural*.
60. Sedgwick, *Tendencies*.
61. Piepzna-Samarasinha, *Care Work*, 192.
62. Suicidism holds that suicide must be prevented at all costs. It pervades minoritarian activism and scholarship in which "suicidality becomes the barometer of oppression: The more one is oppressed, the more one is at risk of experiencing suicidality; the less one is oppressed, the less one might be suicidal." This approach, Baril argues, deprioritizes the needs of suicidal people in order to uphold "compulsory aliveness." By making suicidality less acceptable and speakable, this approach makes it more difficult for those experiencing suicidal ideation to receive support, understanding, and care. Against a narrowly preventionist approach to addressing suicide, Baril offers "accompaniment" as a category through which to think about supporting people through suicidal ideation. See Baril, *Undoing Suicidism*, 13, 11, 21.
63. Nyong'o, *Afro-Fabulations*, 6.

64. Rodriguez, *Suspended Apocalypse*, 105.
65. Stanley, *Atmospheres of Violence*, 21, 24.
66. Muñoz, *Disidentifications*, 74.

CHAPTER TWO. THE RACIALIZED HOLDING ENVIRONMENT

1. Cho, *Office Hour*, 8.
2. Roy, *No Right to Remain Silent*, 36.
3. Roy, *No Right to Remain Silent*, 37.
4. Roy, *No Right to Remain Silent*, 38.
5. Winnicott, *Maturational Processes*, 165. To speak of an "affective architecture" is to speak not only of the felt contours of a space and time but also of all those material and performatic aspects of a spatiotemporal setting that affect the infant, including the mother's literal holding of the infant and the aesthetics of the nursery.
6. Roy, *No Right to Remain Silent*, 265.
7. Roy, *No Right to Remain Silent*, 266.
8. Roy, *No Right to Remain Silent*, 266.
9. Caitlin Yoshiko Kandil, "Play Written after College Shootings Intends to Get People Talking About Safety and Violence," *Los Angeles Times*, April 9, 2016, https://www.latimes.com/socal/weekend/news/tn-wknd-et-0410-office-hour-play-20160410-story.html.
10. My formulation of the racialized holding environment is informed and inspired by the work of other Asian Americanists who have similarly sought to adapt Winnicottian psychoanalysis for critical race theory. For instance, my notion of the racialized holding environment is implied when David Eng and Shinhee Han invoke the Winnicottian holding environment as a shape through which to think the ideal function of Asian American and ethnic studies programs. Additionally, I am inspired by Vivian Huang's notion of the racial "good-enough environment." Positioning the model minority thesis as a "transitional object" and model minority subjectivity as an assimilative mode of "compliance," Huang describes a racial good-enough environment as one that emerges when the subject plays with and seeks to destroy the model minority thesis-as-object, thus recognizing such racialization as external to the self. In this chapter I extend the work that Huang begins by racializing another set of Winnicottian terms, those that pertain specifically to the earliest stage of subject formation—the fusion of mother and infant, the holding environment. If the paradigmatic performance of the racial good-enough environment is "play," the paradigmatic performance of the racialized holding environment is "care." See Eng and Han, *Racial Melancholia, Racial Dissociation*, 178. See also Huang, *Surface Relations*, 124–25.
11. Butler, *Bodies That Matter*, 3.
12. I quote here from a presentation on minoritarian mentorship that Karen Shimakawa and I gave together as part of the State of the Profession plenary panel at the 2017 annual conference of the American Society for Theatre Research, Atlanta, GA, November 18.
13. I thank Kareem Khubchandani for leading my thinking to this point.
14. An important distinction: to indulge in the psychoanalytically situated gender

roles that Winnicott presents is not to reduce oneself to gender essentialism. As Anne Anlin Cheng has written, "far from inscribing essentialism, psychoanalytic thinking recognizes essentialism as but a *guise* of subjectivity. The psychoanalytic subject is universal only insofar as it posits every subjective being as *historical* beings, embedded in time, family, and sociality." When remarking on the categories of femininity and maternity in relation to the psychoanalytic subjects of this chapter, I do so with Cheng's insights in mind. See Cheng, *Melancholy of Race*, 62.

15. Some readers have suggested that the arguments I make in this chapter around Asian American racial care and the racialized holding environment have implications for the way we think about white male mass shooters. If a professor's performance of gendered racial care can calm murderousness in young Asian American men, as *Office Hour* suggests it can, are we not then forced to speculate that we may be able to keep "troubled" young white men from becoming mass shooters with a similar strategy—through the provision of meticulously calibrated gendered racial care? To this I can only answer maybe, as problematic as such a prospect may seem, because isolation and neglect are often found at the root of such men's motives. But the ethico-political problem of care's relation to white male mass shooters is ultimately someone else's to solve.

16. Cho, *Office Hour*, 8.

17. Though the actual events that preceded the Virginia Tech massacre are largely outside the scope of this chapter, it is notable that Genevieve's actions echo, though inexactly, real life measures taken by some faculty and administrators at Virginia Tech in relation to Seung-Hui Cho prior to the massacre.

18. Cho, *Office Hour*, 7.

19. Cho, *Office Hour*, 9–10. In an earlier version of the script, the version used for the South Coast Repertory production, Genevieve also suggests that Dennis "sucks your chi." Alongside the question Genevieve poses around Dennis's language skills, this line wrote a more explicit anti-Asian bias into Genevieve's character. The line no longer appears in the published version of the script.

20. Cho, *Office Hour*, 10.

21. Glenn, *Forced to Care*.

22. For more on adjuncting in the Asian American case, see Khúc, *Dear Elia*.

23. It is not my view that invocations of Nikki Giovanni made by these casting decisions are attempts to frame her as a participant in anti-Asian racism.

24. Cho, *Office Hour*, 8.

25. Cho, *Office Hour*, 10.

26. Winnicott, *Maturational Processes*, 53.

27. Cho, *Office Hour*, 24.

28. Cho, *Office Hour*, 24.

29. Price, *Mad at School*, 154.

30. Price, *Mad at School*, 158.

31. Eng, *Racial Castration*.

32. Cho, *Office Hour*, 27–28.

33. Cho, *Office Hour*, 34.

34. Cho, *Office Hour*, 34–35.

35. Shimakawa, *National Abjection*.
36. Cho, *Office Hour*, 27.
37. My claim that Gina shoots Dennis out of fear is based on the performance of actress Sue Jean Kim, who played the role in the Public Theatre's production of *Office Hour*.
38. Cho, *Office Hour*, 38.
39. Cho, *Office Hour*, 39.
40. Winnicott, *Maturational Processes*, 42.
41. Cho, *Office Hour*, 40.
42. Cho, *Office Hour*, 42.
43. Cho, *Office Hour*, 42.
44. Cho, *Office Hour*, 43.
45. Cho, *Office Hour*, 43.
46. Cho, *Office Hour*, 43.
47. Puar, *Right to Maim*.
48. With "ugly feelings" I am referencing the stubborn, stultifying, and noncathartic quality of Asian American loneliness. For more on ugly feelings, see Ngai, *Ugly Feelings*. Sexton, "People-of-Color-Blindness."
49. My use of the word "annihilation" should surface not only the specter of spectacular violences such as mass murder but also its Winnicottian sense as the alternative to a certain continuity of being that is precipitated by exposure to impingement.
50. Cho, *Office Hour*, 43.
51. My invocation of the theater's effective "feminine side" alludes to a debate that lies between the fields of theater and performance studies about the latter field's masculinist posturing in relation to the former. See Bottoms, "The Efficacy/Effeminacy Braid."
52. Winnicott, *Maturational Processes*, 48.
53. Winnicott, *Maturational Processes*, 54.
54. Engster and Hamington, "Introduction," 3.
55. While I hold onto the language of "empathy" to stay tight to Winnicott's insights, I do so somewhat reluctantly. I very much agree with Saidiya Hartman when she writes that "in making the other's suffering one's own, this suffering is occluded by the other's obliteration." Still, when I use the word empathy briefly here, I mean something nearer to attentive response and resonance, as when a violin is played and another in the same space sounds the same note. See Hartman, *Scenes of Subjection*, 19.
56. Bollas, *Shadow of the Object*, 14.
57. Bollas, *Shadow of the Object*, 17.
58. Kondo, *Worldmaking*, 118.
59. Winnicott, *Maturational Processes*, 31.
60. S. K. Lee, "Staying In," 37.

CHAPTER THREE. RACIAL EMOTIONAL LABOR

1. Muñoz, *Disidentifications*, 189.
2. Muñoz, *Disidentifications*, 188.
3. Muñoz, *Disidentifications*, 189.

4. See Chambers-Letson, *A Race So Different*.

5. Andrew Yang, "We Asian Americans Are Not the Virus but We Can Be Part of the Cure," *Washington Post*, April 1, 2020.

6. S. K. Lee, "Staying In," 29.

7. S. K. Lee, "Staying In," 31.

8. Hochschild, *Managed Heart*, 7.

9. Yao, *Disaffected*, 11.

10. Yao, *Disaffected*, 22–23.

11. Yao, *Disaffected*, 7, 28.

12. See Piepzna-Samarasinha, *Care Work*, 136–48.

13. See, for example, Emma Specter, "'Emotional Labor' Is Not What You Think It Is," *Vogue*, November 20, 2019, https://www.vogue.com/article/what-is-emotional-labor.

14. J. Lee, *Japan of Pure Invention*, xiv.

15. Because curious readers will be able to determine which institution it is that I am writing about, let me clarify here that the racist experience I share in this chapter is not representative of my general experience as an undergraduate. I owe a great deal to many of the teachers and mentors I had the privilege to learn from at my undergraduate institution. It would be wrong to read this chapter as a dismissal of their good work.

16. Hochschild, *Managed Heart*, 37, 56.

17. DiAngelo, *White Fragility*.

18. DiAngelo, *White Fragility*, 1.

19. DiAngelo, *White Fragility*, 2.

20. Sedgwick, *Epistemology of the Closet*, 4.

21. Goffman, *Presentation of Self in Everyday Life*, 19.

22. Nancy Fraser, "Capitalism's Crisis of Care," an interview by Sarah Leonard, *Dissent Magazine*, Fall 2016, https://www.dissentmagazine.org/article/nancy-fraser-interview-capitalism-crisis-of-care.

23. Fraser, "Capitalism's Crisis of Care."

24. Fraser and others working within the tradition of socialist feminism have tended to emphasize, and rightly so, that women have historically been made disproportionately responsible for social reproduction, which includes but is not reducible to what I have in this book preferred to call care work. Gender, by extension, has historically functioned as the primary axis of social difference in relation to which social reproductive labor has been theorized. When race has been taken up as a concern for social reproduction theory, it is usually as an additional variable in an ultimately gender-forward analysis. What emerges are narratives in which women of color become doubly tasked with gendered labor, care work included, by consequence of their social position within a racially stratified world. However, by casting racial emotional labor as a form of care, and thus as a form of social reproduction, I mean to offer a different analysis at the intersection of race and social reproduction theory. My aim is not to unseat gender from its privileged place within that school of feminist thought but to lay bare a racial economy of social reproduction that is rarely marked as such.

25. Fraser, "Contradictions of Capital and Care," 99.

26. The play's premiere was also live streamed by *Howlround*, a prominent online

platform aimed at amplifying progressive discussion about theater and between theater makers. This is how I was first able to access the performance. I have since seen the *The Mikado: Reclaimed* performed many times in its entirety on YouTube.

27. Generic Ensemble Company, "About GenEnCo," accessed November 13, 2024, http://genenco.org/about.html.

28. Lehmann, *Postdramatic Theatre*, 26.

29. A thrust stage is a stage that extends into the audience on three sides and has a backstage area.

30. Here I acknowledge *The Mikado: Reclaimed*'s Arab cast member as a possible exception to the identity category of "Asian American" because the cast member, a friend named Smalls McCoy, does. This ambivalence can also signal the position of "west Asia" vis-à-vis the fiction of Asian American.

31. Shah, *Contagious Divides*, 179.

32. Shah, *Contagious Divides*, 1.

33. Shimakawa, *National Abjection*, 10.

34. Shimakawa, *National Abjection*, 78.

35. Mbembe, "Necropolitics," 24.

36. Eng, *Racial Castration*. To recognize racial castration, as Eng argues, is not to disparage the categories of the feminine and feminization. It is instead to observe the coercive gendering mechanisms endemic to instances of obligatory Asian American hyperracialization.

37. Mengesha and Padmanabhan, "Introduction to Performing Refusal," 2.

38. Tronto, *Caring Democracy*, 72.

39. shorb, "Reappropriation," 1–12.

40. shorb, "Reappropriation," 6.

41. shorb, "Reappropriation," 6.

42. Dean Spade, "We Still Need Pronoun Go-Rounds," December 1, 2018, http://www.deanspade.net/2018/12/01/we-still-need-pronoun-go-rounds/. Importantly, there is principled debate around the pronoun go-round. Jen Manion has argued against the ritual on the grounds that it induces anxiety in and at the expense of trans people, reifies binary thinking, and distracts from more significant trans political causes. See Jen Manion, "The Performance of Transgender Inclusion: The Pronoun Go-Round and the New Gender Binary," *Public Seminar*, November 27, 2018, http://www.publicseminar.org/2018/11/the-performance-of-transgender-inclusion/.

43. Goffman, *Presentation of Self*, 104.

44. Goffman, *Presentation of Self*, 83.

45. Although, as a caveat, it is important to remember that many racial situations are already set up so that everyone is on the same team. People of color and anti-racist allies frequently find themselves upholding putatively post-racial, but no less white supremacist, situations in order to eschew the social consequences of rupturing a scene.

46. V. Huang, *Surface Relations*, 53.

47. Muñoz, "Evidence as Ephemera."

48. Muñoz, *Cruising Utopia*, 6.

49. shorb, "Reappropriation," 6.

CHAPTER FOUR. DEHUMANIST CARE

1. Paik, *Bans, Walls, Raids, and Sanctuary*.
2. The text of the mural is also the title of the public art series from which the mural emerges, a series curated by Adriel Luis for the Smithsonian. Luis is also the curator of *Care Package: Poems, Medications, Films, and Other Cultural Nutrients for Times Like These*, the online exhibit with which this book opened.
3. In an earlier draft of this chapter, I turned to key words other than dehumanism to help me describe the caring relations that can exist between humans and the nonhuman world. I wrote for a time in the language of *queer inhumanism*, an approach Dana Luciano and Mel Chen have crafted in an attempt to answer the question: "Has the queer ever been human?" (See Luciano and Chen, "Introduction," 183.) I was drawn to the term (*queer inhumanism*), in part, because it was built to assist us in studying "transmaterial affections," a category of queer contact certainly capacious enough to include care (186). And because much of this chapter addresses the caring relationships that queer subjects in particular enter into with nonhuman entities, much of what I valued in queer inhumanism was given in what each of its terms gives to one another. *Inhumanism* brings queer studies closer to questioning "what 'sex' and 'gender' might look like apart from the anthropocentric forms with which we have become perhaps too familiar" (189). At the same time, *queer*—"the way it gestures, at once, toward a history of abuse and marginalization and an aspirational expansiveness" (189)—endows inhumanism with a similar gestural life, one that indexes both violence and variance. What is fortunate is that Singh sees the same value in these ideas as I do and has explicitly stated that dehumanism is both "indebted to" and "united with" the project of queer inhumanism. My preference for dehumanism over queer inhumanism and other cognate categories like the perihuman and the posthuman ultimately has to do with the fact that *dehumanism* is the term most pointed in its "aims to bring the posthuman into critical conversation with the decolonial" (Singh, *Unthinking Mastery*, 5, 4). In this spirit, I do not take up dehumanism *instead* of queer inhumanism. I do so, rather, with the recognition that the former term bears the queer trace of the latter always.
4. Singh, *Unthinking Mastery*, 123.
5. What Singh calls *dehumanist solidarity* resonates in an important way with what Donna Haraway and Kim TallBear have from different vantage points called *making kin*. Both concepts restructure the hierarchies that foreclose on the caring relations that are everywhere circulating between human subjects and nonhuman others. See TallBear, "Caretaking Relations"; and Haraway, *Staying with the Trouble*.
6. Puig de la Bellacasa, *Matters of Care*, 20.
7. M. N. Huang, "Ecologies of Entanglement," 98.
8. M. Chen, *Animacies*, 237.
9. Weheliye, *Habeas Viscus*, 8. See also, Wynter, "Unsettling the Coloniality."
10. V. Huang and Lee, "Introduction," 12.
11. Simpson, "Indigenous Resurgence and Co-Resistance," 22.
12. See Hall, "Which of These Things."
13. Iokepa Casumbal-Salazar, "Forum 2.2 // In Ceremony and Struggle: The Lāhui at

Pu'uhonu o Pu'uhuluhulu," *The Abusable Past*, August 14, 2019, https://abusable past.org/forum-2-2-in-ceremony-and-struggle-the-lahui-at-pu%ca%bbuhonua-o-pu%ca %bbuhuluhulu/.

14. See Trask, "Settlers of Color"; and Fujikane, "Introduction."
15. See Byrd, *Transit of Empire*, xix.
16. Day, *Alien Capital*.
17. To say that Asian American racial care plays out "nearly always" on stolen land is to acknowledge that Asian Americans may sometimes provide one another with racial care outside of the borders of the settler colonial United States. Imagine two Asian American friends encountering racism while in Europe or encountering alienation while visiting family in Asia.
18. Hamer and Wilson, *Kumu Hina*.
19. Kauanui, *Paradoxes of Hawaiian Sovereignty*, 124.
20. Kauanui, *Paradoxes of Hawaiian Sovereignty*, 201.
21. Ruddick, *Maternal Thinking*, 65, 22.
22. M. Klein, *Love, Guilt and Reparation*, 307.
23. Sedgwick, *Touching Feeling*, 128.
24. Sedgwick, *Touching Feeling*, 312–13.
25. Eng, "Colonial Object Relations," 10.
26. Eng, "Colonial Object Relations," 11.
27. M. Klein, *Love, Guilt and Reparation*, 334.
28. Eng, "Colonial Object Relations," 13.
29. Wolfe, "Settler Colonialism," 387.
30. There is some debate about what exactly facilitates the movement from the depressive position into a reparative position. For Sedgwick, there is a certain "ethical possibility" in the depressive position produced by the subject's "guilty, empathetic view of the other as at once good, damaged, integral, and requiring and eliciting love and care." See Sedgwick, *Touching Feeling*, 137. But Eng disagrees, arguing that the movement through the depressive position to the reparative position is not a matter of ethics as much as it is an act of self-preservation. In Eng's view, the infant does not seek to repair damage done to the mother in response to the guilt it feels for having been too aggressive. Rather, the infant restores the mother out of a recognition that the mother's death would lead to its own death insofar as the infant is totally dependent upon the mother's care for survival. See Eng, "Colonial Object Relations."
31. Isa Borgeson, "Bio," accessed January 13, 2025, http://isaborgeson.com/bio.
32. I am grateful to Jennifer Nelson for drawing this connection for me.
33. N. Klein, *Shock Doctrine*.
34. Viola et al., "Introduction," 6.
35. Le Conte and Navajas, "Climate Change."
36. Snow, "The Last Words of the Honey Bees."
37. Halberstam, *Wild Things*.
38. Horn, *Bees in America*.
39. Snow, "The Last Words of the Honey Bees."
40. Snow, "The Last Words of the Honey Bees."

41. I am referring here to the work of David Eng and Shinhee Han (*Racial Melancholia*) as well as to the work of Anne Anlin Cheng (*Melancholy of Race*).
42. Haraway. *Staying with the Trouble*, 39.
43. See Butler, *Frames of War*.
44. Snow, "The Last Words of the Honey Bees."
45. Snow, "The Last Words of the Honey Bees."
46. R. C. Lee, *Exquisite Corpse of Asian America*, 65.
47. Eng, *Racial Castration*, 204.
48. Gopinath, *Impossible Desires*, 79.
49. "'Migration Is Natural' by Jess X Snow | Project 1324," posted March 15, 2017, by Adobe, YouTube, 2:36, https://www.youtube.com/watch?v=4rNofdwq3oI.
50. Walia, *Border and Rule*, 215.
51. Muñoz, *Cruising Utopia*.
52. Harney and Moten, *The Undercommons*, 157.
53. Malatino, *Trans Care*, 46.
54. Malatino, *Trans Care*, 45.
55. Harney and Moten, *The Undercommons*, 150.
56. For Ninh, the filial debt owed by the second generation to their immigrant parents locks Asian American daughters into model minority aspiration and suffering. For Nguyen, US empire supposedly liberates (gives the gift of freedom) to the Vietnamese refugee through both war and the provision of refuge, which renders such subjects indebted to empire and therefore ultimately unfree. By reaching toward a notion of unpayable debt, I do not so much disregard these dynamics as gesture to an alternate horizon of caring relations toward which we may strive. But to be sure: there is violence wherever a relation of unpayable debt lacks an aspiration toward reciprocity. See Ninh, *Ingratitude*; and M. T. Nguyen, *The Gift of Freedom*.
57. Harney and Moten, *The Undercommons*, 150.
58. Gagnon, "On Gratitude."
59. Gagnon, "Singing with Nanook of the North," 63.
60. Gagnon, "Singing with Nanook of the North," 67.
61. Gagnon, "Singing with Nanook of the North," 50.
62. Gagnon, "Singing with Nanook of the North," 65.

CONCLUSION

1. Madison365 Staff, "Study Finds Wisconsin Most Segregated State in the U.S.," *Madison 365*, January 16, 2020, https://madison365.com/study-finds-wisconsin-most-segregated-state-in-the-u-s/.
2. Adams, "For Aprina, for Cierra," 262.
3. Frank Vaisvillas, "Native American Tribes Support George Floyd Protests, Provide Security During Riots," *Green Bay Press-Gazette*, June 8, 2020, https://www.greenbaypressgazette.com/story/news/2020/06/08/wisconsins-native-american-tribes-respond-george-floyd-protests/5321672002/.
4. For more on Freedom Inc.'s pursuit of this demand, see D. Wong, "The Future Is Ours."

5. For more on this demand and the internal colony thesis, traceable to Martin Luther King Jr. and Kwame Ture, see Adams and Rameau, "Black Community Control Over Police."

6. Abby Budiman, "Hmong in the U.S. Fact Sheet," Pew Research Center, September 8, 2017, https://www.pewsocialtrends.org/fact-sheet/asian-americans-hmong-in-the-u-s/; and U.S. Census Bureau, "Income and Poverty in the United States: 2015," September 2016, https://www.census.gov/content/dam/ Census/library/publications/2016/demo/p60–256.pdf.

7. Vang and Myers, "In the Wake of George Floyd," 20–34.

8. Vang and Myers, "In the Wake of George Floyd," 25.

9. Boal, *Theatre of the Oppressed*, 122.

10. Anker, *Ugly Freedoms*, 6.

11. Wilderson, *Red, White, and Black*, 38.

12. Lepecki, "Choreopolice and Choreopolitics," 26, 22.

13. Lepecki, "Choreopolice and Choreopolitics," 22.

14. Katie Lee-Yang, Kaozouapa Elizabeth Lee, Mai Nhia Vang, and Pajouablai Monica Lee, "Episode 15: Addressing Anti-Blackness and a Way Forward Ft. Kabzuag Vaj," *Not Your Average Mai Podcast*, June 28, 2020, 1:01:00, https://podcasts.apple.com/us/podcast/episode-15-addressing-anti-blackness-and-a-way/id1476993440?i=1000480070887.

15. Kabzuag Vaj, personal interview with author, May, 27, 2022.

16. Gilmore, "Abolition Feminism," 161–78.

17. P. Nguyen, "Abolition as Durational Performance."

18. Harney and Moten, *The Undercommons*, 42.

19. Ruth Wilson Gilmore, "Making Abolition Geography in California's Central Valley," *The Funambulist*, December 20, 2018, https://thefunambulist.net/magazine/21-space-activism/interview-making-abolition-geography-california-central-valley-ruth-wilson-gilmore.

Bibliography

Adams, M. "For Aprina, for Cierra, and for Me: Questions and Commitment to Abolition." *WSQ: Women's Studies Quarterly* 47, nos. 3–4 (2019): 261–68.
Adams, M., and Max Rameau. "Black Community Control over Police." *Wisconsin Law Review* 2016, no. 3 (2016): 515–39.
Aguhar, Mark. *Call Out Queen Zine*. Edited by Juana Peralta and Roy Pérez. POC Zine Project, 2012. https://issuu.com/poczineproject/docs/calloutqueen-zine.
Ahmed, Sara. *Living a Feminist Life*. Durham, NC: Duke University Press, 2017.
Alidio, Kimberly. *after projects the resound*. Berkeley, CA: Black Radish Books, 2016.
Alidio, Kimberly. "All the Pinays are straight, all the queers are Pinoy, but some of us." In *Q & A: Voices from Queer Asian North America*, edited by Martin F. Manalansan, Alice Y. Hom, and Kale Bantingue Fajardo, 38–39. Philadelphia: Temple University Press, 2021.
Anker, Elisabeth R. *Ugly Freedoms*. Durham, NC: Duke University Press, 2022.
Baril, Alexandre. *Undoing Suicidism: A Trans, Queer, Crip Approach to Rethinking (Assisted) Suicide*. Philadelphia: Temple University Press, 2023.
Berlant, Lauren. *Cruel Optimism*. Durham, NC: Duke University Press, 2012.
Boal, Augusto. *Theatre of the Oppressed*. New York: Theatre Communications Group, 1985.
Bollas, Christopher. *The Shadow of the Object: Psychoanalysis of the Unthought Known*. New York: Columbia University Press, 1987.
Bolton, Sony Coráñez. *Crip Colony: Mestizaje, US Imperialism, and the Queer Politics of Disability in the Philippines*. Durham, NC: Duke University Press, 2023.
Bottoms, Stephen J. "The Efficacy/Effeminacy Braid: Unpicking the Performance Studies/Theatre Studies Dichotomy." *Theatre Topics* 13, no. 2 (2003): 173–87.
Bow, Leslie. *Racist Love: Asian Abstraction and the Pleasures of Fantasy*. Durham, NC: Duke University Press, 2022.
brown, adrienne maree. *We Will Not Cancel Us: An Other Dreams of Transformative Justice*. Chico, CA: AK Press, 2020.
Brown, Wendy. "Neoliberalism and the End of Liberal Democracy." *Theory and Event* 7, no. 1 (2003): 37–59.

Butler, Judith. *Bodies That Matter: On the Discursive Limits of "Sex."* New York: Routledge, 1993.
Butler, Judith. *Frames of War: When Is Life Grievable?* New York: Verso, 2010.
Byrd, Jodi. *Transit of Empire: Indigenous Critiques of Colonialism.* Minneapolis: University of Minnesota Press, 2011.
The Care Collective. *The Care Manifesto: The Politics of Interdependence.* New York: Verso, 2020.
Chambers-Letson, Joshua. *After the Party: A Manifesto for Queer of Color Life.* New York: New York University Press, 2018.
Chambers-Letson, Joshua. *A Race So Different: Performance and Law in Asian America.* New York: New York University Press, 2013.
Chambers-Letson, Joshua. "Reparative Feminisms, Repairing Feminism—Reparation, Postcolonial Violence, and Feminism." *Women and Performance: A Journal of Feminist Theory* 16, no. 2 (July 2006): 169–89.
Chen, Jian Neo. *Trans Exploits: Trans of Color Cultures and Technologies of Movement.* Durham, NC: Duke University Press, 2019.
Chen, Mel. *Animacies: Biopolitics, Racial Mattering, and Queer Affect.* Durham, NC: Duke University Press, 2012.
Cheng, Anne Anlin. *The Melancholy of Race: Psychoanalysis, Assimilation, and Hidden Grief.* New York: Oxford University Press, 2000.
Cho, Julia. *Office Hour.* New York: Dramatists Play Service, 2018.
Chuh, Kandice. *The Difference Aesthetics Makes: On the Humanities "After Man."* Durham, NC: Duke University Press, 2019.
Chun, Wendy Hui Kyoung. *Updating to Remain the Same: Habitual New Media.* Cambridge, MA: MIT Press, 2016.
Cohen, Cathy J. "Punks, Bulldaggers, and Welfare Queens: The Radical Potential of Queer Politics?" *GLQ: A Journal of Lesbian and Gay Studies* 3, no. 4 (1997): 437–65.
Day, Iyko. *Alien Capital: Asian Racialization and the Logic of Settler Colonial Capitalism.* Durham, NC: Duke University Press, 2016.
Day, Iyko. "Being or Nothingness: Indigeneity, Antiblackness, and Settler Colonial Critique." *Critical Ethnic Studies* 1, no. 2 (2015): 102–10.
Dean, Jodi. *Blog Theory.* Malden, MA: Polity Press, 2010.
DiAngelo, Robin. *White Fragility: Why It's So Hard for White People to Talk About Racism.* Boston, MA: Beacon Press, 2018.
Eng, David. "Colonial Object Relations." *Social Text* 34, no. 1 (2016): 1–19.
Eng, David. *Racial Castration: Managing Masculinity in Asian America.* Durham, NC: Duke University Press, 2001.
Eng, David, and Shinhee Han. *Racial Melancholia, Racial Dissociation: On the Social and Psychic Lives of Asian Americans.* Durham, NC: Duke University Press, 2019.
Engster, Daniel, and Maurice Hamington. "Introduction." In *Care Ethics and Political Theory*, edited by Daniel Engster and Maurice Hamington, 1–18. Oxford: Oxford University Press, 2015.
Fawaz, Ramzi. *Queer Forms.* New York: New York University Press, 2022.

Ferguson, Roderick. *Aberrations in Black: Toward a Queer of Color Critique*. Minneapolis: University of Minnesota Press, 2003.
Ferguson, Roderick. *The Reorder of Things: The University and Its Pedagogies of Minority Difference*. Minneapolis: University of Minnesota Press, 2012.
Fisher, Amanda Stuart. "Introduction: Caring Performance, Performing Care." In *Performing Care: New Perspectives on Socially Engaged Performance*, edited by Amanda Stuart Fisher and James Thompson, 1–18. Manchester: Manchester University Press, 2020.
Fisher, Amanda Stuart, and James Thompson, eds. *Performing Care: New Perspectives on Socially Engaged Performance*. Manchester: Manchester University Press, 2020.
Fisher, Berenice, and Joan C. Tronto. "Toward a Feminist Theory of Caring." In *Circles of Care*, edited by E. K. Abel and M. Nelson, 36–54. Albany: State University of New York Press, 1999.
Foucault, Michel. "The Ethics of the Concern of the Self as a Practice of Freedom." In *Ethics: Subjectivity and Truth*, edited by Paul Rabinow, translated by Robert Hurley and Others, 281–302. New York: New Press, 1997.
Foucault, Michel. *Fearless Speech*. Edited by Joseph Pearson. Los Angeles: Semiotext(e), 2001.
Foucault, Michel. *The Government of the Self and Others: Lectures at the Collège de France 1982–1983*. Edited by Frederic Gros. Translated by Graham Burchell. New York: Picador, 2008.
Foucault, Michel. "On the Genealogy of Ethics: An Overview of Work in Progress." In *Ethics: Subjectivity and Truth*, edited by Paul Rabinow, translated by Robert Hurley and Others, 253–81. New York: New Press, 1997.
Foucault, Michel. *Security, Territory, Population: Lectures at the Collège de France 1977–1978*. Edited by Michel Senellart. Translated by Graham Burchell. New York: Picador, 2007.
Francisco-Menchavez, Valerie. *The Labor of Care: Filipina Migrants and Transnational Families in the Digital Age*. Urbana: University of Illinois Press, 2018.
Fraser, Nancy. "Contradictions of Capital and Care." *New Left Review* 100 (2016): 99–117.
Fraser, Nancy. "Women, Welfare, and the Politics of Need Interpretation," *Hypatia* 2, no. 1 (1987): 103–21.
Fujikane, Candace. "Introduction: Asian Settler Colonialism and the U.S. Colony of Hawai'i." In *Asian Settler Colonialism: From Local Governance to the Habits of Everyday Life in Hawai'i*, edited by Candace Fujikane and Jonathan Y. Okamura, 1–42. Honolulu: University of Hawai'i Press, 2008.
Gagnon, Olivia Michiko. "On Gratitude." *Syndicate*, May 27, 2020. https://syndicate.network/symposia/literature/unthinking-mastery/.
Gagnon, Olivia Michiko. "Singing with Nanook of the North: On Tanya Tagaq, Feeling Entangled, and Colonial Archives of Indigeneity." *ASAP Journal* 5, no. 1 (2020): 41–78.
Garlough, Christine L. *Desi Divas: Political Activism in South Asian American Cultural Performances*. Jackson: University of Mississippi Press, 2013.

Gilligan, Carol. *In a Different Voice: Psychological Theory and Women's Development.* Cambridge, MA: Harvard University Press, 1982.

Gilmore, Ruth Wilson. "Abolition Feminism: Ruth Wilson Gilmore." In *Revolutionary Feminisms: Conversations on Collective Action and Radical Thought*, edited by Brenna Bhandar and Rafeef Ziadah, 161–78. London: Verso, 2020.

Gilmore, Ruth Wilson. *Golden Gulag: Prisons, Surplus, Crisis, and Opposition in Globalizing California.* Berkeley: University of California Press, 2007.

Glenn, Evelyn Nakano. *Forced to Care: Coercion and Caregiving in America.* Cambridge, MA: Harvard University Press, 2012.

Glenn, Evelyn Nakano. "From Servitude to Service Work: Historical Continuities in the Racial Division of Paid Reproductive Labor." *Signs* 18, no. 1 (1992): 1–43.

Goffman, Erving. *The Presentation of Self in Everyday Life.* New York: Doubleday, 1959.

Gopinath, Gayatri. *Impossible Desires: Queer Diasporas and South Asian Public Cultures.* Durham, NC: Duke University Press, 2005.

Halberstam, Jack. *Wild Things: The Disorder of Desire.* Durham, NC: Duke University Press, 2020.

Hall, Lisa Kahaleole. "Which of These Things Is Not Like the Other: Hawaiians and Other Pacific Islanders Are Not Asian Americans, and All Pacific Islanders Are Not Hawaiian." *American Quarterly* 67, no. 3 (2015): 727–47.

Hamer, Dean, and Joe Wilson, dirs. *Kumu Hina: A Place in the Middle.* Hawaiʻi: QWAVES and ITVS, 2014.

Hamington, Maurice. "Care Ethics and Engaging Intersectional Difference through the Body." *Critical Philosophy* 3, no. 1 (2015): 79–100.

Hamington, Maurice, and Michael Flowers. *Care Ethics in the Age of Precarity.* Minneapolis: University of Minnesota Press, 2021.

Hankivsky, Olena. "Rethinking Care Ethics: On the Promise and Potential of an Intersectional Analysis." *American Political Science Review* 108, no. 2 (2014): 252–64.

Haraway, Donna. *Staying with the Trouble: Making Kin in the Cthulucene.* Durham, NC: Duke University Press, 2016.

Harney, Stefano, and Fred Moten. *The Undercommons: Fugitive Planning and Black Study.* New York: Minor Compositions, 2013.

Hartman, Saidiya. *Scenes of Subjection: Terror, Slavery, and Self-Making in Nineteenth-Century America.* New York: Oxford University Press, 1997.

Hobart, Hiʻilei Julia Kawehipuaakahaopulani, and Tamara Kneese. "Radical Care: Survival Strategies for Uncertain Times." *Social Text* 31, no. 1 (2020): 1–16.

Hochschild, Arlie Russell. *The Managed Heart: Commercialization of Human Feeling.* 1983. Berkeley: University of California Press, 2012.

Hong, Grace Kyungwon. *Death Beyond Disavowal: The Impossible Politics of Difference.* Minneapolis: University of Minnesota Press, 2015.

Hong, Grace Kyungwon. *The Ruptures of American Capital: Women of Color Feminism and the Culture of Immigrant Labor.* Minneapolis: University of Minnesota Press, 2006.

Hong, Mai-Linh K., Chrissy Yee Lau, Preeti Sharma, and Valerie Soe. "We Go Down

Sewing." In *The Auntie Sewing Squad Guide to Mask Making, Radical Care, and Racial Justice*, edited by Mai-Linh K. Hong, Chrissy Yee Lau, and Preeti Sharma, 2–19. Berkeley: University of California Press, 2021.

Horn, Tammy. *Bees in America: How the Honey Bee Shaped a Nation*. Lexington: University of Kentucky Press, 2005.

Huang, Michelle N. "Ecologies of Entanglement in the Great Pacific Garbage Patch." *Journal of Asian American Studies* 23, no. 1 (2017): 95–117.

Huang, Vivian. *Surface Relations: Queer Forms of Asian American Inscrutability*. Durham, NC: Duke University Press, 2022.

Huang, Vivian, and Summer Kim Lee. "Introduction: Contingency Plans." *Women and Performance: A Journal of Feminist Theory* 30, no. 1 (2020): 1–19.

Jackson, Shannon. *Social Works: Performing Art, Supporting Publics*. New York: Routledge, 2011.

Kapadia, Ronak. "The Downward Redistribution of Breath: Abolitionist Visions of Healing Justice." *Asian Diasporic Visual Cultures and the Americas* 8 (2022): 259–84.

Kauanui, J. Kēhaulani. *Paradoxes of Hawaiian Sovereignty: Land, Sex, and the Colonial Politics of State Nationalism*. Durham, NC: Duke University Press, 2018.

Khubchandani, Kareem. "Critical Aunty Studies: An Auntroduction," *Text and Performance Quarterly* 42, no. 3 (June 2022): 221–45.

Khúc, Mimi. *Dear Elia: Letters from the Asian American Abyss*. Durham, NC: Duke University Press, 2023.

Kim, Jina B. *Care at the End of the World: Dreaming of Infrastructure in Crip-of-Color Writing*. Durham, NC: Duke University Press, 2025.

Kim, Jina B. "Toward a Crip-of-Color Critique: Thinking with Minich's 'Enabling Whom?'" *Lateral* 6, no. 1 (2017). https://csalateral.org/issue/6-1/forum-alt-humanities-critical-disability-studies-crip-of-color-critique-kim/.

Kim, Jina B., and Sami Schalk. "Reclaiming the Radical Politics of Self-Care: A Crip-of-Color Critique." *South Atlantic Quarterly* 120, no. 2 (2021): 325–42.

Kang, Jay Caspian. *The Loneliest Americans*. New York: Penguin Random House, 2021.

Klein, Melanie. *Love, Guilt and Reparation and Other Works, 1921–1945*. New York: Simon and Schuster, 1975.

Klein, Naomi. *The Shock Doctrine: The Rise of Disaster Capitalism*. New York: Picador, 2007.

Kondo, Dorinne. *Worldmaking: Race, Performance, and the Work of Creativity*. Durham, NC: Duke University Press, 2018.

Le Conte, Yves, and Maria Navajas. "Climate Change: Impact on Honey Bee Populations and Diseases." *Revue Scientifique et Technique (International Office of Epizootics)* 27, no. 2 (2008): 499–510.

Lee, James Kyung-Jin. *Pedagogies of Woundedness: Illness, Memoir, and the Ends of the Model Minority*. Philadelphia: Temple University Press, 2022.

Lee, Josephine. *The Japan of Pure Invention: Gilbert and Sullivan's "The Mikado."* Minneapolis: University of Minnesota Press, 2010.

Lee, Rachel C. *The Exquisite Corpse of Asian America: Biopolitics, Biosociality, and Posthuman Ecologies*. New York: New York University Press, 2014.

Lee, Summer Kim. "Staying In: Mitski, Ocean Vuong, and Asian American Asociality." *Social Text* 37, no. 1 (2019): 27–50.

Lehmann, Hans-Thies. *Postdramatic Theatre*. Translated by Karen Jürs-Munby. New York: Taylor and Francis, 2006.

Lepecki, André. "Choreopolice and Choreopolitics: Or, the Task of the Dancer." *TDR: The Drama Review* 57, no. 4 (2013): 13–27.

Levine, Caroline. *Forms: Whole, Rhythm, Hierarchy, Network*. Princeton, NJ: Princeton University Press, 2015.

Lewis, Sophie. *Abolish the Family: A Manifesto for Care and Liberation*. New York: Verso, 2022.

Lewis, Sophie. *Full Surrogacy Now: Feminism Against Family*. New York: Verso, 2019.

Lim, Genny. *"Paper Angels" and "Bitter Cane": Two Plays*. Honolulu, HI: Kalamaku Press, 1991.

Lorde, Audre. *A Burst of Light: And Other Essays*. 1988. Mineola, NY: Ixia Press, 2017.

Lorde, Audre. *The Collected Poems of Audre Lorde*. New York: W. W. Norton, 2000.

Lowe, Lisa. *Immigrant Acts: On Asian American Cultural Politics*. Durham, NC: Duke University Press, 1996.

Luciano, Dana, and Mel Chen. "Introduction: Has the Queer Ever Been Human?" *GLQ: A Journal of Lesbian and Gay Studies* 21, nos. 2–3 (2015): 183–207.

Malatino, Hil. *Side Affects: On Being Trans and Feeling Bad*. Minneapolis: University of Minnesota Press, 2022.

Malatino, Hil. *Trans Care*. Minneapolis: University of Minnesota Press, 2020.

Manalansan, Martin. "Queering the Chain of Care Paradigm." *Scholar and Feminist Online*. 6, no. 3 (2008). https://sfonline.barnard.edu/immigration/manalansan_01.htm.

Marx, Karl. "Critique of the Gotha Program." In *The Marx-Engels Reader*, edited by Robert C. Tucker, 525–41. New York: W. W. Norton, 1978.

Mbembe, Achille. "Necropolitics." *Public Culture* 15, no. 1 (2003): 11–40.

McCracken, Allison, Alexander Cho, Louisa Stein, and Indira Neill Hoch. "You Must Be New Here: An Introduction." In *A Tumblr Book: Platform and Cultures*, edited by Allison McCracken, Alexander Cho, Louisa Stern, and Indira Neill Hoch, 1–22. Ann Arbor: University of Michigan Press, 2020.

McMaster, James. "In Defense of Virtue Signaling." *Journal of Dramatic Theory and Criticism* 35, no. 2 (2021): 125–29.

Melamed, Jodi. *Represent and Destroy: Rationalizing Violence in the New Racial Capitalism*. Minneapolis: University of Minnesota Press, 2011.

Mengesha, Lilian, and Lakshmi Padmanabhan. "Introduction to Performing Refusal/Refusing to Perform." *Women and Performance: A Journal of Feminist Theory* 29, no. 1 (2019): 1–8.

Mingus, Mia. "Moving Toward the Ugly: A Politic Beyond Desirability." *Leaving Evidence* (blog), August 22, 2011. https://leavingevidence.wordpress.com/2011/08/22/moving-toward-the-ugly-a-politic-beyond-desirability/.

Moshe, Liat-Ben. *Decarcerating Disability: Deinstitutionalization and Prison Abolition*. Minneapolis: University of Minnesota Press, 2020.

Muñoz, José Esteban. *Cruising Utopia: The Then and There of Queer Futurity*. New York: New York University Press, 2009.

Muñoz, José Esteban. *Disidentifications: Queers of Color and the Performance of Politics*. Minneapolis: University of Minnesota Press, 1999.

Muñoz, José Esteban. "Evidence as Ephemera: Introductory Notes to Queer Acts." *Women and Performance: A Journal of Feminist Theory* 8, no. 2 (1996): 5–16.

Muñoz, José Esteban. *The Sense of Brown*. Edited by Joshua Chambers-Letson and Tavia Nyong'o. Durham, NC: Duke University Press, 2020.

Nadasen, Premilla. *Care: The Highest Stage of Capitalism*. Chicago: Haymarket Books, 2023.

Nancy, Jean-Luc. *Being Singular Plural*. Stanford, CA: Stanford University Press, 2000.

Nash, Jennifer. *Black Feminism Reimagined: After Intersectionality*. Durham, NC: Duke University Press, 2019.

Ngai, Sianne. *Ugly Feelings*. Cambridge, MA: Harvard University Press, 2007.

Nguyen, Mimi Thi. *The Gift of Freedom: War, Debt, and Other Refugee Passages*. Durham, NC: Duke University Press, 2012.

Nguyen, Patricia. "Abolition as Durational Performance: Mutual Aid Aesthetics in Chicago's Southeast Asian Neighborhood." *Journal of Asian American Studies* 25, no. 3 (2022): 463–92.

Nguyen, Tan Hoang. *A View from the Bottom: Asian American Masculinity and Sexual Representation*. Durham, NC: Duke University Press, 2014.

Ninh, erin Khuê. *Ingratitude: The Debt-Bound Daughter in Asian American Literature*. New York: New York University Press, 2011.

Ninh, erin Khuê. *Passing for Perfect: College Impostors and Other Model Minorities*. Philadelphia: Temple University Press, 2021.

Nishida, Akemi. *Just Care: Messy Entanglements of Disability, Dependency, and Desire*. Philadelphia: Temple University Press, 2022.

Nono, Grace. *Babaylan Sing Back: Philippine Shamans and Voice, Gender, and Place*. Ithaca, NY: Cornell University Press, 2021.

Nyong'o, Tavia. *Afro-Fabulations: The Queer Drama of Black Life*. New York: New York University Press, 2019.

Nyong'o, Tavia. "So Far Down You Can't See the Light: Afro-Fabulation in Branden Jacobs-Jenkins's *An Octoroon*." In *Race and Performance After Repetition*, edited by Soyica Diggs Colbert, Douglas A. Jones Jr., and Shane Vogel, 29–45. Durham, NC: Duke University Press, 2020.

O'Brien, M. E. *Family Abolition: Capitalism and the Communizing of Care*. Las Vegas: Pluto Press, 2023.

Page, Cara, and Erica Woodland. *Healing Justice Lineages: Dreaming at the Crossroads of Liberation, Collective Care, and Safety*. Berkeley, CA: North Atlantic Books, 2023.

Paik, A. Naomi. *Bans, Walls, Raids, and Sanctuary*. Berkeley: University of California Press, 2020.

Parreñas, Rhacel Salazar. *Servants of Globalization: Migration and Domestic Work*. Stanford, CA: Stanford University Press, 2001.

Pérez, Roy. "Proximity: On the Work of Mark Aguhar." In *Trap Door: Trans Cultural*

Production and the Politics of Visibility, edited by Reina Gossett, Eric A. Stanley, and Johanna Burton, 281–91. Cambridge, MA: MIT Press, 2017.

Piepzna-Samarasinha, Leah Lakshmi. *Care Work: Dreaming Disability Justice*. Vancouver: Arsenal Pulp Press, 2018.

Price, Margaret. *Mad at School: Rhetorics of Mental Disability and Academic Life*. Ann Arbor: University of Michigan Press, 2011.

Puar, Jasbir. *The Right to Maim: Debility, Capacity, Disability*. Durham, NC: Duke University Press, 2017.

Puig de la Bellacasa, Maria. *Matters of Care: Speculative Ethics in More Than Human Worlds*. Minneapolis: University of Minnesota Press, 2017.

Raghuram, Parvati. "Race and Feminist Care Ethics: Intersectionality as Method." *Gender, Place and Culture: A Journal of Feminist Geography* 26, no. 5 (2019): 613–37.

Rivera, Takeo. *Model Minority Masochism: Performing the Cultural Politics of Asian American Masculinity*. New York: Oxford University Press, 2022.

Rodriguez, Dylan. *Suspended Apocalypse: White Supremacy, Genocide, and the Filipino Condition*. Minneapolis: University of Minnesota Press, 2010.

Rodriguez, Dylan. *White Reconstruction: Domestic Warfare and the Logic of Genocide*. New York: Fordham University Press, 2021.

Roy, Lucinda. *No Right to Remain Silent: What We've Learned from the Tragedy at Virginia Tech*. New York: Three Rivers Press, 2009.

Ruddick, Sara. *Maternal Thinking: Toward a Politics of Peace*. Boston: Beacon Press, 1989.

Schalk, Sami. *Bodyminds Reimagined: (Dis)ability, Race, and Gender in Black Women's Speculative Fiction*. Durham, NC: Duke University Press, 2018.

Sedgwick, Eve Kosofsky. *The Epistemology of the Closet*. Berkeley: University of California Press, 1990.

Sedgwick, Eve Kosofsky. *Tendencies*. London: Routledge, 1994.

Sedgwick, Eve Kosofsky. *Touching Feeling: Affect, Pedagogy, Performativity*. Durham, NC: Duke University Press, 2002.

Sexton, Jared. "People-of-Color-Blindness: Notes on the Afterlife of Slavery." *Social Text* 28, no. 2 (2010): 31–56.

Shah, Nayan. *Contagious Divides: Epidemics and Race in San Francisco's Chinatown*. Berkeley: University of California Press, 2001.

Shimakawa, Karen. *National Abjection: The Asian American Body Onstage*. Durham, NC: Duke University Press, 2002.

shorb, kt. "Reappropriation, Reparative Creativity, and Feeling Yellow in Generic Ensemble Company's *The Mikado: Reclaimed*." *Journal of American Drama and Theatre* 34, no. 2 (2022): 1–12.

Simpson, Leanne Betasamosake. "Indigenous Resurgence and Co-Resistance," *Critical Ethnic Studies* 2, no. 2 (2016): 19–34.

Singh, Julietta. *Unthinking Mastery: Dehumanism and Decolonial Entanglements*. Durham, NC: Duke University Press, 2018.

Snow, Jess X. "The Last Words of the Honey Bees." In *Nepantla: An Anthology for Queer Poets of Color*, edited by Christopher Soto, 145–46. New York: Nightboat Books, 2018.

Snyder, Sharon, and David Mitchell. *The Biopolitics of Disability: Neoliberalism, Ablenationalism, and Peripheral Embodiment*. Ann Arbor: University of Michigan Press, 2015.

Spade, Dean. *Mutual Aid: Building Solidarity During This Crisis (and the Next)*. New York: Verso, 2020.

Stanley, Eric. *Atmospheres of Violence: Structuring Antagonism and the Trans/Queer Ungovernable*. Durham, NC: Duke University Press, 2021.

Tadiar, Neferti. *Things Fall Away: Philippine Historical Experience and the Makings of Globalization*. Durham, NC: Duke University Press, 2009.

TallBear, Kim. "Caretaking Relations, Not American Dreaming." *Kalfou* 6, no. 1 (2019): 24–41.

Taylor, Diana. *The Archive and the Repertoire: Performing Cultural Memory in the Americas*. Durham, NC: Duke University Press, 2003.

Tongson, Karen. *Relocations: Queer Suburban Imaginaries*. New York: New York University Press, 2011.

trân, ngọc loan. "Calling IN: A Less Disposable Way of Holding Each Other Accountable." In *The Solidarity Struggle: How People of Color Succeed and Fail at Showing Up for Each Other in the Fight for Freedom*, edited by Mia McKenzie, 59–63. Oakland, CA: BGD Press, 2016.

Trask, Haunani-Kay "Settlers of Color and 'Immigrant' Hegemony: 'Locals' in Hawai'i." In *Asian Settler Colonialism: From Local Governance to the Habits of Everyday Life in Hawai'i*, edited by Candace Fujikane and Jonathan Y. Okamura, 45–65. Honolulu: University of Hawai'i Press, 2008.

Tronto, Joan. *Caring Democracy: Markets, Equality, and Justice*. New York: New York University Press, 2013.

Tronto, Joan. *Moral Boundaries: A Political Argument for an Ethic of Care*. New York: Routledge, 1994.

Vang, Ma, and Kit Myers. "In the Wake of George Floyd: Hmong Americans' Refusal to Be a U.S. Ally." *Amerasia Journal* 47, no. 1 (2021): 20–34.

Viola, Michael J., Dean Itsuji Saranillio, Juliana Hu Pegues, and Iyko Day. "Introduction to Solidarities of Nonalignment: Abolition, Decolonization, and Anticapitalism." *Critical Ethnic Studies* 5, nos. 1–2 (2019): 5–20.

Walia, Harsha. *Border and Rule: Global Migration, Capitalism, and the Rise of Racist Nationalism*. Chicago: Haymarket Books, 2021.

Weheliye, Alexander G. *Habeas Viscus: Racializing Assemblages, Biopolitics, and Black Feminist Theories of the Human*. Durham, NC: Duke University Press, 2014.

Wilderson, Frank. *Red, White, and Black: Cinema and the Structure of U.S. Antagonisms*. Durham, NC: Duke University Press, 2010.

Winnicott, D. W. *Maturational Processes and the Facilitating Environment*. New York: International Universities Press, 1965.

Wolfe, Patrick. "Settler Colonialism and the Elimination of the Native." *Journal of Genocide Research* 9, no. 4 (2006): 387–409.

Wong, Alice. *Year of the Tiger: An Activist's Life*. New York: Penguin Random House, 2022.

Wong, Diane. "The Future Is Ours to Build: Asian American Abolitionist Counterstories for Black Liberation." *Politics, Groups, and Identities* 10, no. 3 (2021): 1–10.

Wong, Kristina. "Wong Flew over the Cuckoo's Nest and Almost Dropped Dead (Or World's Most Discouraging Essay About Making Live Art for a Living) (Or Why Performance Art Is the Worst Business to Go Into If You Want to Make Mental Health Problems Go Away)." *Asian American Literary Review* 10, no. 2 (2019): 111–16.

Wu, Cindy. *Sticky Rice: A Politics of Intraracial Desire*. Philadelphia: Temple University Press, 2018.

Wynter, Sylvia. "Unsettling the Coloniality of Being/Power/Truth/Freedom: Towards the Human, After Man, Its Overrepresentation—An Argument." *CR: The New Centennial Review* 3, no. 3 (2003): 257–337.

Yao, Xine. *Disaffected: The Cultural Politics of Unfeeling in Nineteenth-Century America*. Durham, NC: Duke University Press, 2021.

Index

Page numbers in italics refer to figures.

18 Million Rising, 137n29

AAPI Women Lead, 137n29
abandonment, 10–11, 53, 65, 72, 102, 115, 117, 123
abjection, 2, 13, 26, 55, 60, 72, 75, 121, 141n17; Mark Aguhar and, 43–44, 53; national, 19, 67; spatialization of, 90
ableism, 11, 18, 67, 74
abolition, 8, 15, 27, 102, 114, 126–27, 129, 132–34, 141n19
Adams, Ansel, 87
Adams, M., 127
aesthetics, 14, 127, 140n57, 140n10, 144n5; of existence, 43; of Jess X. Snow's works, 102–3, 105, 121, 123; of Mark Aguhar, 31, 33–34, 38–40, 43, 46–47, 53; of *The Mikado*, 82, 87; of *The Mikado: Reclaimed*, 98; minoritarian, 4, 19, 28, 59; performative, 2–3, 18–20, 22–24, 73–74, 99, 102, 121; of social movements, 27–28, 128, 134
affect, 22, 48, 50–51, 106, 119, 121, 141n17, 142n26, 149n3; alien, 41; architecture and, 144n5; of Asian American loneliness, 15, 61, 71; Asian American theater and, 26, 73–76, 93–94; and attachment, 5, 7, 18, 27; dehumanist grief and, 105; in care, 58; emotional labor and, 79–80, 83, 85, 91; labor and, 47, 78; mobilizing, 28; in racialized holding environment, 21, 25, 73, 76; social networks and, 47; suffering and, 2–3, 8, 19, 70, 83, 95; violence and, 4. *See also* emotion
affirmative action, 12
Afterearth, 2, 13, 27, 104–9, 111–12, 114, 123
aggression, 12, 33, 51, 98, 110–11, 113–14, 150n30; micro-, 68, 84, 93; passive, 66; racial, 65, 94
Aguhar, Mark (Call Out Queen), 13, 24, 29–56, 99, 101, 117, 133, 141n10, 142n35
Ahmed, Sara, 41
Alidio, Kimberly, 13, 24, 33, 48–54, 143n48
alienation, 1, 38, 41, 71, 75, 80, 89–90, 107, 120, 150n17
Angel Island, 9, 89, 137n27
Anker, Elisabeth, 130, 141n10
antagonism, 10, 39, 55, 68, 88, 95, 98–99, 101
anti-Asian neglect, 14, 17–18, 21, 101, 128, 133; as Asian American loneliness, 15, 64, 72, 99; of Mark Aguhar, 31, 38; in *Office Hour*, 59, 61, 64–65, 71–72
anti-Asian violence, 1–2, 17, 19, 78–79, 94, 101, 103, 135n9
anti-Blackness, 3, 12, 14–17, 27, 31, 71, 95, 126–29, 131, 133
anxiety, 2, 12–13, 21, 57, 66, 110, 148n42
AQUA, 137n28
Asian American, as term, 10
Asian American Literary Review, 19

Asian American Resource Workshop, 137n29
Asian American studies, 10, 12, 14, 104, 107, 122, 128, 136n18, 138n47
Asian American Writers' Workshop, 137n29
Asian Freedom Project. *See* Freedom Inc. (formerly Asian Freedom Project)
Asianness, 15, 33, 41, 62, 82, 107, 138n46
assaults, 4, 39, 68–69, 110, 129, 132, 135n9
assimilation, 12, 42, 71, 78, 81, 138, 144n10
attrition, 13, 26, 68, 70–71, 94, 101, 117
Auntie Sewing Squad, 20–22
Austin, J. L., 142n26
autonomy, 6, 55, 124
auto-orientalization, 81, 91, 97

babaylan (ritual specialist), 49–50
Baril, Alexandre, 55, 143n62
Bell Scott, Patricia, 48
Berger, John, 49
Berlant, Lauren, 13, 39
BIPOC (Black, Indigenous, people of color), 16, 21
Black liberation struggles, 125–26, 131–32
Black studies, 8; afropessimist, 16; anti-Blackness and, 3, 12, 14–17, 27, 31, 71, 95, 126–29, 131, 133; Black feminism, 30, 48, 126, 136n18
Blake, Jacob, 130
Boal, Augusto, 129
Boggs, Grace Lee, 1, 28
Bollas, Christopher, 74–75
border regimes, 9, 103, 120, 150n17
Brecht, Bertolt, 86
brown, adrienne maree, 141n19
Brown, Michael, 127
brownness, 33, 38, 41, 46–47, 50, 54, 116, 138n46
burden of liveness, 77–78, 91–92, 96
burden of relatability, 78–79, 81, 96
Butler, Judith, 31, 43, 60, 117
Byrd, Jodi, 107

California, 59, 112, 137n28, 139n49; San Francisco, 10, 89–90, 137n27
call-out culture, 13, 40, 48, 141n19, 142n26
Cambodian diaspora, 5, 126–30, 132, 136n11
cancel culture, 6, 13, 141n19

capitalism, 7, 11–12, 14, 27, 52, 122; anti-, 20, 96, 102, 114, 127; communicative, 47; disaster, 114; neoliberal, 4, 133–34; racial, 8, 12–13, 15, 73, 133; settler colonial, 3, 31, 106, 108, 112–14, 116
care ethics, 5, 27–28, 39, 53, 74, 119, 122, 139n47, 145n15; of Auntie Sewing Squad, 22–23; dehumanist, 104, 107, 111, 114, 123–24; emotional labor and, 80; feminist, 6–8, 136n18, 142n35; Freedom Inc. practicing, 127, 129, 131–32; radical, 9, 11, 17, 127, 134
care justice, 8, 123
care of the self, 24, 32, 34, 38–40, 43, 45, 54, 141n10
care theory, 6–9, 23, 111, 114, 119, 122; Asian American studies with, 12, 14, 105; critique of neoliberalism, 11, 12; interdependence and, 17; intersectionality in, 136n18; with performance studies, 19
care web, 23, 117, 119
care work, 3, 23, 80, 85, 122, 140n57, 147n24
caring democracy, 122
caring labor, 7, 14, 18, 60
Cave, Nick, 31
Chambers-Letson, Joshua, 78
Chauvin, Derek, 127
check-ins, 66, 93–96, 133
Chen, Mel, 104, 149n3
Cheng, Anne Anlin, 145n14, 151n41
childcare, 11, 85, 94
China, 1–2, 108; heritage from, 46, 106, 112, 136n11; migrants from, 9–10, 89–90, 137n27
Chinatowns, 89–90, 103
Chinese exclusion, 9–10, 137n27
Chinese Exclusion Act, 137n27
Cho, Julia: *Aubergine*, 73; *Office Hour*, 13, 25, 57–76, 99, 101, 133, 145n15, 145n19, 146n35
Cho, Seung-Hui, 57–61, 63, 65, 67, 70–71, 74, 99, 101, 145n17
choreopolitical plan, 131
Christianity, 45, 50–51, 108
Chuh, Kandice, 23
Chun, Wendy Hui Kyoung, 53
climate crisis, 2, 13, 24, 102, 106, 112–15, 122
Clinton, Hillary, 11

coalitions, 10, 18, 23, 27, 71, 125, 127–29, 132, 136n11, 139n47
Cohen, Cathy, 11
collective care, 13, 24–25, 33, 48, 54, 102
Collins, Patricia Hill, 136n18
colonialism, 14, 18, 49–50, 105, 110, 127, 140n10; anti-, 22, 98, 113, 126; decolonization, 27, 51–53, 102–4, 108–9, 111, 113–14, 116, 122, 134, 140n3; US racial-, 4, 9, 12, 15–16, 129, 131. *See also* imperialism; settler colonialism
colony collapse disorder, 115–17
Combahee River Collective, 48
community agreements, 93–96
concentration camps, 10, 13, 78, 81, 87, 89–90, 99, 101
COVID-19 pandemic, 13, 81, 89, 91, 106, 125, 127, 129, 134; anti-Asian violence during, 1–2, 78, 101, 103, 135n9; Auntie Sewing Squad during, 20–22
Crenshaw, Kimberlé, 136n18
crip of color critique, 8, 32
crisis ordinariness, 13, 102, 134
critical disability studies, 8
critical ethnic studies, 136n18
critical flippancy, 39–40, 46, 51
critical theory, 16, 92, 100
cruel optimism, 39
culture wars, 12–14, 21, 28, 34, 98, 128, 133, 138m39

Day, Iyko, 15, 107, 114
Dean, Jodi, 47
death, 12, 20, 39, 92, 112, 121, 130, 150n30; collective, 99; of honey bee, 27, 105, 115, 117, 119, 122; of Mark Aguhar, 48–49, 53–56, 101; premature, 4, 26, 34, 76, 102. *See also* suicide
debilitation, 5, 8, 15, 25, 28, 71, 117, 122
debt, 48, 149n3; unpayable, 122–23, 151n56
dehumanism, 100, 103, 107, 109–11, 124, 149n3; of grief, 27, 105, 115, 119, 123
dehumanist care, 103–5, 114–15, 117, 124, 134
dehumanist solidarity, 104, 114, 116, 149n5
depression, 2, 5, 12–13, 54–55, 65
depressive position, 110, 150n30
desexualization, 4, 35, 65

desirability, 31, 33, 38–39, 41, 44–46, 48, 98, 113, 137n28
destruction, 39, 73, 108, 112, 132
DiAngelo, Robin, 83
diaspora, 121; Asian, 7–8, 10, 13, 16, 18, 20, 102–5, 120, 123; Cambodian, 126–30, 132, 136n11; Filipino, 17, 24, 30, 33, 48–51, 53, 55, 89, 112–14, 139n53; Indigeneity and, 106–7; Japanese, 10, 78, 82, 90, 94; Korean, 5, 17, 25, 57, 61, 63–64, 72–73
disability justice, 8, 19, 30, 94, 96, 122, 134, 139n53
disablement, 8, 11, 23, 44–45, 48, 60
disaffection, 79
disaffirmation, 33, 39–40, 42, 44, 49, 52
disavowal, 3, 11–12, 47, 53, 61, 63–64
dismissal, 31, 33, 38–40, 49, 52, 68, 138n39, 147n15
displacement, 61–64, 71, 121
dyads, 25, 59, 102

education, 11, 127–28, 131, 138n46; higher, 9, 59; minoritarian, 10
eldercare, 11, 85, 94
emotion, 6, 60, 79–80, 83, 93–94, 97; exhaustion of, 48; management, 80, 92. *See also* affect
emotional labor, 3, 13, 65; racial, 25–26, 79–81, 83–86, 91–93, 95–97, 100, 147n24
emotional support, 9–10, 80, 85
empowerment, 40, 43, 65, 95, 127
Endo, Mitsuye, 10
Eng, David, 65, 91, 110–11, 114, 120, 144n10, 148n36, 150n30
Engster, Daniel, 74
Enriquez, Virgilio, 51
entanglement, 6, 78, 103, 105, 109, 114, 116, 119, 121; ecologies of, 104, 117, 123–24
erasure, 15, 136n18
eroticism, 30, 32, 34–35, 38–39, 42–43, 45, 49
Essar, Qais, 19
ethics, 40, 43, 84, 103, 107, 114, 133, 150n30; of interdependence, 125; of self, 32–33; of unpayable debt, 123. *See also* care ethics
exceptionalism, 16, 27, 104, 124
exclusion, 41, 120; Chinese, 9–10, 137n27
exhaustion, 3–4, 6, 8, 13, 48, 65, 70, 122
exploitation, 4, 51, 74

INDEX 165

Facebook, 20
fatphobia, 17, 30–31, 33, 38–39, 43–45, 47–49, 53
fear, 2, 58, 66–67, 83, 146n35
femininity, 6–7, 69, 108, 145n14, 148n36; of Mark Aguhar, 33, 41, 53; of theater, 74, 146n49; trans-, 30, 41
feminism, 2, 20–21, 38, 49, 53, 95–96, 102, 122, 126, 133; Black, 30, 48, 126, 136n18; care ethics in, 142n35; feminist killjoy, 41; movements, 10; socialist, 84, 147n24; white, 136n18. *See also* care ethics; social reproduction
Feminist Press, 48
femmephobia, 31, 40
femmes, 13, 41, 45, 47, 53–54, 69, 95, 120, 143n48; femme gaze, 49
Ferguson, Roderick, 11
Filipino Americans, 17, 24, 30, 33, 48–50, 53, 55, 89, 112, 139n53
Fisher, Amanda Stuart, 18, 140n57
Fisher, Berenice, 2–3
flippancy, 39–40, 46, 51
Floyd, George, 20, 125, 127–28, 132, 134
Foucault, Michel, 24, 31–34, 38–40, 43, 45, 54, 93, 140n10, 141n17, 142n26
Francisco-Menchavez, Valerie, 48
Fraser, Nancy, 84–85, 142n35, 147n24
Freedom Inc. (formerly Asian Freedom Project), 27, 126–31, 133–34
Fujikane, Candace, 107
Fung, Richard, 31

Gagnon, Olivia Michiko, 123–24
GAPIMNY, 137n28
Garlough, Christine, 40
gender: in *Afterearth*, 108, 114; colony collapse disorder and, 116; divisions of labor and, 7, 19, 120; essentialism, 145n14; Generic Ensemble Company and, 86, 88, 93–94, 96; hyperracialization and, 148n36; justice, 27, 126; Kimberly Alidio and, 49–51; Mark Aguhar and, 31, 41, 47, 49; misgendering and, 49, 143n48; neglect and, 15; in *Office Hour*, 59–63, 65–67, 71, 74; queer inhumanism and, 149n3; in racial care, 25, 59–62, 65, 69, 107, 134, 145n15; in racial emotional labor, 81, 84; in service work, 80; in social reproduction theory, 147n24; in theater, 76. *See also* femininity; feminism; masculinity; nonbinary identity; queerness; transgender people
Generic Ensemble Company (GenEnCo), 13, 17, 133; *The Mikado: Reclaimed*, 25, 76, 81, 86–91, 93–94, 97–99
genocide, 16, 55, 111
Georgia: Atlanta, 2
Gilbert, W. S., 76; *Mikado, The*, 25, 81–88, 90–91, 97–99
Gilligan, Carol, 6
Gilmore, Ruth Wilson, 4, 132–33
Ginsburg, Ruth Bader, 20
Giovanni, Nikki, 58, 63, 145n23
Glenn, Evelyn Nakano, 3
Goffman, Erving, 79, 84, 95–96
Gopinath, Gayatri, 120
grief, 2, 19, 34, 50, 54–55, 117; dehumanist, 27, 105, 115, 119, 123
grievability, 105, 119

Halberstam, Jack, 116
Hamington, Maurice, 26, 74
Han, Shinhee, 144n10
Haraway, Donna, 117, 149n5
harm, 51, 65, 92, 95, 109, 113, 122, 133–34, 141n19; racial, 4, 6, 14, 23, 46, 93–94
Harney, Stefano, 122, 133
Harris, Kamala, 11
Hartman, Saidiya, 146n53
Hawaiʻi, 123; culture of, 106–8; Kanaka Maoli people, 104, 106–7, 123; Native Hawaiian studies, 107
health care, 11, 127
heteropatriarchy, 28, 108, 113; anti-, 20
hierarchies, 13, 33, 48, 79, 85, 104, 141n10, 149n5; racial, 3, 31, 135n5
Hmong Americans, 126–30, 132
Hobart, Hiʻilei Julia Kawehipuaakahaopulani, 8
Hochschild, Arlie, 79–80, 83, 85
Ho-Chunk people, 126–27
holding environment, racialized, 21, 25–26, 58–70, 72–76, 133, 144n10, 145n15
home, 10, 65–66, 96, 108, 112–13, 124, 128, 134; during COVID-19 pandemic, 22, 106; in Jess X. Snow's work, 105, 115, 119–23

homelessness, 112, 120, 122
homophobia, 18, 122
honey bees, 27, 105, 115–19, 122–23
Hong, Grace Kyungwon, 11
HowlRound, 89, 147n26
Huang, Michelle, 104
Huang, Vivian, 97, 104, 106, 144n10
Hull, Gloria T., 48
Hu Pegues, Juliana, 114
Huxtable, Juliana, 31
hypersexualization, 2, 4

Illinois: Chicago, 17, 31
immigration, 16, 21, 59, 65, 86, 107–8, 121, 126; Chinese, 9, 89, 120, 137n27; loneliness and, 71; migrant justice and, 102–3; of migrant workers, 48, 139n53; Vietnamese, 151n56
imperialism, 8–10, 14, 89, 97, 107–8, 112, 122, 126, 128, 136n11, 151n56. *See also* colonialism; settler colonialism
incarceration, 8–9, 14, 88, 90, 93, 97–98, 101, 127, 132, 137n28; call-out culture and, 141n19; wartime, 10, 78, 87. *See also* internment
inclusion, 12–13, 16, 38, 48, 94–95, 121
incompossible, 55
Indigeneity, 15–16, 52–53, 106–7, 139n47
Indigenous people, 2, 15–17, 21, 27, 52, 103–9, 111–14, 121–22, 126–27, 133, 138n49. *See also individual nations, communities, and tribes*
Indigenous resurgence, 106–9, 111, 113–14
Indigenous studies, 8, 27, 104, 136n18
individualism, 11–12, 32, 39, 51, 53, 105, 123, 125
individualization, 24, 65, 67, 122–23
inequalities, 3, 14, 31, 63, 65
interactions, 6, 20, 61, 66, 71, 83, 87, 95, 103–4; social, 3, 19
interdependence, 5, 7–8, 11, 17, 23, 28, 96, 105, 125, 133–34
internment, 4, 76; Japanese, 9–10, 78, 87, 90
intersectionality, 7, 11, 60–61, 136n18, 147n24
Inuit people, 123
invisibility, 8, 15, 21, 23, 86
isolation, 24, 47–48, 64, 73, 87, 90, 98; amid COVID 19 pandemic, 21, 125; anti-Asian neglect and, 17, 19, 145n15; Asian American loneliness and, 71, 139n49

Jackson, Shannon, 21
January 6, 2021, insurrection, 20
Japan: diaspora of, 10, 78, 82, 90, 94; misrepresentation of, 82–83, 88
Japanese wartime incarceration, 9–10, 78, 87, 90

Kanaka Maoli people, 104, 106–8, 123
Kang, Jay Caspian, 18
kapwa (Filipino concept), 51–54
Kauanui, J. Kēhaulani, 108
Kay-Trask, Haunani, 107
Kenny, Matt, 127
Khmer Americans, 126–27
Khubchandani, Kareem, 144n13
Khúc, Mimi, 8, 138n37; *Open in Emergency*, 19–20
Kim, Jina B., 32
Kim, Sue Jean, 146n35
King, Martin Luther, Jr., 152n5
King and I, The, 86
Klein, Melanie, 27, 105, 109–12, 114
Kneese, Tamara, 8
Kondo, Dorinne, 4, 74
Korean Americans, 5, 17, 25, 57, 61, 63–64, 72–73
Kristeva, Julia, 67
Kumu Hina, 106, 108

labor, 4, 6, 15, 18, 44, 61, 65, 107, 122–23; affective, 47, 78; care and, 7, 14, 18, 60, 63, 135n5, 142n35, 147n24; Chinese, 9, 137n27; divisions of, 7, 19, 120; emotional, 3, 13, 25–26, 65, 79–81, 83–86, 91–93, 95–97, 100, 147n24; feminized, 21; forced, 78–79; invisibilized, 21; pedagogical, 62, 68–69, 71; reproductive, 3, 10, 13, 85, 116, 119, 139n53, 147n24
Lange, Dorothea, 78, 87
Lavender Phoenix, 137n28
Lee, Corky, 20
Lee, Josephine, 82
Lee, Rachel C., 119–20
Lee, Summer Kim, 16, 76, 78, 106
Lehmann, Hans-Thies, 86
Lenapehoking territory, 103
Lepecki, André, 131

Lim, Genny: *Paper Angels*, 9
Lin, Wiena, 103
logic of elimination, 111. *See also* genocide
loneliness, 15, 19, 48; Asian American, 61, 64, 69, 71–72, 75–76, 99, 139n49, 146n46
Lorde, Audre, 32, 140n1
Lowe, Lisa, 13–14
Luciano, Dana, 149n3
Luis, Adriel: *Care Package*, 2, 149n2
Luna, Caleb, 141n15

māhū (transness), 108
making kin, 149n5
Malatino, Hil, 7, 122
male gaze, 49
Manalansan, Martin, 135n6
Manion, Jen, 148n42
Manzanar internment camp, 10
marginalization, 45–46, 84, 126–27, 141n19, 149n3
Marx, Karl, 27
masculinity, 6, 33, 38, 44, 61, 95, 108, 146n49; Asian, 65–67; white, 34–35, 41, 46, 68–69, 116. *See also* femininity
maternity/maternal care/motherhood, 6, 49, 58, 60, 74–75, 105, 109–10, 145n14, 150n30
Mbembe, Achille, 90
Melamed, Jodi, 11
melancholia, 56, 117; racial, 19
Mengesha, Lilian, 92
mental health, 65, 67, 138n37. *See also* unwellness
microaggressions, 68, 84, 93
migrant workers, 48, 139n53
migration. *See* immigration
Mikado, The, 25, 81–88, 90–91, 97–99
Mikado: Reclaimed, The, 25, 76, 81, 86–94, 97–99, 101, 147n26, 148n30
Mingus, Mia, 8, 43
Minnesota: Minneapolis, 127, 132
minoritarian team, 26, 81, 92–96
misogyny, 18, 40, 86
Miss Saigon, 86
Mitchell, David, 11
modalities of the human, 105

model minority, 11–12, 14, 16–17, 42, 49, 71, 128, 138n37, 144n10, 151n56; masochism, 19, 138n47
morality, 6, 10–11, 83, 122
moral masochism, 139n47
Moten, Fred, 122, 133
Movement for Black Lives, 127
movements, 39, 79, 117, 121, 139n48, 150n30; Asian American, 138n47; decolonization, 113; disability justice, 8; Indigenous resurgence, 109, 113; liberation, 10–11; organizing of, 4, 28; political, 8, 73; racial justice, 126–28, 132; social, 12, 27, 102–3, 122, 134
multiculturalism, 11–12, 14–16, 30, 53, 94
multiply marginalized people, 4, 8, 18, 24–26, 61, 93, 102, 123; in *Afterearth*, 113–14; art of, 30–31; check-ins of, 94–95; in ecologies of entanglement, 104; labor of, 60, 78–79; social movements of, 134; in *The Mikado: Reclaimed*, 81, 99; view category of home, 105, 120
Mulvey, Laura, 49
Muñoz, José Esteban, 31–33, 45, 56, 77, 97, 121, 138n46
Myers, Kit, 128–29

Nancy, Jean-Luc, 53
Nash, Jennifer, 136n18
National Conference of Third World Lesbians and Gays, 137n28
nationalism, 11–12, 42, 61, 89–91, 100
National Liberation Front of North Vietnam, 10
Nayeem, Sham-e-Ali, 19
necropolitics, 70, 90
neglect, 16, 19, 23, 145n15; carceral, 9; Mark Aguhar's work and, 33, 35, 38–39, 45, 47, 53; need for racial care and, 2, 4–5, 15, 17–18, 28, 31–33, 59, 123; state, 101. *See also* anti-Asian neglect
negligence, 26, 46, 70, 116, 134
neoliberalism, 11–12, 25, 49, 60, 63, 122, 125; capitalism and, 4, 73, 133–34; individualism and, 32, 39, 51, 123; multiculturalism and, 12, 15, 30
New York Theatre Workshop, 20–21

Nguyen, Mimi Thi, 122, 151n56
Nguyen, Patricia, 133
Nguyen, Tan Hoang, 35
Nguyen, Viet Thanh, 139n48
Ninh, erin Khuê, 11, 122, 139n49, 151n56
Nishida, Akemi, 8
nonbinary identity, 30, 94, 102
Nono, Grace, 49
normative ideality, 38–39, 42–46
NQAPIA (National Queer Asian Pacific Islander Alliance), 95
Nyong'o, Tavia, 55
NYU Asian/Pacific/American Institute, 103

Obama, Barack, 11–13, 16, 30, 138n46
Obama-Trump years (2007–21), 12–13, 16, 138n46
Office Hour, 13, 25, 57–76, 99, 101, 133, 145n15, 145n19, 146n35
ontology, 16, 54, 104–5, 117, 121, 123; of interdependence, 5, 7, 11, 17, 133–34
Open in Emergency, 19–20
oppression, 7, 16–17, 24–25, 60, 77, 84–85, 93, 98, 122, 138n46; hierarchies of, 79; liberation movements against, 10; Mark Aguhar and, 40–41, 44–45; suicidism as, 55, 143n62; theater of the oppressed and, 129
orientalism, 9, 64, 81–82, 86, 91, 97
Oshiro, Wan Ping, 108–9

Pacific Islanders, 2, 95, 106–7
Padmanabhan, Lakshmi, 92
Paik, A. Naomi, 102
pandemic. *See* COVID-19 pandemic
Parreñas, Rhacel Salazar, 139n53
parrhesia, 40, 45, 142n26
patriotism, 42, 78, 81
people of color (POC), as term, 16
people of color blindness, 71
Pérez, Roy, 35, 39–40
performance studies, 19–20, 72, 142n26, 146n49
performance theory, minoritarian, 77
performativity, 5, 22, 52, 79, 85, 121; alienation and, 71; of care, 18, 27, 40, 102, 128, 130; of holding environment, 60, 69, 74; normative ideals and, 38–39, 96; J. L. Austin's, 142n26; queer, 23; reappropriation and, 93
Philippines, diaspora and culture of, 17, 24, 30, 33, 48–51, 53, 55, 89, 113–14, 139n53
Piepzna-Samarasinha, Leah Lakshmi, 8, 54, 80; *Care Work*, 23
poetry, 2–3, 19–20, 23, 27, 112–13, 117; of Chinese immigrant detainees, 9; of Jess X. Snow, 17, 102–3, 105, 115–16, 119–21, 123; of Kimberly Alidio, 17, 24, 33, 48–54, 143n48
policing, 9, 13, 95, 103, 126–27, 129–30, 132
pornography, 30, 34, 41
posthumanism, 8, 149n3
preservative love, 109
Price, Margaret, 65
psychoanalysis, 8, 19, 25, 58, 105, 109, 144n10, 145n14
psychosocial suffering, 2, 18–20, 25, 31, 44, 133–34
Puig de la Bellacasa, Maria, 27, 104

queerness, 7–8, 10, 20, 33, 60, 77–78, 81, 86, 101, 126–27; in *Afterearth*, 2, 112–14; dehumanist solidarity and, 104; GenEnCo and, 17, 81, 86, 95–99; historical activism in, 137n28; home as concept in, 120–21; in Jess X. Snow's work, 102; Kimberly Alidio and, 48–51, 53–54; Mark Aguhar and, 17, 24, 30–31, 35, 38, 44–46, 48, 52–53, 55; neoliberalism and, 11; queer inhumanism, 149n3; queer performativity, 23

racial care, definition of, 2–3, 31, 135n5
racial castration, 65, 67, 91, 148n36
racial culpabilities, 3, 25, 96
racial emotional labor, 25–26, 79–81, 83–86, 91–93, 95–97, 100, 147n24
racial impingement, 68, 70, 74, 146n47
racialization, 3, 8, 16, 65, 85, 96, 116, 120, 131, 135n5; of Asian Americans, 15, 17, 31, 46, 63, 71, 91; of care, 71, 73, 79, 84, 99, 130, 134; desirability and, 44; hyper-, 148n36; model minority, 11, 14, 17, 144n10; of sexuality, 42; of violence, 70, 74. *See also* racialized holding environment
racialized holding environment, 21, 25–26, 58–70, 72–76, 133, 144n10, 145n15

INDEX 169

racism, 135n5, 147n15, 150n17; anti-, 5, 12, 67, 81, 96, 135n5, 138n47, 148n45; anti-Asian, 2, 15, 18, 46, 66, 99, 145n23; anti-Black, 3, 12, 14–17, 27, 31, 71, 95, 126–29, 131, 133; brownness and, 138n46; cancel culture and, 141n19; definition of, 4; emotional labor and, 83–84, 86, 96; of *The Mikado*, 25, 81–82, 90; *The Mikado: Reclaimed* and, 87, 101; in *Office Hour*, 68; sexual, 137n28; structural, 126; surviving, 17
racist love, 19
radical care, 8
refugees, 16, 126, 128, 133, 151n56. *See also* immigration
refusal, performance of, 92
relationality, 5–8, 17, 23–24, 47, 49, 128, 131, 139n47; of Auntie Sewing Squad, 20, 22; dehumanism and, 104; in emotional labor, 79, 85
remote intimacy, 33
reparation, 10, 20, 27, 105, 109–14, 123, 150n30
representation, 8, 12, 15, 21–23, 61, 107, 129, 147n15; Asian American sexual, 35, 39; burden of, 64, 71; identitarian, 74; in *The Mikado: Reclaimed*, 82, 86–87, 90; of minoritarian self, 33; of model minority, 128
reproduction, 123; of emotional support, 85; psychosocial, 13, 26; social, 7, 18, 84–85, 115–16, 120, 127, 136n18, 138n39, 147n24; of suicidism, 55
reproductive justice, 8
reproductive labor, 3, 10, 13, 85, 116, 119, 139n53, 147n24
responsibilities, 15, 73, 88, 115, 141n19; care, 2, 4, 6–7, 11, 14, 22, 32, 116, 123; in caring coalitions, 27; holding environment and, 61, 63–64, 76; in minoritarian teams, 96; performance studies and, 20; for social reproduction, 147n24
revolting self-care, 24–25, 33, 38–41, 44–48, 50–51, 53–54
revolt of conduct, 39, 141n17
Rittenhouse, Kyle, 130
Rivera, Takeo, 138n47
Robinson, Tony, 127
Rodriguez, Dylan, 12, 55
Ross, Loretta, 141n19
Roy, Lucinda, 58–61, 63
Ruddick, Sara, 109

San Francisco State University, 10
Saranillio, Dean, 114
saviorism, 131–32
Schalk, Sami, 32, 139n53
Searle, John, 142n26
Sedgwick, Eve, 20, 54, 84, 110, 150n30
selective mutism, 65
self-care, 2, 13, 54, 59, 76, 94; Audre Lorde on, 32; Foucauldian, 32; Mark Aguhar and, 17, 24, 32–33, 39–40, 43, 54, 133, 141n10; minoritarian, 24, 33, 44, 49; in Naoko Wowsugi's meditation, 2, 19; problem of, 24; on *The Real World*, 33. *See also* revolting self-care
separatism, 13, 33; virtual, 44, 46–48, 51, 53–54
September 11, 2001, attacks, 78
settler colonialism, 1, 3, 27, 31, 102–3, 116, 121, 126, 133, 150n17; *Afterearth* on, 106–8, 111–14; Asian, 107, 138n47; violence of, 15–17
Sexton, Jared, 71
sexuality, 15, 34, 57, 61, 65–66, 94, 97, 134, 137n28, 149n3; decolonizing, 108; dehumanism and, 107; desire, desirability and, 25, 31, 35, 38, 41–42
sexualization, 30, 41–44, 46, 67, 86, 141n19; de-, 4, 35, 65; hyper-, 2, 4
sex work, 45, 86
Shah, Nayan, 89
Shimakawa, Karen, 60, 67, 75, 90
shootings, 2, 13, 58, 62, 65, 67, 73, 130, 132
shorb, kt, 81, 86, 93–95, 99
Simpson, Leanne Betasamosake, 106
Singh, Julietta, 27, 103–4, 123–24, 149n3, 149n5
Smith, Barbara, 48
Smithsonian Asian Pacific American Center, 102, 105, 137n29; *Care Package*, 2–4, 13, 19–22, 106, 149n2
Snow, Jess X., 102–3, 133; *Afterearth*, 2, 13, 27, 104–9, 111–12, 114, 123; *Funeral for the Honey Bee*, 115, 117–18; "Migration Is Natural," 120–21; "The Last Words of the Honey Bees," 115–17, 119, 122
Snyder, Sharon, 11
sociality, 6, 13, 33, 51, 64, 78, 97–98, 125, 131, 145n14; white, 79, 85

social media, 13, 16, 24, 30, 33, 39, 41, 46–48, 141n10, 141n19
social reproduction, 7, 18, 27, 84–85, 115–16, 120, 127, 136n18, 138n39, 147n24
solidarity, 3, 11, 13–15, 17, 20, 50, 71, 95, 100, 138–39n47–48; Asian-Indigenous, 103; in Auntie Sewing Squad, 22; dehumanist, 104, 114, 116, 149n5; Freedom Inc. and, 27, 129–30
sovereignty, 40, 49, 53; dehumanism and, 27, 103–4, 111, 124; Indigenous, 16, 106, 108, 133
Spade, Dean, 94
Stanislavsky, Konstantin, 85
Stanley, Eric, 55
Stop AAPI Hate Project, 2, 135n9
stress, 12, 83
student strikes, 10
suicide, 26, 34, 54, 66, 100–1, 132; femme, 13; ideation of, 5, 12, 19, 143n62; suicidism and, 55, 143n62
Sullivan, Arthur, 76; *Mikado, The*, 25, 81–88, 90–91, 97–99
Sweatshop Overlord, 20–23

Tadiar, Neferti, 51–52
Tagaq, Tanya, 123
TallBear, Kim, 149n5
Taylor, Diana, 26, 142n26
terrorism, 4, 14, 67
Texas, 17, 139n49; Austin, 25, 81, 86, 99; Houston, 31
Thao, Tou, 128–29
theater, 3, 57, 60, 94, 96, 146n49, 147n26; Asian American, 6, 13, 17, 21–22, 26, 72, 75; ethnic, 61, 73–74, 76; musical, 81, 86–89, 98; of the oppressed, 129; postdramatic, 86
Theatre of the Oppressed, 86
Third World Liberation Front (TWLF), 10
Thompson, James, 140n57
Thoroughly Modern Millie, 86
Tongson, Karen, 33
trần, ngọc loan, 141n19
transfemininity, 30, 41
transformational objects, 74–75
transformative justice, 8, 133
transgender people, 2, 7–8, 10, 60, 106, 108, 114, 120, 127; anti-, 17, 102; burden of liveness of, 77; historical activism of, 137n28; immigrant, 21; minoritarian team and, 94–96, 148n42; transphobia and, 18, 122
trauma, 5, 21, 52
Trecartin, Ryan, 31
Trikone, 137n28
Tronto, Joan, 2–3, 6–7, 20, 92, 122, 140n57, 142n35
Trump, Donald, 2, 12–13, 16, 89, 132, 138n46. *See also* January 6, 2021, insurrection
Tsang, Wu, 31
Tumblr, 13, 24, 30–31, 33, 39, 42, 46–47, 50
Ture, Kwame, 152n5

ugly freedom, 130, 141n10
unpayable debt, 122–23, 151n56
uprisings, 20, 126–29, 132
unwellness, 20, 132, 138n37

Vaj, Kabzuag, 126–27, 132
valorization, 38–39, 42–45, 120
Vang, Ma, 128–29
Vietnam, 10, 86, 126, 128, 151n56
Viola, Michael J., 114
violence, 9, 25, 40, 51, 131, 134, 142n26, 146n47, 149n3, 151n56; affective, 4; in *Aftermath*, 107; after September 11 attacks, 78; anti-Asian, 1–2, 17, 19, 78–79, 94, 101, 103, 135n9; anti-Black, 15–16; anti-migrant, 102; of aspiration, 12; cisheteropatriarchal, 28; domestic, 66, 126; Freedom Inc. activism against, 126, 129, 134; in *Funeral for the Honey Bee*, 115; and George Floyd murder, 20, 125, 127–28, 132, 134; interpersonal, 141n19; *The Mikado: Reclaimed* and, 81, 90–93, 97–99; of misgendering, 49; model minoritism, 12; in *Office Hour*, 57–58, 61, 64–68, 70, 72, 74, 76, 99; police and vigilante, 130–31; psychosocial, 31; racial, 31, 61, 67, 70, 80, 83, 96, 129, 131; racial care and, 84, 102, 135n5; racial-colonial, 12, 129; of racial emotional labor, 97; racial-gendered, 81; settler colonialism, 15–16, 112, 114; of slavery, 77; of white supremacy, 14, 40
Virginia Tech massacre, 25, 57, 63, 65, 72, 145n17

Walia, Harsha, 121
Walker, Alice, 48
wars, 2, 5, 48, 112, 132; culture, 12–14, 21, 28, 34, 98, 128, 133, 138n39; imperial, 9, 18, 126, 128–29, 136n11, 151n56; World War II, 10–11, 90
Weheliye, Alexander, 105
white fragility, 3, 13, 25, 64, 83–85, 92, 94, 135n5
whiteness, 7, 12, 25, 33, 41, 44–45, 75, 79, 96, 130–31; non-, 16
white supremacy, 3, 9–10, 27, 31, 55, 119, 131, 133, 135n45; emotional labor and, 83, 85; Mark Aguhar on, 40, 44; multiculturalist, 12, 14–15, 30, 94; neoliberalism and, 4, 11–12, 15, 30, 134
Wilderson, Frank, 131
Winnicott, D. W., 25, 58, 60, 68, 74–76, 144n10, 145n14, 146n47, 146n53
Wisconsin: Kenosha, 130; Madison, 1, 27, 126–31
Wolfe, Patrick, 111
Wong, Kristina, 13, 133, 136n11; Auntie Sewing Squad, 20–22; *Sweatshop Overlord*, 20–23; *Wong Flew over the Cuckoo's Nest*, 5–6, 14, 22
Wong-Kalu, Hinaleimoana Kwai Kong, 107, 109, 114; *Kumu Hina*, 106, 108
World War II, 10–11, 90
w.o.w. Project, 103
Wowsugi, Naoko, 2, 19
Wu, Cynthia, 41
Wynter, Sylvia, 116

xenophobia, 1, 14, 18, 97

Yan, Kit: *Afterearth*, 2, 13, 27, 104–9, 111–12, 114, 123
Yang, Andrew, 78
Yao, Xine, 79
yellowface, 4, 81–82, 86
Yellowjackets Collective, 95
yellowness, 138n46
Yew, Chay: *Sweatshop Overlord*, 20–23

Zamora, Pedro, 33

www.ingramcontent.com/pod-product-compliance
Lightning Source LLC
Chambersburg PA
CBHW020256170426
43202CB00008B/400